Lick Me

Lick Me

How I Became Cherry Vanilla

(by way of the Copacabana,
Madison Avenue, the Fillmore East, Andy Warhol,
David Bowie, and the Police)

Cherry Vanilla

Foreword by Rufus Wainwright

CHICAGO
REVIEW
PRESS

An A Cappella Book

Library of Congress Cataloging-in-Publication Data

Cherry Vanilla.

  Lick me : how I became Cherry Vanilla / Cherry Vanilla.

    p. cm.

  Includes index.

  ISBN 978-1-55652-943-6 (hardcover)

  1. Cherry Vanilla. 2. Singers—United States—Biography. I. Title.

ML420.C47218A3 2010

782.42166092—dc22

[B]

2010024849

Although the characters and events in this book are all real,
certain names have been changed.

Interior design: Monica Baziuk

Published by Chicago Review Press, Incorporated
814 North Franklin Street
Chicago, Illinois 60610
ISBN 978-1-55652-943-6
Printed in the United States of America

5 4 3 2 1

Dedicated to all of the dancers in the make-believe ballroom

Contents

Foreword

FIRST MET Cherry Vanilla at a McGarrigle sisters show in L.A. My mom and aunt were performing, and most likely I was there to do bits of Stephen Foster and French folk music. I was happy to be there but also a little antsy since, at that point, I was in California to make my own album, which was going to be decidedly *not* folk. On first sight of her, I was completely hooked: the shock of red hair, the old Hollywood–style makeup, the haute couture ensemble all mixed with a general enthusiasm and understanding for what my mother and aunt's rustic world was all about. She was the most glamorous person in the room but made no attempts to dominate the space; she happily waited for her victims, and I was reeled in by her elegant and sexy kindness.

Something inside of me that evening exclaimed: This is it! This woman is the bridge! A bridge over a river, a bridge in a song, the Rainbow Bridge to Valhalla, home of the gods. Banjo players suddenly became Hollywood players, coffeehouses turned into bathhouses, and song stylings transformed into Paris styles.

Thanks to Cherry's work with the composer Vangelis, a few years later I was in Greece on one of the most glamorous European trips of my life. There a close friend of hers pointed out to me that she is, in fact, not a woman, not a man, not even a deity—Cherry Vanilla is a whole state of mind, a kind of mental field which, once reached, graces your life with more perspective and thus a grander vision. I understood what this man was saying instantly. Since our fateful meeting that night in L.A., I'd definitely experienced several "Vanilla Fields." ("Cherry Fields" I suppose would be more apropos due to the Lennon song "Strawberry Fields Forever"; still, it sounds too much like a real name, and we definitely don't want that!) I had begun to transform myself through my constant and ever-present hunger for discovery, and Cherry was right there, spoon-feeding me ambrosia, poisoned apples, sweet nectar, and all the good and bad elements of heaven and earth required for the creation of a true rock and roll spirit.

Throughout my artistic life, and the lives of many others, she's remained a beacon of uncompromising sensuality and freedom of expression while at the same time maintaining an avid interest in the now, a woman certainly formed by the '60s but in no way chained to them. I hope that you, the reader, will experience some of the same inspiration we lucky many, a cast of thousands, have gained from her perspective for many years. I also hope that you will keep one more thing in mind as you discover her fantastically wild story: behind the sex, drugs, and rock and roll is one of the kindest and most loyal human beings the world has ever known. Despite becoming the glorious Cherry Vanilla, onstage tornado and backstage bad girl, little Kathy Dorritie from Queens has always remained and is never far behind—always excited, always enthralled, and always pleased to meet you, whoever you are. In the end, a good little girl dressed in a tutu.

—RUFUS WAINWRIGHT

1

The Bridge to Oz

A S THE warm pee ran down my legs and into my socks and brown leather oxfords, a trance-like state ensued, rendering me helpless to stop the flow of liquid emanating from my body. A momentary flash of guilt was quickly overcome by the hypnotic and liberating rush. Standing in the kitchen by the fridge, only steps away from the bathroom, I was powerless to move my feet at all—and what's more I had no desire to do so. There'd be a price to pay for my behavior, I knew. But as the pee made a puddle all around me, I was miles above my fear, excited by what were probably the first stirrings of intoxication and sensuality in me, and feeling, though unintentionally so, quite rebellious.

My mother was naturally alarmed. I was a chronic bed wetter and had suffered from kidney infections, but I had long since outgrown the practice of peeing in my pants. She was gentle and forgiving as she cleaned up both the mess on the floor and me, even though I could offer no explanation as to why it had happened. But when my father got home from work and heard about it, he became enraged, saying I was "disgusting" and scowling "shame on you." I cried myself to sleep that night and prayed that I would die, 'cause he said he was going to tell everyone what a "dirty girl" I was. But I know now that through those tears, an inner strength was born in me, an *I'll show you* determination to decide for myself what was shameful or not and to never again give a shit about what names either he or any other insensitive dumb-fuck like him would ever call me again. It's my earliest memory. I was five years old at the time.

I WAS born Kathleen Anne Dorritie on October 16, 1943, in New York City. World War II was on, and it must have been hard on my parents, who already had three other mouths to feed—Margaret, Johnny, and Mary. But my mother worked, and my father, in addition to his job with the Department of Sanitation, drove a truck part-time for Sam's Ninth Avenue Meat Market. So there was always plenty of food on the table, especially meat. And there was always the mungo—perfectly good items salvaged from the trash that the sanitation men would bring home and recycle. My parents were also the supers of the six-unit tenement building in which we lived, and we thereby paid a much reduced rent. (Ya gotta hand it to 'em; they worked every angle.)

My father's father came from a long line of New Yorkers and owned speakeasies in Hell's Kitchen. Some ancestors on his side were French, from New Orleans, name of Ritchie. My mother's sister, Lucinda, had once been crowned "The Belle of Harlem" and my Scottish grandfather bought both her and my mom two-hundred-dollar dresses (a fortune in the 1920s and '30s). But aside from that, there was never that much family history talk around our house. I knew my other grandparents had come from County Clare and Galway in Ireland, but that's about it. They were all dead by the time I was six.

Except for a few medical problems (eye, ear, and kidney) and the violent side of my father that erupted now and then, my early life in Woodside, Queens, didn't seem so bad. We prayed for lots of snow in the winter, 'cause it meant overtime hours for the sanitation men to plow the streets and more money in the kitty for Christmas presents and summer vacations. And we somehow managed to have the first-ever television set on all of Skillman Avenue—a Stromberg-Carlson "with a twelve-and-a-half-inch screen and forty-two tubes," as my father so incessantly pointed out to all who would listen. (It had probably come from my Aunt Rita, who was well over four hundred pounds and who always had a bunch of "hot"—which in those days meant stolen—items for sale.) When the baseball game was on, our living room was filled with cheering, jeering friends and neighbors— the beer, highballs, cold cuts, and dirty jokes flowing. And when the *Friday Night Fights* were on, my father turned into a fanatical, red-faced, leaping lunatic of an authority on boxing—throwing phantom punches and yelling things at the TV like "Hit 'im with the left!" and "C'mon, get up, ya bum!"

I knew that some people, like my Aunt Lizzy's family, the Dona-hues in Elmhurst, and my parents' friends, the Kents in St. Alban's (both of whom I often stayed with for weeklong visits without my mom and dad), lived life with more than one bathroom and doors on their bedrooms, but I figured there really wasn't much more to aspire to than what we had in Woodside at the time.

ON SATURDAYS, while my mother was at work, my dad would often take me to the Department of Sanitation's huge incinerator out by Flushing Bay. It had gigantic metal doors, and when they opened, it was like looking into hell, the heat from the flames burning your skin like a dozen summer suns. It was a fire so big that if you were to throw a couple of Mack trucks in there, it would swallow 'em whole. Then he'd take me to a landfill the department was making out there, a giant mountain of garbage with seagulls flying all around it. Other Saturdays, we would visit my dad's friend Mr. Gruber at his pigeon coop on the roof down the street, or else maybe the coop on the roof of the sanitation garage in Long Island City.

And on Sundays—even though he drove all week long as a chauf-feur for the Department of Sanitation's borough superintendent of Queens—my dad loved taking long drives to places like Rockaway

Beach, Coney Island, Graymoor (an upstate religious retreat), and even Washington, D.C. My mom would be at work or at home cooking, and my brother and sisters were usually busy with homework, so it was often just the two of us, my dad and me, who went for the rides. We didn't talk much on the road, so I got to listen to a lot of AM radio, at first in the pearl grey '47 Nash Ambassador, and later in the forest green '52 Buick Roadmaster. The music they played on shows like the *Make Believe Ballroom* was what my father liked best. But as the 1950s approached, I noticed a new sound seeping onto the airwaves, one that was way hotter than "She Wore a Yellow Ribbon" by the Andrews Sisters or "Lavender Blue (Dilly Dilly)" by Burl Ives. Not that I didn't love some of that 1940s pop stuff: "Far Away Places" by Perry Como made me dream of the exotic travel I'd do when I was older, and "Powder Your Face with Sunshine," besides being a good philosophy to follow, was sung by Dean Martin, probably my first celebrity crush. Once I heard that newer, grittier sound, though, by artists like Fats Domino, Johnny Otis, Ruth Brown, Percy Mayfield, the Ravens, the Swallows, and Sonny Til and the Orioles, I was hooked on it and would search it out on the dial.

At first, this new sound was referred to as "race music," but it soon became known as rhythm and blues. And in Queens, whenever you went into a subway station, a public bathroom, or any place with an echo, there'd be groups of teenage boys there, singing the songs a cappella, making up their own harmonies and calling it doo-wop. This new music spoke directly to me somehow, and told me that something really big was coming, something maybe even bigger than the music itself.

LADY WAS our family dog, a purebred Dalmatian. She was so smart, we never even had to walk her. She would just jump out the back window, go down the cellar door, through the garden, over the cyclone fence, and into the huge vacant lot behind our row of flats to do her duty. All of Skillman Avenue used to walk their dogs back there, and there were always a few strays around as well. (And in those days, nobody picked up the poop.) When she was finished, Lady Clauheen (her full name) would run the whole course in reverse, coming right back up the cellar door, through the window, and into the kitchen. And she did it all as one smooth piece, beautiful choreography. She was so elegant, with a lightly spotted body and an almost all-white face. She was the first living thing I can remember loving. She made me know what love was. I hadn't particularly recognized that emotion yet with people, at least not the way I knew it with Lady.

One night my father came in very angry and everyone at home was acting really strange. Lady was cowering in the corner of the living room and shaking like a leaf. She seemed to sense that something bad was about to happen—and so did I. After a lot of whispered stuff about some big black mutt, then some loud angry curses and shoving around of chairs and such, my father made my brother help him grab a hold of Lady and carry her into the bathroom. She was yelping and howling, convulsing and fighting to get free. I thought her beautiful long legs were gonna break.

I didn't understand. Why were they hurting her so? What could she have done that was so bad? And what were they going to do to her in the bathroom? My father made my sisters take me to my parents' bedroom at the far end of our railroad flat, as if that would prevent me from hearing all of the horror. Nobody would tell me what was happening, but after a while I pretty much figured it out. No, he didn't kill the dog, but he did kill any puppies she may have had inside of her, or at least the sperm that might have turned into those puppies. Yes, my father performed a scalding–hot water rubber-hose abortion on Lady while my brother held her down in the tub.

This, in a way, was my introduction to the birds and the bees, and it very well may have scarred me for life. I hated all men in that moment. And the sounds wouldn't stop. All I could do back in the bedroom was curl up in a fetal position and sob from the deepest part of my six-year-old soul. I never wanted to feel so helpless again. I tried so hard to make myself disappear, to escape from the pain. If only I could get out of there, I thought, go live in the woods on my own, everything would be all right. But there was no way. I simply had to find a place inside my mind where I could hide at moments like these.

Lady was never the same after that night. She stayed under the bed constantly and became very nervous. And when my parents started keeping her down in the cellar, she went for my sister Margaret (at least that's what Margaret said) and seemed to go insane. They had her put down after that, though they told everyone that what Lady really died from was "a broken heart over never having had any puppies."

Without knowing if the Lady trauma was the cause, I soon developed a condition that would plague me for the rest of my life—a shameful, secret thing I did, which was diagnosed decades later as obsessive-compulsive disorder (OCD).

THERE WAS a place we went to every summer. It was a kind of camp for employees of the Department of Sanitation and their families. When the old Second Avenue El was taken down in Manhattan at the end of the '30s, the Department of Sanitation bought up all of the trains and, in 1941, turned the individual cars into modern compact houses with built-in beds, kitchens, and bathrooms. They added big front porches onto them; placed them here and there around the mountains and lakes of a multi-acre property in Holmes, New York, they'd named Sanita Hills; and rented them out very inexpensively to the sanitation workers for their family vacations.

For some reason, my parents, who were always so cautious and strict with me back in Queens, let me roam around Sanita on my own, even when I was as young as six or seven. There were lakes with swim-cribs, lifeguards, floats, and boats—and all for free. And the trails and meadows were all marked with signposts, so you couldn't get too lost. I loved being alone in nature, just me and the earth and the sky. I found a secret little spot by a pond that I returned to over and over, where I just sat silently, entranced by the willow trees, the water lilies, the frogs, and the birds. I was too young to know that what I was actually doing there was meditating. I just knew that all of the time I sat there, I felt good and I wanted for nothing—except, maybe, for a slice of the divine, warm peach pie from the bakery nearby. And so, it was nature that comprised my first real fantasy world, whether the actual time I spent in it in the summers or the memories of it I could call to mind the rest of the year when faced with one of those "God, please get me out of here" moments.

If that didn't work, I would escape any painful situations via the OCD route, manically picking at any cut, scratch, bite, or blemish on my body, alternating constantly between letting a scab form and picking it off, keeping the wounds open and bloody for weeks, sometimes months, on end. I guess I was just substituting one kind of pain for another, and punishing myself for whatever wasn't right with my life. But all I knew was that I was learning how to slip into a kind of trance at will, honing my zoning-out skills in whatever ways possible, to the point where I almost *could* disappear.

MY SISTER Mary and her girlfriend Roseanne used to put on little variety shows underneath our front stoop. The audience was made up of the neighborhood kids who paid ten cents, sat on the cellar steps, and got one free glass of Kool-Aid each. Mary and Roseanne were the producers and a few young starstruck kids like me and my next-door neighbor Joannie Jackolovsky were the performers. We each knew one routine and we did it for every single show.

Joannie was always the ballerina. She had long blond braids and a whole wardrobe of pink crepe-paper ballet costumes that Mary and Roseanne had made her. The 78 of "Dance Ballerina Dance" by Vaughn Monroe would come on, and Joannie would invariably chicken out and freeze. Mary and Roseanne would be there, pushing her out from the cellar, and the kids would all laugh like the Little Rascals. Then, after a quick jolt of courage, which prompted a pirouette or two, Joannie would burst into tears and crouch in the corner.

The kids loved it. Some of 'em threw their Kool-Aid at her, which kind of melted her crepe-paper costumes. And I guess that's why she had so many of 'em.

I was always Leilani, the hula girl. I wore a flower-printed towel as a sarong, with my fanciest panties underneath and a toilet-tissue carnation tucked behind one ear, while strumming a plastic ukulele and singing along with either "Sweet Leilani" or "Johnny Brings Leilani Home." About halfway through the number, I used to get rid of the ukulele and start to wiggle (I thought I was doing the hula). Mary, Roseanne, and the kids would go bananas, cheering me on, making me gyrate wildly. And eventually, the towel would work its way loose and fall to the ground. Once everyone got a good look at me dancing topless in my panties, I would clutch my breasts, act embarrassed, and run off into the cellar. But even at age six or seven, I kind of knew what I was doing.

Joannie and I were always doing secret, sick little things, like pooping together behind the hedges in the backyard instead of in the toilet. And for most things we never were caught. But on Valentine's day in 1951, we really got into trouble for the cards we sent some neighborhood ladies who always sat on the front stoops chatting when the weather was nice. Sam's Candy Store on Skillman Avenue used to sell "penny Valentines," though they actually cost around a nickel. They were printed on a single sheet of paper, and each one had a theme expressed in a rhyme, along with a garish illustration. We knew they were naughty but didn't realize just how vicious they actually were. And not having money for lots of them, we only bought one of each of our favorites—"The World's Biggest Cheapskate," "The World's Biggest Gossip," and "The World's Biggest Pig." We used tracing paper and crayons to make multiple copies of them and anonymously left them in the women's mailboxes.

There probably wouldn't have been such a huge hullabaloo about them had we not nailed the women with exactly the right theme for each, according to the way we'd heard our parents talk about them. Mrs. Sayles, who lived on the top floor of our building, made the biggest stink of all, and she knew right away who had sent them. Joannie and I owned up to doing it and had to apologize to each and every woman in person. Our parents scolded us, but they couldn't help but laugh at what we'd done—saying things that they themselves only wished they had the balls to say to those women. Mrs. Sayles was indeed known as "the neighborhood gossip" and here's what her Valentine said.

> *You always put folks in a hole*
> *With talk that's vile and cheap*
> *I'd like to see you in a hole*
> *A big one six feet deep*

We knew what we'd done wasn't nice—naturally, we didn't really want Mrs. Sayles to die—and I, for one, learned a few lessons by getting caught. I realized the importance of owning up to one's mistakes (of course, making the copies instead of sending the originals was our first mistake) and that the things adults say behind each other's backs are often different than the things said to their faces. Mostly, though, I learned a lot about the power of words, especially poetry. And I believe this may have been the beginning of my lifelong love affair with the form.

MY SISTER Margaret was the governess for the actor Don Ameche's two adopted daughters, Bonnie and Connie. They were my age, so Margaret often took me to spend weekends with them at the Ameche's posh Manhattan apartment in the Croyden Hotel. This was yet another fantasy world for me, the world of luxury living. We girls were like three little Eloises running around that hotel. We could sign for ice cream in the coffee shop, order club sandwiches from room service, hang out on the couches in the lobby playing grown-up, have the doormen get us taxis (when Margaret was with us), and let the bellhops carry our bags.

Mr. and Mrs. Ameche were so sophisticated and glamorous compared to every other adult I'd ever known. Often in the evenings they'd get all dressed up in formal clothes to go out on the town. Before that, I had only ever seen people dressed in formal clothes for weddings or proms. I knew Mr. Ameche was a big movie star, but at home he was just a regular dad. Of course, he was exceptionally handsome, well groomed, and well spoken, but he was also very easy going, down to earth, and kind. It was because of Don Ameche, I think, that I came to realize that not all men were as crude and coarse as my father—and also because of him that I learned to feel comfortable around the biggest of stars.

The Ameches treated me like one of the family. On Saturdays Bonnie (who always wore blue), Connie (who always wore pink), and I (who mostly wore yellow or green when with them) had our usual routine. First, Margaret would take us to FAO Schwartz and let us play with the life-size toys. Then she'd take us to Toots Shor's for lunch, where she would put it on the Ameches' tab. Little did I realize that the nice people stopping by our table, saying things like "Give my best to Don and Honora," may have included the likes of Frank Sinatra, Jackie Gleason, Joe DiMaggio, Judy Garland, Ernest Hemmingway, Orson Wells, and Marilyn Monroe, all of whom hung out there and were friends of the Ameches. I was too engrossed in the shrimp cocktails and the maraschino cherries in the Shirley Temples to take that much notice. And then, to end the day, we'd always go for a hansom cab ride through Central Park.

Because of my bed-wetting, I was often embarrassed when I slept over at the Ameches'. But, bless their hearts, they were as kind as the Donahues and the Kents had always been. They simply got out the rubber sheets, brushed off my "little accidents" as insignificant, and always invited me back. It was because of my relationship with the Ameches that I began to realize how lucky I was, instead of how misplaced, disconnected, and alien I felt as a member of the Dorritie family. God, if the Ameches ever saw us at home having dinner, passing one dishtowel around for us all to wipe our mouths on instead of using individual napkins, then using that very same towel to dry the dishes—ugh! Even at an early age I wondered: was I really meant to be so shanty Irish? Could there have been a mix-up at the maternity ward?

MY MOTHER was a telephone operator at the Hotel Fourteen in Manhattan. And she mostly worked the late shift, which meant she was rarely at home in the evenings. My father hung out down the block, in the back room of Gus Arnold's delicatessen and on the street corner outside of it. So he wasn't around that much either. The neighbors had him pegged as a nosy windbag because he loved being in on all of the dirt that was dished around Gus's. My sister Mary did most of the cooking and housekeeping, even when she was as young as eleven or twelve.

We kids fought like cats and dogs and were constantly calling my mother at work. So, to keep us in check, she devised a little game she called Listening In. She'd tell us that if we were absolutely quiet and put our hands over the mouthpiece, she would let us "listen in" on the hotel guests' telephone calls. Though the conversations we heard were never really that interesting, there was something so secretive and exciting about it. It was better than doing homework or even watching TV in those days. And there'd be some peace and quiet around the house for a while. The best thing about it, though, was feeling the connection with my mother, even if it was only over the phone.

My mom's shift ended at 11:00 p.m. during the week, and my father used to drive into the city to pick her up from work. (We called Manhattan "the city," even though Queens is technically the city too.) Some nights he'd let me stay up late and—wearing my pajamas underneath my coat—ride in with him. It was the biggest thrill of my life at the time because of two things: getting to listen to late-night radio, when the raunchiest songs were played—like "Rollin' Stone" by Muddy Waters, "Sixty Minute Man" by Billy Ward and His Dominoes, "Rocket 88" by Jackie Brenston, and "Dust My Broom" by Elmore James—and getting to visit the most magical, musical, theatrical, glitzy, glamorous place I could ever have imagined, the Copacabana, which just happened to be located in the basement of the Hotel Fourteen.

On the weekends my mother's shift ended early, and that's when, standing with my dad by the Copa's kitchen doors, I'd get to see performances by the biggest stars in the world—Martin and Lewis, Jimmy Durante, Tony Bennett, Carmen Miranda, Eartha Kitt, Billy Eckstine, Danny Thomas, and more. But it wasn't just the shows that were so enthralling; it was the whole atmosphere of the Copa. There were plush booths and palm trees and ladies in strapless gowns, their mink stoles draped over the backs of chairs. The room sparkled with cocktail glasses, diamond bracelets, and Brylcreemed hair, and reeked of scotch, cognac, French and Chinese food, and fine perfumes. Cigarette smoke filled the air, and when the lights went down, the joyous buzz from everyone talking and laughing would give way to whistles, warm-hearted cheers, and wild applause.

The Copa had its own entrance at 10 East 60th Street, but the stars who, as a rule, stayed at the Hotel Fourteen at 14 East 60th Street (and even, like Jimmy Durante always did, gave my mother hundred-dollar tips) could take the elevators right down into the Copa's kitchen, and get to the show room and the dressing rooms from there. And so could we, thanks to my mom's relationship with the management and her fellow employees, especially with Jimmy the bellhop who usually escorted us down to the shows. Jimmy wore electric blue eye shadow and my father said he "flew," which in those days meant he was a fairy. But I really loved Jimmy and so did my mom. And my dad did too, in his own somewhat homophobic way. And the stars especially loved Jimmy, because he would do anything for them and always made them laugh with his flamboyant mannerisms and his practical jokes.

One Saturday night Jimmy had a special little treat planned for me. So I took the elevator with him to a room on one of the Fourteen's higher floors. He opened the door with his passkey, let me in, and told me to sit at the foot of the bed and wait for my surprise. And then he left me there all alone in the room. I must've sat there like that for a good fifteen or twenty minutes before I finally heard the elevator opening down the hallway and the key in the door. And in walked the most handsome man I had ever seen in my life, even more handsome than Don Ameche, or maybe just another whole kind of handsome. This was surely the first time that I was ever truly aware of the sexual chemistry that exists between a man and a woman, though I didn't know the name for it then. You see, this wasn't just any six-foot-something gorgeous specimen of a man before me; it was none other than Dean Martin, one of my biggest idols! I had prayed that I would meet him one day, and there I was, little Kathleen Anne Dorritie from Queens, hanging out with him in his hotel room.

Up close and in person, Dean Martin seemed taller than the tallest man I knew and his hair was blacker and shinier than any I'd ever seen. His shirt looked blindingly white against his deeply suntanned skin. And his brown wool slacks and brown tweed sportcoat were perfectly coordinated and showed off his broad shoulders and slim body so well. "Oh hi, and who are you?" he greeted me, not seeming at all shocked or flustered by the trick that was obviously being played on him—though I could sense an edge of laughter behind his kind brown eyes. I told him I was Mary the telephone operator's daughter and we talked for a while about God knows what. I wanted so badly to be older, so he would fall in love with me right then and there. Every minute felt like heaven. Then Jimmy came to get me so Dean could change for his show. Of course, I never let on to Dino that I had often listened in on his telephone calls. I knew my mother would lose her job if anyone ever found out about that.

All I could think of back then was the Copacabana—that and the Latin Quarter, where my mom also arranged for me to get a glimpse of the shows. I forget if it was the Copa Girls or the Latin Quarter Girls who had their hair dyed pale pink, baby blue, lavender, and mint green (at the twenty-four-hour Larry Mathews salon) to match their showgirl costumes, but that image really struck me as the height of showbiz chic—a look I hoped to emulate one day. On New Year's Eve

I would always wait up for my mom to come home with the incredible Copa party hats, which were so imaginative and lavish, it was hard to believe they were made to last for just one night. I kept mine for years and dressed up in them often when I wanted to dream my big show business dreams.

Of course, the Hotel Fourteen itself was just as entertaining and seductive as the Copacabana—totally Damon Runyon—what with the people who lived there and the things that my mom said went on. There was Jules Potnick, a friendly gangster type, who "ran a hot fur and diamond ring" and from whom my mom got a full-length sable coat for two-hundred-and-fifty dollars; Miss Chadwick, a size-twelve "model," whose bookings were always at night and for whose child my sisters often babysat; Pierre Matisse, "a strange little pack rat," who was actually a major art dealer and the son of Henri Matisse, his suite stacked with paintings by some of the greatest modern artists of the day; and Lady Mountbatten, "a royal with a past."

They were each so intriguing, mysterious, and unique. I was insatiably attracted to them all—the musicians, the Copa Girls, the hookers, gangsters, cardsharps, artists, lords and ladies, and, naturally, the stars. I couldn't wait to be an adult—to sip cocktails, smoke cigarettes, wear eye makeup—and to truly be a part of this wondrous world of madcap Manhattan nightlife. And there it was waiting for me, just across the Fifty-ninth Street Bridge, so close and yet so far—the Emerald City, the Land of Oz. I could see its lights from our Skillman Avenue fire escape, where I hung out on hot summer nights. And one day I would grow up and make it my own. But unlike Dorothy, I knew that once I got there, I would never go back to Queens—which was such a world apart from Manhattan in those days, it might just as well have been Kansas.

2

Rock and Roll

I WAS EIGHT when I began classes at Betty Watson's Dancing School in Queens. I took tap and ballet and eventually worked my way up to toe. I was hooked on the show business rush there from the moment I climbed the rickety old staircase and entered the studio—the thick, humid air... the rosin on the floor... the frail old maestro at the upright piano... the mirrors and the ballet barre. This was a fantasy world even more important to me than the Copacabana, because now I'd no longer just be watching the shows, I'd be *in* them—well, in Miss Betty's annual dance recitals at the Bryant High School auditorium in nearby Astoria, Queens, anyway.

My sister Mary used to take me to Miss Betty's twice a week. By the time she was thirteen, Mary had really assumed the Cinderella role around our house—cooking, cleaning, shopping, and babysitting me. She also made my costumes for the recitals, because my mother said we couldn't afford the six dollars each that Miss Betty's seamstress charged. The workload must have been hard on Mary, a quiet, slightly chubby teenage girl with little or no social life. But there was no way I was gonna give up my lessons. I loved them. And either the dancing itself or knowing how bare my body would be in the costumes kept me from indulging too heavily in my OCD. Of course I couldn't tell Mary or anyone else about that. It was my deepest, darkest secret, and I carefully hid the sores or made excuses for them.

I hated it when my parents would ask me to dance for friends and family at home. I was so shy when it came to doing it in front of a handful of people; I used to lock myself in the bathroom and cry. Sometimes I'd tap dance on the tile floor so they could hear me but couldn't see me. On stage, however, in front of hundreds of people—done up in a fuchsia tutu and tights, wearing makeup and feeling the warmth of the lights—I was a natural-born little performer with no inhibitions at all. So I told everyone that if they wanted to see me dance, they would have to buy a ticket to Miss Betty's recital. Of course, I was aware that a big turnout of my *fans* in the audience would assure me lots of applause, whether I danced fabulously or not. And I figured they'd be more likely to come if I didn't give it to 'em for free at home.

MY MOTHER was in the hospital a lot. Within the space of a few years, she'd had a bout of pneumonia, a gall bladder operation, a hysterectomy, a couple of discs removed from her spine, and a stroke. Our family doctor, whom we'd gotten through my dad's boss, was a kind of upper-class one on Manhattan's east side and, I'm pretty sure, an alcoholic. He used to put his patients in Madison Avenue Hospital, a private chi-chi place right near the Carlyle hotel. The hospital didn't allow young children in for visiting hours, so when my mother was there, I would have to stand across the street, on the other side of Madison Avenue, and wait for her to come to the window and wave to me. Sometimes it was in the dead of winter and with all of the concrete, granite, and glass around there, it just seemed like the coldest place on earth.

Even though I felt like I didn't really belong in the Dorritie family, in those moments I longed to be up there, standing by my mom's bedside, holding her hand, especially when I saw her at the window with tubes coming our of her nose and looking so bad. My mother had a great attitude, always saying things like "everything happens for the best" and "shit them" (her version of "fuck 'em"). She was also a lot smarter and kinder than my father—I always wondered why she married him—and I was really afraid that she was gonna die. Oh God, and then where would we be, without her to balance out the craziness? I don't know if that was love I felt there or only fear. But I do know that on those days I was desperately sad.

I WAS ten in 1953 when I bought my first record from Sam's Candy Store (the same place where Joannie and I got the Valentines)— "Rock Around the Clock" by Bill Haley and His Comets. I played it on our brand-new RCA 45-rpm turntable, which plugged into the back of the Stromberg-Carlson TV, along with the other current hits my brother Johnny had bought: "Cry" by Johnnie Ray, "Night Train" by Jimmy Forrest, "Earth Angel" by the Penguins, "Pledging My Love" by Johnny Ace, "Shake, Rattle, and Roll" by Big Joe Turner, and "Cool Water" by an artist I've forgotten but which was pressed on the most beautiful shade of green vinyl.

Johnny was in college at the time. My parents believed that only boys should go to college; it wasn't worth wasting the money on girls, who would only turn out to be secretaries or housewives anyway. There was a ten-year difference in age between Johnny and me, too much for us to ever be close. He was always pretty conservative and straight anyway, so it was probably just as well he didn't know that much about what I was getting up to. 'Cause by the time I was eleven, I'd tried smoking cigarettes and had let a boy stick his fingers up my pussy. I knew right away that cigarettes were not for me, but the fingers up the pussy stuff, I decided, had possibilities.

MY SUMMERS at Sanita Hills were over. The Department of Sanitation couldn't get enough tax dollars from the city to afford its upkeep, so they gave it away to the Boy Scouts. But, lucky for me, my dad and Mr. Kent had already built us a summerhouse right across the street from the Donahues' in Lake Carmel, about ten miles from Sanita. And my parents had that same uncharacteristic, easygoing attitude about letting me roam free there as they did in Sanita. Margaret was in Shawnee with the Ameches in the summertime, and Mary and Johnny often stayed in the city. So I spent lots of time alone in Lake Carmel—picking blackberries in the woods, skipping across rocks in a crystal-clear stream, taking all-day walks around the lake and leisurely swims across it, drinking icy cold water from a natural spring, and riding my beautiful, powder-blue Ross bicycle to the frozen custard stand. "Living in her own little fantasy world," my parents would say, but it was my freedom in the real world I was actually celebrating there, in my own little loner-weirdo way.

DURING THE school year at St. Mary Help of Christians, I really got into the stories of the saints—especially St. Lucy with her eyeballs on a plate (my patron saint, because I'd had an eye operation at seven), and St. Sebastian, tied to a tree, half-naked, bloody, and shot up with arrows. And the mandatory daily mass (in Latin in those days), with its candles, incense, chanting, and holy communion, always held such mystery for me. It was really just a necessary evil, though, this thing with Catholicism and me. It was shoved down my throat so heavily at home and at St. Mary's that I figured I might as well enjoy and appreciate whatever I could about it. Besides, it was the first live dramatic theater I knew, and the music was often stirring, especially the bass vibrations from the big church organ.

I had, of course, already found God through my love of nature and showbiz. And I was getting more and more addicted to what I knew to be my true religion, rock and roll—which, thanks to the DJ Alan Freed, was beginning to explode all over the airwaves. It was in 1954 that Freed, who originally called himself Moondog, brought his rhythm and blues radio show from WJW in Cleveland to WINS in New York and gave the music I'd been digging for so long that new name, the name that would finally stick: rock and roll. In 1955, I got a turquoise-and-black Motorola portable radio for my twelfth birthday. It was at least twenty times bigger and heavier than an iPod, but it was state of the art and I carried it with me wherever I went. I was obsessed with being constantly in touch with the music, know-ing instinctively somehow that—much like the fingers in the pussy—rock and roll would figure heavily in my future... maybe because both things seemed to touch me in the very same place.

EDDIE ROCK (his real name) was the boy next door (literally) and my very first crush. His mom, Mary Rock, was my mother's best friend. She was also the neighborhood drunk, often found passed out in the gutter, stinking of urine and wine. But that was only when she'd go on a bender. Otherwise, she was very together. Eddie's legs had been badly burned in a fire when he was a baby and the neighborhood kids made fun of us both, Eddie for his scars and his mother, me for my eyeglasses and my dad. My mom always took care of Eddie when Mrs. Rock was incapacitated, and I often hung out at the Rocks' when she was sober. She was the nicest, smartest woman I knew, an avid reader and baker of the best Irish soda bread I ever tasted, cooked in a black iron frying pan in her long out-of-fashion coal oven.

Eddie had been my friend and playmate from birth. But by the time we were teenagers and could have been sweethearts, Eddie said he didn't really like me in that way. And I never even got as far as making out with him. The Teen Queens released "Eddie My Love" around that time, so I naturally clung to it as "my song." Years later, when I heard that Eddie had been killed in Vietnam, the song, of course, came to mind. It'll always remind me of Eddie. I only wish it contained within it the memory of Eddie's kisses.

I WAS around twelve when the Ameche girls, being highly valued customers at B. Altman and Company (a department store too pricey for the Dorritie budget), managed to get me invited to the Saturday morning fashion shows at the store's Charleston Garden. For me, it was like being invited to the White House or the Academy Awards. I'd wear my most expensive-looking outfit, take the subway to 34th

Street, and meet Bonnie and Connie at the store. The shows were free of charge. They served breakfast (including the first croissants I'd ever tasted) and they had girls our age modeling the clothes. Of course, I would never be able to own any of them. My clothes came mostly from bargain stores on 14th Street like S. Klein on the Square. But that didn't matter. I felt so privileged and so chic just being there, and nobody, except Bonnie and Connie, knew that I was only acting the part of a rich girl.

They once had a three-Saturday charm school there that I attended as well, where they taught things like how to tweeze your eyebrows, shave your legs, practice good posture, hold your teacup, and use your knife and fork. And at the end of it you got a B. Altman's Charm School diploma. Man, I just ate that stuff up—along with all the croissants my little tummy could hold.

WHEN ELVIS Presley released "Hound Dog" in 1956, it was as if the whole world really did get *all shook up*. Elvis was the first white man to truly convey the soul and sexuality of rock and roll. If a black man had flaunted those suggestive hip gyrations and bedroom eyes back then, it would have been too much for most of the American public to take. Black men, even in showbiz, were still thought of as dangerous, especially for young white teenage girls. But Elvis, with his clean-cut rockabilly style, his obvious good manners, and his mama's boy reputation, was so appealing a package that even my parents— thank God—realized the futility of putting up any kind of resistance. I adored him, had kerchiefs, wallets, and pillowcases depicting his likeness, and bought every record he made. My mother's stories about the jazz babies and Harlem nights of the 1920s and '30s had always sounded so unbelievably wild and freewheeling to me, especially compared to the ultraconservative mind-set of the 1950s. But with the emergence of Elvis, I knew an even wilder era was at hand.

I WAS fourteen when my sister Mary got pregnant. She was nine-teen and single. All hell broke loose in our house over that, my father screaming he would "kill the guinea bastard" who had knocked her up, while brandishing a butcher's knife to make his point. Mary and her boyfriend had a quickie civil ceremony and moved into an apartment of their own—more major drama, since they'd gotten married "outside the church." My brother Johnny, who was twenty-four, recently discharged from the army, and close with Mary, came to her defense and moved out then as well. You would've thought a murder had been committed the way my parents carried on. They were never going to speak to any of them again, "Jesus, Mary, and Joseph" were being constantly implored, and a parish priest was even brought into the fray to mediate.

Margaret was still living at home, and my parents were driving her almost as crazy as they'd driven poor Lady. She was working as a secretary for the YMCA, the Ameche girls having outgrown their need for a nanny. She gave all of her salary to my parents, as they demanded, and at twenty-five was still a virgin. They knew that without money, she couldn't afford to do anything but stay put. And their rule—though broken by Mary and Johnny—was that you lived at home until you got married.

Of course, much of the excessive drama around our house at that time was due to the fact that we were all on Preludin Endurettes, a brand-new diet pill that Johnny was bringing home by the hundreds, thanks to his job as a drug rep for Sandoz Pharmaceuticals. They were the new "miracle pills," and everyone in our family took them because everyone was overweight, except for me. But I took 'em anyway, because they gave me so much energy and they were free. We didn't think of them as speed back then, but in reality we were all speeding our brains out.

Being the baby of the family, watching all of this go down, I was determined that, when the time came, I would stand up to my parents—especially my blowhard, dictatorial father—and get out from under their tight, oppressive reins. Johnny soon got married, Mary had the baby, and eventually all was forgiven. Margaret lost fifty pounds, got down to a size twelve, and married the first poor Irish schlump who came along. I immersed myself in fantasies of romance with Tab Hunter, Ricky Nelson, Elvis Presley, and James Dean.

I HAD my heart set on going to Immaculata High School in Manhattan, and I'd aced their entrance exam and gotten accepted. But Immaculata was coed, which my parents thought would lead me into sin. So they made me go to all-girls All Saints Commercial High School, where my sister Margaret had gone—and where I got to see girls making out with each other for the first time in my life. All Saints (or "All Sluts," as the Bishop Loughlin boys on the GG local used to call it) was in Williamsburg—at that time the hellhole of Brooklyn—and was situated between a Pfizer chemical plant, vacant lots, and burned-out buildings. And the rats I saw there daily made my blood run cold.

Getting to know a very ethnically diverse group of girls, playing trumpet in the St. Patrick's Day parades, and portraying one of the wives in *The King and I* were probably my favorite things about All Saints, though I also enjoyed learning the art of writing a business letter and taking a course in basic business law. If encouraged, I might well have pursued a law career. I just loved the way that words could be manipulated to mean so many things and could then be challenged for their meanings. And I quite enjoyed typing class too, the keyboard being somewhat like a musical instrument to me. Who knows, had I gone to Immaculata I might have met a nice young Catholic boy, gotten married early, and had a bunch of kids. Instead, my parents set me up for the life I wound up living, and I guess I should be grateful to them for that.

AS A teenager, the Woodside boys didn't go for me at all—maybe 'cause I had no tits when the other girls my age did or maybe 'cause they feared my know-it-all, buttinsky father from the corner. I was a cheerleader for the Woodside Chiefs football team, and I drummed up the idea for the first ever Pop Warner League cheerleading competition (though we didn't win it). Dotsie Corrigan was the Chiefs' blue-eyed, black-haired quarterback, and I was madly in love with him. But Dotsie was not in love with me. Once a week, however, at the after-game party in a nearby Sunnyside church basement, I got to dance at least one slow dance with Dotsie. I always prayed he'd ask me when they played "Tonite, Tonite" by the Mello-Kings, my favorite song at the time. And when it worked out that way, those three or four minutes of bliss were enough to keep me happy for the whole week that followed. "Tonite, Tonite" became synonymous with the live-for-the-moment attitude I knew I'd have to develop if I didn't want to suffer the constant heartbreak that I realized love could bring.

MY AUNT Rita's four sons were all practically lifers, in and out of prison from the time they were kids. As teenagers, they were taught by their mom how to roll drunks outside of bars under the guise of selling flowers. Then each of them, besides procuring the hot appliances and phony driver's licenses, birth, and baptismal certificates that Aunt Rita sold, went on to develop further skills and scams of their own. Charlie, Aunt Rita's second oldest son, needed a sponsor to get paroled from a long stretch on a manslaughter charge. So my parents decided they would volunteer for it and take him in to live with us. (What were they thinking?)

I was around fifteen, and since my brother and sisters were no longer living at home, my parents—after a brief, disastrous attempt to live in Yonkers—had taken a two-bedroom, nonrailroad apartment for us right across the street from where we used to live on Skillman Avenue. So there I was, a schoolgirl, with my career-con cousin of maybe thirty-five sleeping in our living room. I got nervous when Charlie and I were there alone, but I kind of liked it. It felt sexy. And he was into the same kind of music I was into, which I thought was pretty cool.

My sexuality was beginning to emerge at that time, and maybe not in the healthiest of ways. Using my lunch money and a girlfriend's address, I ordered a black satin push-up bra—not that I had any tits to fill it out yet—and matching bikini panties from the Fredericks of Hollywood catalog. After school, I would lock my bedroom door (thrilled to finally have one), put on the bra, clip six or eight metal hair clips onto the outer lips of my labia, pull the panties on over them, and sit there in bed like that doing my homework, usually with the radio on. Of course, the hair clips painfully pinched and poked my pussy, but in my secret, sick little way, I somehow got off on that.

On nights when my parents and Charlie were all at home, I would sit at the kitchen table with them for dinner wearing my jeans and a big sweater over the clips and undies. Sometimes I would stay like that for hours, watching TV, inwardly gloating over the S&M I was practicing right under their noses, and getting off on my ability to not show any pain. I haven't a clue where I got the idea for it. Like my OCD, it was just another form of torture that, for whatever reason, I was fond of inflicting on myself. From the intense looks he had begun to shoot my way, I was starting to worry that maybe Charlie had caught on to what I was doing. Then, one day when I came home from school, Charlie was gone—moved out, never to be seen or heard from again. My parents would only say that he had gone upstate, but I think it was more likely that cousin Charlie had once again been sent up the river.

In the late nineteen fifties, WWRL played the hottest black music on the dial, and the station was located, strangely enough, just a few blocks from home, in the middle of Woodside, a neighborhood that had absolutely no black people living in it at all. I used to sneak down there (my parents had forbidden it, of course) and stand outside with my Motorola, waiting for the DJs to go in and out. I just wanted to see what they were like, make contact, and request a song or two by some of my favorite groups of the day, like the Charts, the Elegants, the Flamingos, the Falcons, and the Drifters. I had this insatiable need to feel connected with anyone who had anything to do with the music. And I never got caught by my parents or any of the neighborhood snoops, because St. Sebastian's Church (a converted movie theater) was right down the street from the station, and I used to tell my mother I was going there to light candles or go to confession.

It was also around the end of the fifties, during the Christmas and Easter breaks, when I started sneaking off to the Alan Freed and Murray the K (New York's other big rock and roll DJ) shows at the Brooklyn Fox and Brooklyn Paramount Theatres. The music, the glitzy outfits, the dance steps, the acts like Frankie Lymon and the Teenagers, Buddy Holly and the Crickets, Chuck Berry, Little Richard, and Jerry Lee Lewis, as well as the DJs and the thousands of excited young fans like me all gave me the feeling that I was becoming part of a movement, finding my crowd, my passion. I had gone to my first Broadway musical, *Bells Are Ringing* starring Judy Holliday, a couple of years earlier, and though I enjoyed it immensely, it didn't give me anything like the incredible rush and sense of belonging that I got at those rock and roll shows.

AROUND THE end of the fifties and beginning of the sixties, girl groups were starting to enter the mostly male-dominated rock and roll world in a big way. And some of them began appearing at, of all places, the Lakeview Inn in Lake Carmel. Groups like the Chantels, the Chiffons, and the Crystals, in their satin sheaths and bouffant wigs, were performing right there in the banquet room of our local pizzeria/restaurant/tavern, and making me dream again. A few years earlier, I had organized a girl group of my own with Joannie (the reluctant ballerina) and my other neighborhood friends Doodoo Devers (who looked like Elizabeth Taylor) and Irene Sayles (whose mom was the recipient of the gossip Valentine). For weeks on end, up on the roof, we diligently practiced an a cappella version of the Four Lovers' "You're the Apple of My Eye." And I even got us an invitation to audition for Ted Mack's *Original Amateur Hour* TV show. But when the time came, our parents all got together and forbade us to go. I'd let my dream of being a singer die for a while after that, but having these girl groups so close at hand certainly rekindled the flame.

I knew I was never gonna sound like Maxine Brown did on "All in My Mind," my favorite song at the time, but I figured my voice could be doctored up like so many of them were. I had already learned about double tracking, echo, and reverb from the DJs, and also about the fact that the real money in the music biz was in the writing. I loved writing poetry, so I figured at least maybe I could be a lyricist one day. I spent most of my All Saints typing classes churning out little verses and choruses. But whenever I showed them to my mother or anyone else to elicit support, I pretty much always got the same response, "Never mind the poetry; just make sure you learn how to type."

I USED to take the bus over to Palisades Amusement Park in New Jersey when I was maybe fifteen or sixteen. One of my favorite TV shows, a kind of local version of *American Bandstand*, was *The Clay Cole Show*. It originated from Palisades Park in the summer months and they had just begun the Miss Teenage America Pageant there, with Clay Cole as the host. I entered my picture and received an invitation to compete. I was so nervous on my way to the contest that I fell and scraped my knee and had to go on stage with a big bloody bandage peeking out from beneath my mint green summer dress. I was chosen as a semifinalist, which was a rush beyond belief. And I immediately started envisioning all kinds of doors opening for me.

A few weeks later, I went back for the finals and got to dance with Clay Cole on TV. But when I wasn't chosen as a finalist, my heart sank and I decided to give up on the idea of beauty contests forever. I figured maybe I really wasn't pretty enough and that they had, perhaps, only chosen me the first time because they felt sorry for the girl with the bandage. Oh well. I was still so young, and I was confident that I'd get into showbiz some day. It was the dawn of a new decade, and I was open to whatever was about to come along.

3

On Becoming a Mad Woman

NEVER PLAYED hooky until my junior year at All Saints, in 1960. I was in and out of the hospital so much with appendicitis and kidney infections that the nuns got used to the idea of me not being around. So I'd leave home in the morning in my uniform and saddle shoes, but instead of going to school, I'd go down to Greenwich Village and walk around all day. The girls I saw there were what I wanted to be—kohl-eyed beatnik beauties in berets, black tights, and ballet slippers, sipping espressos and having intense conversations with men in beards, boatneck sweaters, and sandals. In the afternoon I'd go to the Cafe Wha? on MacDougal Street, drink vanilla ice-cream sodas, and swoon over Tommy Rey and his Trade Winds Steel Drum Band.

I met this guy in his mid-twenties named Fred there once. He wore Zizanie cologne—this was before all of the downtown dykes starting using it—and I went with him to a three-story walk-up apartment a few blocks away. First thing I noticed was a guitar, which struck me as so beat-cliché-perfect, propped up like it was against a bare brick wall. But then I saw a gun on the mantelpiece, which kind of freaked

me out. I was scared, but putting myself in dangerous situations was
fast becoming a turn-on. I was alone with a grown-up beatnik man,
nobody knew where in the world I was, and I had no idea what was
going to happen.

Bless him, though, he never laid a hand on me, and I don't know
what I would have done if he had. We just talked, drank some instant
coffee, and then went back to the Wha. Whatever he'd brought me
home for, he must've changed his mind about it once he realized how
young and dumb I was. Years later, I got into the incredible music and
poetry of Fred Neil ("Love for any time at all is worth the price you
pay to fall") and read that he'd at one time been the MC at the Wha.
And it really made me wonder if it had been him whom I was with.
But then, even though it was a hip scent at the time, I just couldn't
imagine the great Fred Neil ever having worn that awful Zizanie.

ELEANOR GALUCCI was my best friend at All Saints, especially during our senior year. I used to hang out with her after school at Jacobi's
ice cream parlor in Astoria. Eleanor was in love with an adorable Irish
guy named Gil McFarland, who worked as a media buyer at SSC&B
(Sullivan, Stauffer, Colwell & Bayles), a prestigious Manhattan ad
agency. He was a couple of years older than us, and though he loved
Eleanor as a friend, he wasn't attracted to her in a romantic way. Eleanor was quite heavy and was always going on hard-boiled-egg diets
to try to shed the pounds. Meanwhile we consumed vast quantities
of Coca-Cola, banana milk shakes, French fries, and English muf-
fins (the Preludens I shared with her no longer doing much to curb
our appetites), while listening to Carla Thomas, Etta James, Dick
and Deedee, the Shirelles, the Dovells, and the Marcels on Jacobi's
jukebox.

When I could get away with it by telling my mother I was at band
or play practice, I would stay at Jacobi's with Eleanor until 5:30 P.M.
or so, when Gil would stop in on his way home from work. Because of
Eleanor's crush, Gil and I tried hard not to fall in love, but we did any-

way. Eleanor was heartbroken. And though she said she accepted and understood the situation, she soon grew more and more distant from both Gil and me. It was the first time I had ever lost a girlfriend over a boy and I missed her. (I also missed the incredible lasagna her mother used to make when I went over to her house sometimes on Sundays.)

Gil took me to the 82 Club in the East Village for my seventeenth birthday. I put my hair up in a French twist and wore a cobalt-blue-and-black-print jersey sheath and lots of makeup, and nobody asked me for proof of age. The management, waitstaff, and performers at the 82 Club were all drag queens and transsexuals. I had never seen a show like it in my life or been in such a delightfully deceptive atmosphere. You really couldn't tell who was what sex, and many of them were extraordinarily beautiful. My favorite number was done by an older, fat, Sophie Tucker–type drag queen, who wore an evening gown adorned with plastic tomatoes at the bustline and sang "Please Mister, Don't Touch Me Tomatoes."

Gil also took me to my first jazz club, the Village Gate, to see Nina Simone. She completely blew my mind. She was so strong, militant, confrontational, and soulful. I had never seen such a fearless woman or heard such heavy music in my life. Thanks to Gil, my ideas about both showbiz and acceptable female demeanor were being greatly expanded.

Though my cherry had gotten broken somehow on the monkey bars when I was nine, I was still, for all intents and purposes, a virgin and petrified of getting pregnant. So Gil and I only went so far, mostly making out and getting off on the good old fingers stuff I'd tried with a couple of different boys since that first time when I was eleven—especially at Lake Carmel (if my parents only realized), where the boys all had cars to fool around in.

In May of '61 Gil took me to my senior prom, after which we caught Connie Francis's show at the Copacabana. My mom didn't work at the Fourteen anymore and most of the old Copa staff was gone, but it was still a dream come true to be there in my white strapless gown (designed by me and made by my sisters), getting completely wiped out on daiquiris, with a handsome Madison Avenue adman on my arm. I'd thrown a bit of a hissy fit earlier that evening when Gil brought me white baby orchids instead of the pale pink camellias I had so clearly specified. I eventually accepted that camellias were out of season in May, but poor Gil spent much of the night trying to make amends. And, for the first time, I realized how much a little diva power doth humble a man—something I filed away in my brain for possible future use.

When I graduated from All Saints that June, Gil set me up with a Manhattan employment agency and made me promise him one thing—that I wouldn't take a job at SSC&B. But, of course, that's exactly where I wound up, working in the radio/TV traffic department, supplying prints and tapes of SSC&B commercials to radio and TV stations, for a starting salary of sixty-five dollars a week. It was the best job being offered and I figured Gil would understand. Advertising wasn't exactly show business, but it was at least a field with some creative possibilities, showing up more and more in Hollywood movie scenarios back then, so I imagined myself as a kind of Doris Day character and got off on the glamour of it all.

I started at SSC&B a few days before the Fourth of July and Gil was so pissed off, he broke up with me. A sweet, very pretty, and obviously well-bred young woman named Gail Keating, who had been working at SSC&B for a year or two, invited me to spend the holiday weekend with her and a group of the agency's young staffers at a house they had rented on Fire Island. I grew up in Queens on Long Island and had never even heard of Fire Island, which is just off Long Island's southern shore. That's how unsophisticated and uninformed I was. But I was only seventeen and I was always very honest and up-front about how little I knew, which, thankfully, people seemed to find refreshing.

I was still living at home, so I told my parents, with the help of Gail's very chic and modern mother, that I was spending the weekend at the Keatings' summerhouse in the Hamptons. This was one of the many lies I'd tell my parents, having realized that lying was easier than standing up to them. I did, however, lay down the law when it came to my salary: I gave them fifteen dollars a week for room and board and that was it. I was determined to manage my own money—what little there was of it—and not be treated like my poor sister Margaret, who, by then, was pregnant with her second child and saddled with a husband who was drinking.

I fell in love with Fire Island the minute I stepped off of the ferry at Davis Park. And even though I spent almost every weekend there that summer, wearing little more than a bikini, hanging out with suave and swinging Mad men (Madison Avenue ad men)—most of whom were hot to seduce me—I managed to remain a virgin. I almost gave it up once to the writer Nelson Algren (*A Walk on the Wild Side*), because he was so much older (around fifty) than any guy who had ever come on to me, and I found the age thing temptingly perverse. I was a bit of a cock tease, I guess. But I was still hoping to get back together with Gil, and I was still so scared of getting pregnant. (No one ever mentioned condoms back then.) Also, I didn't know anything about oral stuff or even how to give a good hand job, so I was kind of insecure about all of that. I was a Madison Avenue ad woman but I was still such a babe in the woods.

Gil soon forgave me for working at SSC&B, and we got back together and had some steamy moments there, sneaking off to the broom closets, fire exits, and elevators to grab a few kisses and feels. Mad Ave. people got away with murder in the sixties, coming in around nine-thirty, leaving at five, and almost always taking two hours for lunch. So sometimes Gil and I would take the subway to Astoria to make out at his home while his parents were at work. His father was a major jazz fan and we used to play his Dave Brubeck, Wes Montgomery, and Bill Evans records while we were doing it. Oh God, it got me so hot, being naked in his bed, with the chance that any minute we might get caught in the act. I had begun to let him put his penis just a little bit inside of me but always with great fear and never when an orgasm was too near. Poor Gil must have been frustrated, but, in a way, the danger and restraint made it that much more erotic.

✦

THE FIRST time I heard the word *discotheque* was in the fall of 1961, when an SSC&B account exec took me to dinner at a little French restaurant on East 55th Street called Le Club. It was a totally new phenomenon, and I dug the idea of it immediately. A live DJ (called a *discaire* back then) played soft French sounds during dinner and then gradually raised both the volume of the music and the intensity of the beats as everyone took to the dance floor. New York had such restrictive cabaret laws up until then, dictating where you could and couldn't dance, but Le Club called itself *a private club* and got away with it. The fad soon caught on, the laws eventually changed, and a plethora of discotheques followed.

Meanwhile, over on West 45th Street, another phenomenon was just beginning. Those West Side streets were previously infamous for their little dive bars, where sailors, hookers, hustlers, traveling salesmen, and various and assorted manner of regular folks hung out. But in 1961, a club there called the Peppermint Lounge was suddenly playing host to the likes of Judy Garland, Tennessee Williams, Merle Oberon, Truman Capote, Noel Coward, Norman Mailer, and Jackie Kennedy, all happily groovin' together on the tiny dance floor with what they might once have referred to as "a pretty seedy crowd."

Unlike Le Club, the Pepp featured live bands for dancing. Joey Dee and the Starliters was the house band and their song "The Peppermint Twist," and the dance craze it ignited, drew everyone in. My coworker Dolores and I often danced our Friday nights away there, then rolled in to my sister Mary's at 4 A.M., tipsy and exhausted. My parents thought I was staying at Mary's on the weekends in order to help her with the baby, but it was really just so I could stay out late and party. It was the very beginning of the golden age of discos and rock clubs in Manhattan. And, having just turned eighteen, the legal drinking age then, I was at the perfect place in my life to enjoy it.

BY THE start of 1962, Gil had joined the army and I was moving on. I spent his first weekend furlough with him at Fort Dix in New Jersey and then never saw him again. I had a short romance with Bobby Arcaro (son of famed jockey Eddie Arcaro), almost going all the way with him in Bermuda while there with Gail Keating for spring break. (Flying down there was my first commercial airplane trip, and I remember getting all dolled up for it in a navy blue suit, white hat, white gloves, black patent-leather high heels, and nylon stockings.) I dated a couple of art directors from SSC&B—one because he had a sports car and one because he had a plane (a Piper Cub)—but I still kept my virginity intact… well, sort of, anyway.

I WAS happy at SSC&B, but I soon set my sights on being a radio/TV producer. I enrolled in a film production course at the New School for Social Research and decided to move to a smaller agency, where I might stand a better chance for advancement. I liked SSC&B's location at 51st and Lexington; it was convenient for the IRT to Queens and had both a Chock Full o' Nuts (loved their cream cheese on date-and-nut-bread sandwiches) and a great after-work hangout right off the lobby. So I looked on the building's directory for any other ad agencies that might be in the building. There was one called Kastor, Hilton, Chesley, Clifford & Atherton a few floors above SSC&B, and I literally took the elevator up there on a coffee break one day and got a new job. Turned out the friendly, portly gentleman I had started chatting up on the elevator just happened to be Kastor Hilton's personnel manager and within less than fifteen minutes I was hired.

Paradoxically, I think it was my naivete that gave me the confidence people responded to. I knew that women had a hard time being accepted in the ad world, but I somehow just didn't think that it applied to me. And with my long, straight, shiny hair, expensive-looking clothes (I was always able to pluck a gem from the bargain bin), good grooming, and tasteful makeup (B. Altman's Charm School), most people seemed to think I was some sort of debutante. And the more I insisted I wasn't, the more they seemed to think that I was. Without fostering it, I had an air of mystery about me that most other eighteen-year-old career girls did not. I think that may be why so many doors seemed to open so easily for me—that and the fact that because I had already been around such big stars in my life, I had no problem being totally at ease with Madison Avenue ad execs.

I took up my new radio/TV trafficking position at Kastor Hilton and—being immediately efficient at it thanks to my training at SSC&B—had time to begin assisting the radio/TV producers there as well. The people in Kastor Hilton's radio/TV department seemed a bit different somehow, more artsy and bohemian than my coworkers at SSC&B. And it never occurred to me at first, nor did it make any difference when I soon realized, that they were all gay.

One of Kastor Hilton's producers, Macs McAree, was out sick the whole first week I was on the job. By Friday I had spoken with him on the phone a few times and he seemed like a really cool guy. So I asked if I could bring him a pizza for lunch and he was delighted by the idea. Since I was going to Fire Island for the weekend, I had my bikini with me in my overnight bag. I stuck it in my purse and got Dolores to go downtown to Macs's apartment with me. We picked up a pizza in his neighborhood and I changed into the bikini in the hallway of his tenement building, while Dolores hid in the stairwell with my belongings. When Macs opened the door, there I was, someone he'd never met before, dressed only in a yellow-and-white-check bikini and holding a pizza. And all he said was "Oh hi, you must be Kathy. How did you get down here on the subway like that?" It was the beginning of what would turn out to be a lifelong friendship.

ONE SUNDAY at Fire Island, Dolores and I met a really nice guy who invited us to stay at his house in Davis Park for the following weekend. He said he had a roommate, who he was sure wouldn't mind. The next Friday night we arrived, and from the moment I met Alan, the roommate, I just knew what was going to happen. He was Italian, around thirty-five, an ex-army trumpet player, and a Mad man. Alan devoured me with his eyes but took his time with the rest. The whole evening became a kind of erotic ballet. We had dinner at the house, went dancing at the Casino, and then hit a couple of late-night house parties—all the while sending each other sexual vibes that could not be denied. I just couldn't believe what this guy was stirring in me. I was dying to kiss him and to feel his cock inside of me, all the way inside of me. But I also loved the way he was making me wait for it. It was a form of foreplay that lasted for hours. And it really did its magic on me.

Eventually Dolores and I went to our separate single beds in the guest room, but sensing what was coming, neither of us fell asleep—though Dolores did a pretty good job of pretending. My heart was beating so fast as Alan entered the darkened room, slipped into my bed, and took over the choreography from there. He was a sexual master—with my limited experience, at least, he sure seemed to be. The incredible release I felt from letting him lead me further and further into complete sexual rapture was miraculous, a major awakening for me. I was eighteen and I had finally gone *all the way*, without any thought of the taboos and with what I recognized right away to be an insatiable hunger for more.

Alan went back to his regular thirty-something girlfriend the next weekend, but I was into being a free spirit anyway. So, though my ego was momentarily crushed, I really didn't mind all that much, and I proceeded to go on an all-out sexual spree. Of course, it took a while before I gained any real finesse at it. With the first guy I fucked after Alan, I was on top and had come with such gusto that I didn't realize I was actually pissing all over him as well. He freaked out something awful and got really prissy and mean. And I was devastated. Of course, later on in life, I learned that there are guys in this world who quite enjoy a nice warm golden shower now and then.

FATE HAD smiled on me when I sought out Kastor Hilton. It was the first ad agency to ever be charged with fraud, resulting from a historic court case over their ad campaign for the enormously successful Regimen Diet Pills—which, when tested, were proven to be totally ineffective for weight loss. It gave the place a kind of weird, offbeat cachet that really made me feel like I belonged there. And I blossomed there in both my social and professional life. I even dropped out of my film production classes, because I was learning so much more and so much faster on the job.

My coworkers became like family, the kind of family I craved—exceedingly liberal, completely supportive, well informed, creative, cheerful, and totally kooky. There was Macs, of course, who, after the bikini/pizza incident, introduced me to marijuana, underground filmmaking, and the downtown art scene. But there was also Louise, who set me up with a gynecologist to get my first diaphragm and whose brother used to playfully whip and fuck me in front of everyone at the after-work get-togethers we'd have at their apartment; Tom, with whom I drank Thunderbird wine, made 8mm movies, and tried, unsuccessfully, to have sex; Dick, the head of the department, who tolerated and encouraged us all in our craziness; and Nancy, who got me into Herbert Berghof's scene study class without an audition (the showbiz bug still in my blood) and gave me the biggest break of my advertising career.

Nancy was a radio/TV producer and also the agency's casting director, one of the very few females (if not the only one) to hold that dual position on Madison Avenue at the time. She took me under her wing at Kastor Hilton, and I assisted her on all of her shoots and voice-over, editing, casting, and sound-mixing sessions. She even gave me one of her accounts as my own, the *New York Journal-American,* a popular newspaper of the day. When Nancy decided to leave the agency to become an actress and a social worker, she recommended to Dick King that I get her job. I think what my coworkers liked most about me was that I was simply too young to have become jaded yet and I got off on making even the most mundane radio and TV commercials—that and the fact that I was such an open-minded little freak when it came to all of our sex and social lives.

So there I was, at nineteen, a full-fledged radio/TV producer and casting director with my own accounts (Orafix Denture Adhesive,

Ora Denture Cleanser, Yodora Deodorant, and the *New York Journal-American*), an office with a window, and a paycheck in the hundreds—not to mention an assortment of male model boyfriends. I was hanging out at PJ Clarke's, wearing dresses from Bloomingdale's Y.E.S. (Young East Sider) shop and shoes by Roger Vivier, and being wined and dined by models, actors, announcers, and the heads of jingle houses, production houses, and recording studios. Barely two years out of high school, I must have been the youngest producer/casting director in the biz, certainly the youngest female. Though I didn't even realize what a miracle that was at the time.

Meanwhile, I was still living at home with my parents, though I was rarely ever there. When I was, I hardly ever spoke to them. And when I did, I lied, saying that on all of the nights I was away from home, I was either sleeping over at a girlfriend's apartment or on a location shoot for Kastor Hilton. I felt bad about shutting them out of my life, but my mom had already suffered another stroke—and knowing even half of what I was getting up to would probably have given her a fatal one. My sister Mary was the only family member I confided in. And even then, I didn't tell her everything.

BY THE summer of 1963, I had already become quite familiar with booze, grass, hash, coke, speed, opium, uppers, downers, and hallucinogens—mostly hallucinogens, like mescaline, peyote, and psilocybin, because they were my favorites. There was still a lot of innocence to the sex stuff I was doing, one-on-ones for the most part and some lighthearted hetero group scenes with my Fire Island roommates. Our geodesic dome was known as the Whipped Cream House because of the notorious whipped cream parties we held there every weekend, as evidenced by the cases of ReddiWip waiting for us at the loading dock each Friday night and the many empty cans in Sunday's trash.

One night out there I encountered two famous male models, Michael Welch and Farrell Connor, as they were getting off of the ferry—and within minutes found myself fucking Michael in the sand dunes. Afterward, he decided I was more suited for his buddy Farrell. So I went with them to the house where they were staying and fucked Farrell all night long. Farrell and I proceeded to have a steady, but open romantic relationship over the next few years. He once brought a beautiful high-priced hooker home to bed with us in the city, but I wasn't yet ready for that. However, when he brought a black man named Mal Stevens to the beach house one day, I was more than ready for what he had to offer. No, not sex (Mal had a gorgeous platinum-blonde girlfriend) but the sacred elixir of life—pure, clear, liquid LSD.

I can still see Mal standing at the kitchen counter in the middle of the dome, carefully dropping the acid onto the tiny sugar cubes with an eyedropper. He was putting so much on them that the cubes were partially breaking down and dissolving onto the aluminum foil beneath them. Mal promised that I'd get way higher with acid than with organic hallucinogens and that I wouldn't even have to throw up. It was the start of a love affair with LSD, which lasted about ten years. Along with pot, it was my number-one drug of choice. Of course, I still had a huge supply of Preludins, which I continued to take every day as if they were vitamin pills. I just layered all of the other drugs on top of 'em.

History has painted a picture of the initial LSD boom as starting among the artistic hippie fringe, and it might have been that way in L.A. and San Francisco. But in New York, it was the advertising community—the clean-cut, buttoned-up, Brooks Brothers types, who years later would be labeled "yuppies"—that first embraced LSD. They may have been upstanding junior account executive trainees during the week, but on the weekends, especially on Fire Island where so many of them partied, they were tripping the heights fantastic on LSD. Outsiders often looked to their Mad Ave. friends to score, because they knew the supply on the Avenue was abundant and pure. And that, of course, was due in large part to Mal Stevens.

Mal was highly visible, because he was the only black man at that time in Fire Island's Davis Park. And pretty soon he was supplying

LSD to our friends and fellow Mad Avers in the houses all around us. You could tell who was on it when we went to the beach, because we all used to lie on top of each other forming what we called a human pyramid, and we'd stay like that for what seemed like hours on end. We were so obviously and blatantly stoned out of our heads. But LSD had yet to be declared illegal, so we felt free to be as freaky and outrageous as we liked. What a great time it was to be so young, so free, and so high.

AROUND 1963 or '64 I started heading down to the Bitter End, the Gaslight Cafe, Gerde's Folk City, and the Cafe Au Go Go in the Village to check out the folk musicians I'd been hearing about, like Bob Dylan, Eric Andersen, Phil Ochs, Bob Gibson, and Tim Hardin. I was especially enamored with a trio of brothers (later a duo) called the Dalton Boys, and I wound up having sex more than a few times with Jack, the youngest one, for whom I really had the hots. Competing with the other girls in the audience for Jack's affections and getting to sleep with him after the shows added a whole new dimension to lovemaking for me. It was with Jack Dalton, I guess, that my sexual addiction for musicians really began to take hold.

IN 1964, not long after the Birmingham riots, Kastor Hilton sent me to what were still being called "Negro radio stations" in five Southern cities to produce local radio commercials for Yodora Deodorant, which we claimed in our ads was "especially made for black skin." Can you imagine how controversial a claim that would be today? Kastor Hilton would be looking at its second major lawsuit for sure. But Madison Avenue's political incorrectness was nothing compared to the segregation that was still going on in the South back then. Being there and seeing for the first time those "whites only" signs and the degree of hatred that went along with them really drove home the fact that the *soul* I related to in the best rock and roll was the result of someone's deep emotional pain ... but the music was also, of course, a way to exorcise it.

One night, the station owner in the Dallas–Fort Worth area—a white Colonel Sanders–type with a big Cadillac (all of the Negro station owners were white and had big Cadillacs)—took me to a nightclub run by one of his DJs. It was in a double-wide trailer along the highway between the two cities. He and I were the only white people there and it was the sexiest atmosphere I had ever experienced—lit only by black light, the air a purple haze of marijuana and cigarette smoke, and couples bumping and grinding unabashedly to recordings by Theola Kilgore, Solomon Burke, the Earls, Baby Washington, Bobby Bland, Sunny and the Sunglows, Dale and Grace, Ruby and the Romantics, and Garnet Mimms and the Enchanters. Of course, the Colonel didn't think it would be right for me to join them, so I just sat there in my whiteness, sipping my 7 and 7, and taking it all in.

The whole scene had gotten me so horny that, within minutes of the Colonel dropping me off at my hotel, I picked up the leader of a Boy Scout troop (the hotel was hosting a Boy Scout convention) in the bar and fucked him for hours. But more important than the effect it had on my libido, being at that nightclub had really put a fire under me. Despite the racial prejudice they had to endure, everyone there seemed to know how to rise above it all and have a good time. And the major driving force that lifted their spirits was, of course, the music. I really liked making radio and TV commercials; in its most creative aspects it was almost like being in showbiz. But I made a secret vow that night that one day, no matter how long it took, I'd be working in *real* show business, maybe even in the area of it I loved the most—music.

4

Out There

NEW YORK was a microcosm of the whole hip world in the sixties, and Fire Island was a microcosm of the microcosm ... a string bean of white sand jutting brazenly eastward into the Atlantic ... wild, windswept, and pulsating with bass riffs and rock beats from the glass and bleached-wood houses. Fire Island was our Atlantis—with no cars, no roads, no neon signs, and no attitude about whatever you were into. Walking the well-worn boardwalks in the early August sun, barefoot and naked except for a tiny bikini and big sunglasses, your acid aura connecting, colliding, coalescing like a sex act in the air with everyone you passed, wanting for nothing but whatever came your way—man, that was my idea of an ideal summer day.

When the tide was low, I'd walk for hours along the hard-packed sand at the water's edge, the warmth of the sun on my body and the cool of the waves at my feet—heaven on earth for me. One day at low tide, I walked with Farrell and Michael to Fire Island Pines, a community about four miles down the beach to the west of Davis Park. They had a friend there named Hal Fredericks, an artist who was confined to a wheelchair for life as the result of a jeep accident he'd had while in the army. Hal was gay, as was just about everyone in the

Pines, it seemed. I was both fascinated and fine with that and my model boys seemed quite comfortable with it as well.

We stayed at Hal's that night and by the next day I knew I'd never be content with Davis Park again. The Pines was so much richer, prettier, more sophisticated, more glamorous, and more intriguing. Its inhabitants came from more diverse and artistic fields of endeavor, not just Madison Avenue. And they seemed to be indulging in just as many drugs as we were in Davis Park, except maybe for LSD—a situation I would soon remedy, of course, by taking many of them on their first acid trips.

I was welcomed into the Pines with open arms, especially by a handsome gay man named David Barrett. David was a prominent interior decorator with an antique shop on Manhattan's Upper East Side. He and his older lover, George, had a house on the bay, complete with swimming pool, guesthouse, and grand piano. I wound up staying there a lot during those early sixties summers. David had such an elegant, gracious, yet totally relaxed style of living and entertaining, and he was delighted that I was always up for helping him out in the kitchen and playing "cohostess" (as he called it) for his many laugh-filled luncheons and parties.

One of George and David's best friends was the burlesque star Gypsy Rose Lee. She had given them a few trunks filled with her old costumes, which they stored downstairs at the house and let their friends rummage through for drag. At some point during almost every one of their parties, you could count on at least one of the guests—usually a balding, pudgy queen—teetering up the spiral staircase in high heels, long gloves, pasties, and a G-string. It always got a laugh, and it always got me thinking about showbiz again. Unfortunately, I never did meet Gypsy, but I once spent a lovely weekend there with the actress Claudette Colbert.

The most beautiful boys in the world were at the Pines in those days, including some very horny hetero ones like Super Surfer and Super Sidekick. And David and George, besides treating *me* so graciously, always welcomed them and all of my numbers, gay and straight alike, to their house. When it came to our sexcapades, David had only one rule. And we'd all laugh when he'd say it—"No jism in the pool."

ON MY twenty-first birthday in 1964, I finally moved out of my parents' apartment—against their wishes, of course. I had mostly been staying at Farrell's until then, but the situation with him eventually got to be more than I could handle. Farrell was the funniest, sweetest, most entertaining guy you could ever dream of, especially when stoned on pills, pot, or psychedelics. But when he drank too much, he would often snap and turn into a monster. And he'd taken to demanding strange things of me, like that I strip naked and scrub his bathroom from top to bottom each night before he'd fuck me. Stupid me, for a while I thought it was exciting to be dominated like that, to be dabbling in S&M. But then one night, after numerous Irish coffees at PJ Clarke's, Farrell went a bit too far. I often wore his clothes when I stayed over unprepared, and that night he got physically violent with me because I couldn't kick-start his motor scooter while wearing his flip-flops, which were, of course, way too big for me.

I was mortified, because everyone near the front window in PJ's had seen him manhandle me and shove me hard. And I was afraid that when we got to his place, he was gonna hurt me even more. So, as soon as we got there, I started to change into my own clothes to go home. But before I could, he grabbed me, pushed me out into the hallway, and locked the door. He lived on the ground floor, so I was actually in the building's lobby, and I was totally naked. I begged him for my clothes and purse, but he just opened the door, quickly threw out my trench coat and one of my shoes, and ignored my further pleas. Luckily, my keys were in my coat pocket and, miraculously, I found a sympathetic cab driver, who took me home to Queens on the promise that I'd send him the fare in the mail. And, bless his heart, when he dropped me off, he told me to forget about it. Thank God my mom and dad were asleep when I got in.

The next day, Farrell claimed he couldn't remember any of it and accused me of making it all up. Then he called my parents and asked them if he could marry me. And my parents, not knowing anything about him, except that he was Irish, Catholic, successful, and good looking, said of course. This was my second marriage proposal, Gil having asked me upon his going into the army. But I still wasn't ready to marry anyone. I wanted to be free to revel in the new wave of permissiveness and promiscuity that was just taking hold, when at last a lusty young woman like me could play the sex game the way men had been playing it for so long.

I soon began a new phase of my life, living at last in my own apartment—well, one I shared with two roommates. Finally, I could come and go as I pleased without having to lie to anybody or scrub anyone's bathroom to get laid. I could blast the Ronettes, the Beach Boys, the Rolling Stones, the Dave Clark Five, Marvin Gaye, Rufus Thomas, Otis Redding, Chuck Berry, Darlene Love, and, most of all, the Beatles on my own stereo. And I could smoke all of the pot, take all of the acid, and have all of the sex I wanted. The sexual revolution had just begun, though, so young women like me still had to be quite brave to take on the label of "playgirl"—which, in polite society, of course, still definitely had the connotation of "whore."

ONCE IN your life you should have the white-light acid trip. It's the one that shows you nirvana and the one that prepares you for your eventual and inevitable moment of physical death, when the act of letting go is of the utmost importance. The only way I've ever been able to describe it is that it's both nothingness and everything-ness all at the same time. There is absolutely no want, only absolute bliss. I had mine there in my very first apartment at 250 Riverside Drive in Manhattan.

Michael Welch was dating my roommate Andrea at the time, and they were tripping in the living room along with my other roommate, Andrea's sister Gail. Andrea and Gail were kind of on the hippie side when it came to housekeeping, so the huge, rambling apartment was pretty much a mess—not really dirty, just jumbled and chaotic. But my room was spotless and orderly, an incense-scented sanctuary with very little furniture, and, since it was at the deep end of the U-shaped building, it also had a wonderfully framed Hudson River view. Horizontally, boats passed through it rather quickly; vertically, the sunsets lasted long and tinted the white walls a lovely pink.

The acid was just coming on, always the strongest part of the trip. I was curled up in a fetal position on my bed. Death or the other dimension—whatever you wanna call it—beckoned me more strongly than ever before. And I was, as always in that first phase of a trip, really scared. But I let go, surrendering completely, allowing myself to free-fall into the abyss, to go wherever the forces wanted to take me. And once I did, I became totally fearless, totally bodiless, and totally happy. I don't know how long it lasted. Even time did not exist there. But in those few seconds, minutes, or hours, I believe I got a glimpse of what's on the other side. And, cliché as it may sound, it was truly nothing but light—just pure, white, all-encompassing, all-fulfilling, all-knowing, all-loving light. I had never experienced any trip quite like that one and I never traveled as far out there again. It was the trip I would hold in my heart forever, the one that made me unafraid to die, which in turn, I believe, made me unafraid to live.

THE PARTIES at the Pines were amazing affairs, complete with fanciful themes, Hollywood-like sets, giant sound systems, DJs, booze, and drugs. And in the summer of '65, a couple of older queens named Sam Hadad and Royal Marks decided they would throw the most elaborate and decadent party of the season, calling it "The Bacchanal." I was staying at a rented house with my friends Dick Villany, a decorator in the David Barrett mode, but with a less affluent clientele; Franklyn Welsh, the best, though as-yet-undiscovered, makeup artist and hair stylist in the world; Barry dePrendergast, a wily wheeler-dealer and model from Ireland; and Loy Mazor, a notorious speed freak. Loy mainlined methedrine to the point where his skin had taken on a pallor that was decidedly gray.

Franklyn made me the most divine toga from one of the lightweight linen bedspreads and did my hair in a curly Grecian updo adorned with baby's breath from Dickie Decorator's living room flower arrangement. We were just about ready to leave for the party and already tanked-up on pot and God knows what, when Loy asked if I'd like to try some speed. Never having shot it, I was, of course, up for the adventure.

Franklyn held the belt tightly around my arm while Loy stuck the needle in my vein. The rush was immediate. I slumped to the floor in a moment of orgasmic ecstasy, pulled Franklyn, a rather shy homo-sexual, to me and French kissed him so deeply he was in complete shock. "That good, huh?" he marveled, realizing how high I must have been. Everyone else was yelling that we should hurry up lest we miss the party. But I was so on fire with sexual desire, I just wanted to fuck somebody, anybody, right then and there before leaving the house. Alas though, it was a house full of homos and none of them were into girls. So I pulled myself together, hit the boards with them, and headed for The Bacchanal.

It was a daytime party, and as we neared the house, we saw legions of scantily costumed boys on the various boardwalks leading to it, their muscular sun-kissed bodies as tempting as Greek gods' in the afternoon light. I was still rushing and so incredibly horny; I just had to quickly find a straight or bi one to fuck me. We were greeted with some magic punch at the door of the party—just what I needed on top of the speed!

Upstairs in the main room there was a huge table, the centerpiece of which was a stunningly beautiful boy, reclining naked except for a laurel wreath in his hair and some grapes covering the lower part of his torso. He poured wine for the guests from an ancient-style urn, and as I offered my glass to be filled, I looked into his eyes and caught the hetero vibe. "Ah, a real woman," he cooed. And that was it. Within seconds, his fruit and my toga pushed aside, I was up on the table having sex with him. Suddenly, as if seen through a fish-eye lens, there were hordes of sex-hungry faces looking down at us, their hands all over his ass as he was thrusting his cock into me. I found it all so excitingly surreal, so Fellini-esque, and so fitting with the theme of the party. I felt no shame or contrition at all.

But Sam and Royal were outraged and decided I had ruined their party. They intervened before either of us got to come, and they took the boy away before I even got to know his name. He was ordered to stay in a downstairs bedroom until they sent him back to the mainland on the next boat, and I was ordered to leave the party, never to see my sweet momentary Adonis again. The next day I was the talk of the island, and everyone was divided into two camps: those who congratulated and high-fived me, and those who scolded and scorned me. But I felt I had taught them all a lesson. You throw a bacchanal, you put a naked boy on the table, and you give out magic punch—what do you expect?

I think the only problem anyone there really had with it is that I was a woman. Had it been two boys going at it, it might have been OK. But apparently, they had hired the boy through an ad in the *Village Voice* and had no idea that he was straight. Anyway, Sam and Royal should have been eternally grateful to me for my performance and to Loy for supplying the speed. Their party became the stuff of Fire Island legend, not only for that summer, but for many summers that followed.

MY ADVERTISING career was rolling along quite nicely in 1965, but what I really reveled in was Manhattan nightlife, which was in super–high gear at the time. Except for my little forays to the Village for my acting classes with Herbert Berghof and my folk music, underground movie, and art fixes, I was pretty much an uptown girl. So I mostly hit the uptown clubs like Shepheard's, Il Mio, Ondine, and L'Interdit, eventually narrowing it down to my two favorites, Arthur and Aux Puces. They were all in easy walking distance from my new apartment at 404 East 55th Street—a tiny $85-a-month studio in a prewar building with an elevator and doorman and no roommates. With its alternate entrance at 405 East 54th Street, the building was known as "the four out of five," meaning four out of every five of its tenants were gay.

Farrell lived a block and a half away, and I still slept with him on and off. I even cast him in a Tiger aftershave commercial for Kastor Hilton. He asked me to marry him again, and when I said no, he told me he was going on a trip to Miami (where he'd been a pool boy at the Fontainebleau before becoming a model) and would pop the question to the first girl he met. Sure enough, he proposed to the stewardess on the plane going down there and she accepted. After a week or so of married life, Farrell took his bride's brand-new Mustang, drove thirty-six-hours straight through from Florida to New York, and came knocking at my door. He was all speedy from uppers and wanted to take me out to dinner at PJ Clarke's. As soon as we got there, the waiters and regulars started coming by our table and congratulating us both on the marriage, to which Farrell delighted in replying, "No, my wife's in Florida. Kathy's still my girlfriend." Afterward, we went to his place and made love as though nothing had changed.

A couple of months later, he talked me into accompanying him and his wife, Mary, on a trip to his hometown of Waterbury, Connecticut, to introduce Mary to his family. I took my friend Cliff Jahr along. Cliff was an in-the-closet ad man I'd nicknamed "Cookie Jahr" (who, years later, as an out journalist, got Elton John to admit that he was bisexual). I figured Cliff's presence would keep me from succumbing to any sexual scenarios Farrell might have had in mind, though none ensued. I did hook up with him one more time after that, though, at the swanky Palm Bay Club in Miami, where we soon got thrown out for creating such a ruckus with our druggy sex romp.

Farrell and Mary stayed together and had a son. I remained friends with Farrell and ran into him now and then when he was in New York. And then one day I got the news that he had died in a car crash in Miami—the way he always wanted to go, fast.

❧

AUX PUCES means "of the fleas" or "flea market," and Nilo dePaul named his discotheque that because everything in it was for sale. If you liked the chair you were sitting on, the table you were at, or the birdcage hanging over your head, you could buy it and take it home with you. Nilo was truly a Renaissance man. There was nothing that he couldn't do and do well—sing, dance, play piano, draw, paint, cook, design buildings, make couture clothing, breed and break horses, whatever. He was also a major sensualist, savoring and teaching his friends to savor the finest of everything, be it wine, food, fashion, ballet, Broadway, limos, or good lighting. And, of course, Nilo and I shared an appreciation for the beautiful boys he had working at his club.

Frank Loverde was Aux Puces's DJ and he played a much more ballsy, bluesy, and eclectic mix of music than was being played at the other New York discos—mostly Motown, funk, Philly sound, and soul but often mixed with a French pop or English rock track, an operatic aria, or a momentary waltz. Aux Puces became known for its opulence and intimacy, its gay, straight, hooker, drug-dealer, socialite, and celebrity clientele, but most of all for its fabulous music. Since I spent lots of time there and had become close with both Nilo and Frank, they welcomed my offer to spin the records for free for an hour or two each night, allowing Frank a couple of nice long cigarette (or whatever) breaks.

Eventually, I became the official DJ on Wednesdays and Sundays, earning fifty dollars a night and never having to pay for food or drinks. I still worked full-time in advertising and also part-time at Bloomingdale's on Thursday nights and Saturdays (where I got an employee discount on my Young East Sider outfits), but I had finally made that all-important shift. I was a professional DJ, the only female spinning at a New York club at the time. I was, to some degree anyway, in the music business! Before long, Frank Loverde moved on to a recording career of his own and I was spinning five nights a week, with a cute young guy named Jay Martin filling in for me here and there. And, thanks to Nilo's generosity, I was also learning the epicurean

pleasures of Chateau Margaux '62, Chateau Latour '55, Chevalier-
Montrachet '61, and Chateau d'Yquem '59.

WITH ALL of the sex, drugs, and rock and roll in our lives, most of
us New York twentysomethings had hardly noticed that the war in
Vietnam was escalating to the point of pure carnage. But by 1965 or
'66, even party girls like me followed the lead of activists and college
students around the country and took to the streets to protest. I knew
I wasn't educated or dedicated enough to be any kind of leader in the
antiwar movement, but when the marches were held in Washington,
D.C., and New York, I felt a great sense of worth just being there and
being counted. I was a part of what Allen Ginsberg had just named
"flower power."

     The stars of the movement, in addition to Ginsberg, were guys like
Abbie Hoffman, Jerry Rubin, Tom Hayden, David Dellinger, and
Lawrence Ferlinghetti. We were finally looking up to these intellec-
tual, civilly disobedient peaceniks as our idols, not just to rock stars
and actors anymore (though the rock stars and actors usually tended
to be cuter). Our values were changing, and, naive though it may
have been, we thought the whole world was changing too—the much
hoped-for commodity at the end of the rainbow no longer being gold,
but rather peace. Of course, this didn't mean we were doing any less
drugging or fucking. Our motto, after all, was "Make love, not war."
And I, for one, was determined to live up to that credo.

KEEPING UP with the schedule I was on back then would have been
impossible were it not for the drugs. And in 1966, I got introduced
to the in-crowd's newest elixir, Dr. Bishop's vitamin shots. At thirty-
five dollars a pop, they were pretty expensive, but one or two a day
would keep you up forever and keep you looking fresh and vibrant the
whole time. I forget who first introduced me to Dr. Bishop. It might
have been Joel Schumacher (one of the original Paraphernalia design-

ers), whom I'd recently met at the Pines, or Wally Graham, a friend of Joel's I knew from Mad Ave. Anyway, someone had to bring you there. You couldn't just walk in off of the street.

Dr. Bishop's office was located on the ground floor of a high-rise near First Avenue and later in a mansion at 53rd and Madison. It was a scene so quintessentially *sixties,* you just couldn't even imagine a doctor's office like it today. The clubby drug buzz in the waiting room was so dense and intense, you got high on anticipation just walking in there. The "nurses" (none of us knew or cared if they were really nurses or not) wore seductively modern sportswear and often pulled down your pants and gave you your shot in the hallway, while the examining rooms might be occupied by Dr. Bishop giving someone the sixty-dollar special and/or somebody "having a bad reaction." Everyone was always in a rush, wanted to be seen first, had somewhere to be, had a taxi waiting, whatever. But then once they got that shot in the ass, they often couldn't tear themselves away from the chemically and socially charged atmosphere and would get caught up in the speed-rap session that was always going on among the patients.

When the taste of the iron, or whatever it was, hit your mouth, you started getting off on the shot. And as long as the soreness in your ass lasted, your stamina pretty much lasted too, a good six to eight hours anyway. The first half hour after the shot was dangerous, because you often got a sudden urge to shop, buy someone a gift, spend the rent money on something pretty. And right across the street from the 53rd Street office was a shop called Hunter's World and, oh my God, how many elephant-hair bracelets and zebra-skin notebooks could anyone possibly need? (This was long before PETA, of course.) The other temptation was a nearby crystal and rock shop, where it was especially hard to resist the colorful sparklers.

Dr. Bishop had his favorite patients, especially the one male and one female he'd singled out from each sign of the zodiac. I was his Libra girl. I can't believe I actually had a huge sense of pride about that. It meant that, along with the vitamins and speed, my shot might get an extra dose of whatever he was experimenting with that week—

things like adrenaline stimulants, niacin, and even LSD. And he'd have his favorites call him about an hour after getting the shot to let him know what we were feeling. This guy was using us all as guinea pigs, and I thought he was some kind of savior, freeing us from the need for food and sleep.

One night Dr. Bishop came by Aux Puces while I was spinning and offered me a free shot of something special if I'd come to his office after work. All night at the turntables my mouth was watering with the prospect of what was to come. And as soon as we closed I ran the two blocks over there to take him up on his offer. As his building's open-sided elevator rose through its Day-Glo painted, black-lit shaft, I felt positively dizzy with excitement. A minute later I was alone with Dr. B. in his fabulous office space, with its high ceilings, mahogany paneled walls, dance studio, and all of those delicious drugs in the cabinets. He loaded the needles and instructed me to slap his ass, poke him fast, and slowly push the plunger on the first one. And then he shot me up with the second. A few minutes later, he had his fingers up my pussy and I was rushing beyond belief.

Pretty soon, I was going kind of numb all over, even in my brain. Then, all of a sudden there was blood everywhere and Dr. Bishop just laughed and said rather flippantly, "My dear, you're bleeding. Maybe you should see a doctor." I knew I didn't have my period and I didn't feel any pain, but the shock of seeing the blood running down my legs made me come to my senses. Even though the bleeding seemed to be subsiding, I just wanted to get out of there and get away from him as fast as I could. It wasn't easy, since he'd become quite perturbed and paranoid about the fact that I was leaving.

I went back to Aux Puces, where the new maitre d', David Smith, was tripping after hours with Jay Martin and a couple of friends. I banged desperately hard on the locked front door and, luckily, they heard me above the loud music they were playing. My shaken state and gory story must have been a real bummer for them on their LSD high, but they snapped into action immediately and got a limo to take me to the emergency room. Turned out I had cuts and scratches inside my vagina, maybe made by a ring or a more sinister object, though the doctors said no major damage had been done. By that time the bleeding had stopped, and I still wasn't feeling any pain. Though questioned, I refused to rat out Dr. Bishop and was quickly released. I went back to join the gang at Aux Puces, where we opened a few bottles of Chateau Lafite Rothschild '61, smoked some hash-oiled joints, and partied until dawn.

I HADN'T really fallen in love with anyone since Farrell and, despite some of the situations I'd gotten myself into, I was thoroughly enjoying being single and free. I'd met some darling guys and had some wonderfully sensual affairs, but I often took stupid chances and cheapened myself just to get laid. There were times when I'd be out on the town for the night without scoring a number. So I'd hail a cab to go home but reject each one that stopped until I found one with a fuckable driver I could invite upstairs for a quickie. I was emulating the behavior of the gay boys I knew who romanticized their anonymous sexcapades, telling me tales of orgy rooms at the baths and the shadowy scene at "the trucks." I was trying to be as debauched and decadent as they were, forgetting the fact that I was a twenty-three-year-old, rather vulnerable, heterosexual woman.

And then there was Carlos. I met Carlos at El Morocco, which was two blocks away from my apartment. He was a luscious Latino in an impeccably tailored suit, and I immediately invited him to come home and have sex with me. He insisted we take his car, and right away I should have realized that something was up. There was a really big dog in the car, barking his head off. Carlos started horsing around with him in what appeared to be a very brutal manner. I brushed off my suspicions, though, chalking it up to some macho man/beast game the two of them were used to playing, and got in the car for the two-minute ride to my apartment.

Carlos locked the dog in the car and came upstairs. He was a powerfully built young man and extremely aggressive. Within no time he'd ripped off my clothes, pushed me onto the sofa, and was mounting me from behind. He still had all his clothes on and was dry-humping with no penetration. I liked to play rough and weird sometimes, so I didn't complain. But all too soon, his hands were around my neck, getting tighter and tighter, making it increasingly hard for me to breathe. And while that seemed to be getting him more and more excited, it was scaring the hell out of me. I thought to myself, this is it, you've gone too far, this is how you're gonna die. I dug my nails into his wrists, tried to pry away his hands, and begged him to stop, but it was difficult to get out the words, and he really wasn't paying attention anyway. Then, with every ounce of strength in me, I managed to squirm out of the chokehold he had me in, grab my coat from the floor, and run out of my apartment and down the eight flights of stairs to the lobby, afraid of waiting for the elevator lest he follow me.

I asked the doorman if he would call the police for me from the phone booth on the corner. He said he couldn't leave his post, but he gave me a dime to make the call. It was three in the morning, but barefoot and naked except for my coat, I walked the half block to the corner. There had been snow, then freezing rain, that night, so each step felt like I was breaking through the glassy sugar topping of a crème brûlée. And my feet were going completely numb.

New York City cops are so great. Without treating me like the dumb slut I obviously was, they escorted me back up to my apartment to deal with Carlos, who was just sitting there waiting as though nothing had happened. Their presence seemed to shock him into a kind of obstinate sobriety. He started ranting and raving that his father was with the Colombian consulate and that nothing I'd say against him would stick. But once he realized I wasn't pressing charges, he shut up and left pretty quickly.

One of the cops escorted Carlos down to his car, while the other stayed behind to give me a little pep talk about being more careful in the future. But all the while he was talking to me, I just couldn't help but think how cute the cop was and how naked I was underneath my coat. I had possibly just come close to dying, thanks to my addiction to sex—and what was I thinking about, more sex. No wonder I was no longer picking at my skin and mutilating my body. I had simply traded one OCD for another. I never saw a shrink back then or was diagnosed as such, but it would certainly seem I had become a nymphomaniac.

5

Thistle

DROPPED OUT of Herbert Berghof's scene study class, because Mr. Berghof said pretty much the same thing every week—that we had to be "like children playing make-believe," behaving like kids do when they think no adults are watching. He said that once children know that someone is watching, they become little fakes, *acting* their roles instead of *playing* them. I totally understood what he meant. I also noted that he always gave high marks to any female student doing a scene where she had to take her clothes off, provided she did it unself-consciously. And that was something I had already mastered.

I was working at a small production company called Anglofilms, but I was hanging out with Macs McAree from Kastor Hilton more than ever. Macs had moved to a top-floor, East Village loft, decorated with white silk parachutes, beanbag chairs, and mattresses on the floor. It was a great place for group tripping and for making Macs's underground movies. Plus, we could climb up the fire escape and hang out on his roof in good weather. It was on an acid trip at Macs's that I chose my first fantasy name, Thistle. Taking on a new name was a way of giving myself permission be a bigger-than-life version of who I already was, to live in real life as the character I wanted to play. It was supposed to be just a one-name name, but Macs's downtown friends mostly wound up calling me Thistle Dorritie.

Macs was a part owner of the New York Six Art Gallery on St. Marks Place, and he himself painted in a style he called "determinate plasticism." I occasionally posed nude for Mel Leipzig, one of the New York Six artists. He once gave me a painting of myself standing naked in the kitchen of his downtown flat. And I actually threw it away some years later, because I was living out of a suitcase at the time and because I thought it made me look too fat. What an asshole I was about art. Mel's works now hang in the White House, the Whitney, and the Cooper-Hewitt National Design Museum. Oh well. At least I knew the romance of a pre-gentrified, pre-commercialized SoHo, when it was all about the factories by day and the A.I.R. (Artist in Residence) parties by night. A painter named Lucio Pozzi threw the biggest and best of 'em. And yes, Thistle took her clothes off at a few.

RUDOLF NUREYEV, Margot Fonteyn, Gary Chryst, Jackie Kennedy, Salvador Dalí, Francesco Scavullo, Michael York, Franco Zeffirelli, Miles Davis, Judy Garland, Odetta, and newlyweds Peter Allen and Liza Minnelli were but a few of the stars who came to Aux Puces on a regular basis. And thanks to David Smith's relationship with Peter Allen (they were former lovers), I too became friends with Peter and Liza. Many nights after Aux Puces closed around 2 A.M., the four of us would run over to Arthur to catch the last few dances there and then go to the brasserie on 53rd Street for breakfast or to Peter and Liza's apartment on 57th Street to drink champagne.

The real stars of Aux Puces, however, as far as we on the staff were concerned, were the waiters and waitresses, all of whom Nilo had handpicked for their beauty and charisma. And the biggest star of them all was Richard (pronounced Ree-shard) Thuilliette. Richard had just come to the United States from France. He modeled under the name Christian Cau in the daytime and worked at Aux Puces at night. He had big, dark, innocent eyes, spoke almost no English, and was completely adorable. I soon fell madly in love with him. Only problem, besides the language barrier, was that Richard was totally gay. And—unlike with other gay boys I'd drugged into sexual surrender—because I was so in love with him, I just couldn't be that aggressive with Richard. I wanted to be around him as much as possible, without him ever having to fear that I'd embarrass him in that way.

Richard's English improved quickly, and the more I got to know him, the more in love with him I fell. We became extremely close, even going away for weekends together, often sleeping in the same bed, our warm, naked bodies entwined. But it never went any further than him kissing the back of my neck, the side of my face, or the top of my shoulder. I wanted to make love with Richard so badly. It was frustrating as hell not to, but it was also heaven just being in his arms. People told me I was crazy, that he was terminally gay and I was deluding myself with the fag-hag romance. But I felt free to follow my heart, confident that the love Richard and I had for each other was deep and real. Still, I prayed like crazy that we would one day consummate it.

AS MUCH as art wasn't exactly my thing, music was becoming more and more my everything—especially with the explosion of incredible albums released around 1967: *Sgt. Pepper's Lonely Hearts Club Band* by the Beatles, *Between the Buttons* by the Stones, *The Piper at the Gates of Dawn* by Pink Floyd, *Surrealistic Pillow* by Jefferson Airplane, *Are You Experienced* by the Jimi Hendrix Experience, *Disraeli Gears* by Cream, *Days of Future Passed* by the Moody Blues, *The Mamas & the Papas Deliver*, as well as the self-titled debut albums by the Doors, Buffalo Springfield, Grateful Dead, Moby Grape, and Procol Harum. But the soundtrack of my life wasn't made up exclusively of psychedelic rock. Soul artists were also topping the charts and their records were what I played at Aux Puces to make people dance—Marvin Gaye and Tammi Terrell, Otis Redding and Carla Thomas, Jr. Walker and the All Stars, Aretha Franklin, Wilson Pickett, Lee Dorsey, the Temptations, the Marvelettes, and the Four Tops, to name a few. And there was one pop

artist I loved so much, I thought I might be turning lezzie over her—
Linda Ronstadt. Linda and her band, the Stone Poneys, had a hit song
I adored called "Different Drum." I was attracted to Linda's sweet,
sincere voice and Keane-eyed cuteness, but what really intrigued me
about her was the career and lifestyle she had created for herself—
singing and hanging out with all of those hetero male musicians in
the rock and roll world.

That same year, 1967, New York got something truly revolutionary in radio—WNEW-FM, a twenty-four-hour rock and roll station
that, in addition to the customary singles, played full album cuts, even
whole albums, no matter how long or non–Top 40 they were. The
news there was presented with a different slant too. And with all of
us twentysomethings tuning-in to the same messages and the same
sounds, it instantly became "our station." WNEW served to connect
us, unite us, and make us feel that we were becoming a force to be
reckoned with.

And apparently we were. Because soon radio stations all over
the country were copying WNEW's format, and Madison Avenue
couldn't help but take notice. My generation had suddenly become
the demographic to which the corporate world had to cater. We really
were having a "Youthquake" (a term Diana Vreeland had coined in
Vogue a few years earlier). It was a powerful feeling. And it occurred to
us that if we could make the airwaves and the commercial world bend
to our desires, maybe we could make the government bend too, to end
the war in Vietnam. That deeper sense of purpose is what energized
and kind of tribalized us.

SPINNING RECORDS, like advertising, had become my business. So
on my evenings off, I was naturally drawn to clubs that featured live
music. Uptown, it was Steve Paul's Scene, where the Velvet Underground, Jeff Beck, Jimmy Page, and Jim Morrison performed and
jammed. Downtown, it was Jerry Brandt's Electric Circus (formerly
Andy Warhol's Dom), where experimental composers and early

synth bands like Terry Riley, Morton Subotnick, and Silver Apples played. But my favorite downtown club at the time was Salvation, on Sheridan Square. Bradley Parks, Bobby Woods, and Jerry Schatzberg (Faye Dunaway's fashion-photographer boyfriend) owned Salvation. Bradley was the manager, Richard Roundtree (later famous for his role in *Shaft*) worked the door and Terry Noel (whom I knew from the Peppermint Lounge) was one of the DJs.

It was either Terry or my friend Kelly O'Hara (artist's model and Aux Puces waitress) who first brought me to Salvation. Because of the bridge-and-tunnel crowd invading from the boroughs and New Jersey, Manhattan clubs were beginning to get a bit picky, so you had to either know somebody or be somebody to get in. Bradley was a doll and always treated me like a star. He really loved girls and used to coax Kelly and me into showing him our panties and breasts in his office. We never did anything really dirty with him, though, just that slightly naughty stuff. (Not too many years after Salvation's heyday, Bradley Parks became a Catholic priest.)

The night I saw the Jimi Hendrix Experience perform live at Salvation sticks in my mind like no other. I remember exactly what I was wearing—a white silk-crepe sleeveless turtleneck minidress (originally long, with an accompanying white ostrich-feather coat, that I designed and my sister Mary made me for a chic David Barrett event), chartreuse Day-Glo tights, clear plastic Queen Ann heels, a mango-colored Afro wig, and big, round, clear plastic sunglasses with orange lenses. And I wasn't even on acid when I put that look together!

Salvation was so small, I could've reached out and touched Jimi a number of times throughout the evening, but I didn't. I held him in such high esteem that I was kind of awestruck in his presence. I'd been comfortable around performers ever since I was a kid, and I had no trouble seducing folkies like Jack Dalton in the coffeehouses, but these rock musicians were different somehow. And Jimi was dazzlingly different. He was the only black man playing psychedelic rock, and you just knew he was gonna be major. Though I desired him intensely and could have easily met him through my friend Colette

Mimram (a girlfriend of his at the time), I guess I just wasn't ready
yet to bring my love for these guys down to a sexual level. There were
plenty of other boys around for that and I was getting off already
anyway by simply worshiping at the feet of my idols. Or maybe I just
wasn't confident enough yet to go after them.

ON EASTER Sunday 1967, we had the first New York City be-in.
Unlike the antiwar protests, the be-in had no stage, no speakers, and
no apparent organizers, except maybe for a group called Experiments
in Art and Technology that had distributed flyers and posters stating
the date and location—March 26, Sheep Meadow in Central Park.
About ten thousand people showed up, including Allen Ginsberg,
Abbie Hoffman, and most of my friends and me—all of us there simply to *be* (unless we were part of some secret social experiment we've
yet to find out about).

It was like a scene out of a fairy tale and a lovely way to celebrate
spring—flower children, hippies, and Easter paraders strolling around
or sitting on the grass in their pastel-colored finery, sharing their
sandwiches and jelly beans, giving out daffodils and daisies, playing
flutes, flying kites, and tossing frisbees. It was blissful and magical—
especially on acid, as so many of us were. Looking back, I realize how
deluded we all were then, to imagine that the whole world had been
spiritually awakened by psychedelics and would soon become one big
peaceful, harmonious, communal garden like Central Park was on
that day. But it was that very absence of cynicism that made being
young and high in the sixties so especially great.

The be-in launched a new era of partying in the park, which had in
prior years been relatively underused by hip young New Yorkers. And
soon more be-ins, love-ins, smoke-ins, and human-be-ins followed.
But the grooviest Central Park happening of them all was made up of
a smaller, more local NYC crowd than any of the other -ins, which
tended to attract as many tourists as they did trippers. It was a totally
spontaneous, unstructured gathering that took place every week in

good weather just north of the Sheep Meadow and south of the lake at Central Park's Bethesda Fountain.

On any given Sunday, there'd be maybe five or six hundred people meandering around the fountain and along the lakeshore and paths that adjoined it. And what mostly set the tone there was the music. Emanating from various nooks and crannies near the edges of the area were the usual amorphous strains of acoustic guitars, penny whistles, and portable radios. But the dominant sound at Bethesda Fountain was the beat of the drums—bongos and congas played mostly by Latino guys from Spanish Harlem, sometimes in groups as big as ten or more. It was utterly impossible for me to be there and be high and not dance like a crazed voodoo woman to the rhythm of those drums.

I DIDN'T want to miss a trick in the sixties, a *trick* being what we called a sexual liaison or a guy with whom we would have a sexual liaison. So I went to Tiffany & Co. and had some elegant little cards printed that said, "You are beautiful, so am I," with my name and phone number at the bottom. Then, whenever I spotted a really cute guy on the subway, the street, or wherever, instead of letting him disappear from my life, I simply handed him a card. Nine out of ten called me and we took it from there. It was one of my most brilliant ideas ever and it paid off in spades as far as getting laid.

PAUL MCGREGOR had a hair salon in the penthouse of a high-rise at 57th and Sixth. I've read for years that Warren Beatty's character in the movie *Shampoo* was based on the hairdressers Jay Sebring and Jon Peters, but a bit of Paul McGregor was surely in there as well. Paul introduced the shag haircut to America, "by turning the Sassoon cut upside down." He was hetero and cute and wore the shortest possible cut-off jeans you could imagine, with no underwear. And since his crotch was right about level with your shoulders when you were in his chair, his package would often brush against you while he was cutting your hair.

Julie Christie, Goldie Hawn, Donald Sutherland, Roger Vadim, Warren Beatty, and Bob Crewe were already among Paul's clients, and he later became famous for that tough little haircut he gave Jane Fonda for the movie *Klute,* the same one she wore during her activist days as "Hanoi Jane." It was whispered that Paul was having affairs with a good many of his female clients, but he also had a wife and six young kids in the Pines. And that's where I got to know them. They were a welcome refuge in the midst of the sometimes overwhelming gayness out there.

Paul's brother Richie was killed in Vietnam in '67, and that summer Joel Schumacher (who had just been named style director at Revlon), Wally Graham, and I took Paul and his wife, Carol, on their first acid trip. We wanted it to be a fabulous experience for them, so we spent the whole day preparing their beach house for it—cleaning every surface, covering the lamps with colored fabrics to soften the light, making sure the fridge contained nothing potentially monster-making like a chicken carcass or heads-on shrimps, choosing the perfect music, incense, candles, and outfits for the night.

The McGregor kids were fast asleep downstairs and used to loud parties, so we got to trip with complete abandon—laughing our asses off, facing our monster-selves in the mirror, and freaking out over the millions of stars in the sky. We were just at that mellow, coming-down part of the trip at sunrise when those six little towheaded angels came upstairs, jumped into bed with Wally, Joel, and me, and started climbing all over us. Childhood is like a natural acid state, and they were totally in tune with our playful vibe. Amazingly, with all of us in that bed, it was so completely comfortable—more than comfortable, it was entrancing, their little fingers touching us everywhere. It was the most beautiful feeling in the world. Later that morning, at their persistent prompting, I did what had become my signature striptease dance, and they giggled their heads off, as always. Paul and Carol were rather open-minded parents, I guess, but those kids all turned out just fine.

Joel (who, I soon discovered, had grown up only three blocks away from me in Queens) and I took many more acid trips together, mostly in the orange lacquered bedroom of his Gramercy Park apartment. I was straight and he was gay, so we didn't have sex per se, but at least once in every trip we'd have sex in what we jokingly called "our way." We'd brush our strikingly similar and always freshly washed long brown hair together in the mirror, so that the strands intermingled and you couldn't tell which were his and which were mine, and it would crack us up every time.

I'd have dinner with Paul in the city sometimes while Carol and the kids were at the beach. He picked me up one night after doing Jane Fonda's hair in her suite at the Warwick Hotel—where, he said, Black Panther leader Huey Newton had answered the door. We went to Max's Kansas City to have the surf and turf and mix with the artists Paul said hung out there, like Larry Rivers, John Chamberlain, and Robert Rauschenberg. I really didn't know one of those artists from the other, though. I was mostly there to check out the food, the jukebox, and the reasonable prices, all of which Paul had been raving about. When I went to the ladies room, I noticed just beyond it a red-florescent-lit backroom that really intrigued me. It seemed private, like the domain of a certain select crowd or clique. There was an invisible but definite wall of intimidation at its entrance, so I didn't attempt to go in. Though I had the distinct feeling that one day I would.

PSYCHEDELIA SEEMED to reach its peak in 1968. The thrills of LSD (which had just been declared illegal) and other hallucinogens, along with pot, pills, and vitamin shots, were still enough to keep most people I knew high and satisfied. And everything still seemed to be moving in a positive, consciousness-expanding direction. *Hair* was on Broadway, with Dr. Bishop as its "official cast doctor." (On opening night, my friend Hiram Keller, who later starred in Fellini's *Satyricon*, sat on my lap when he and the rest of the cast came out into the audience naked for the act one finale—the first time nudity was ever featured on Broadway.) The antiwar and civil rights movements were going full speed ahead. And it was looking like we would soon have another Kennedy in the White House. (I got to shake Robert Kennedy's hand one night at PJ Clarke's.) And most importantly for me, Bill Graham had just opened the Fillmore East—two shows a night, three bands per show, one tab of acid—priceless.

Franklyn Welsh was living with Dick Villany, and he'd become quite successful, doing hair and makeup for magazine shoots, TV ads, and album covers. He loved the Fillmore and usually escorted me to the shows. I could have gone with Richard or Annie, but then I would have felt obligated to stay with them. I wanted to be free to leave whomever I was with in case I ran into a rock star and was asked to go back to his hotel room. It was a bit of a fantasy, but both Franklyn and I believed it could happen. And Franklyn, whose promiscuity surpassed even mine, was fine with our arrangement if it did.

Over the course of our seeing Big Brother and the Holding Company, Tim Buckley, the Doors, Richie Havens, the Who, Traffic, Iron Butterfly, Jefferson Airplane, Jimi Hendrix, Jeff Beck, Vanilla Fudge, Paul Butterfield, Ravi Shankar, the Mothers of Invention, and the Grateful Dead, I didn't even try to get backstage to score, though I did abandon Franklyn a couple of times for guys I met in the Fillmore's lobby. Talk about a scene—you could barely walk up the staircase between sets, it was so filled with trippers. The air was thick with marijuana smoke and bodies were packed so tightly together on both floors that it was hard to avoid getting instantly intimate with the strangers around you. But most nights Franklyn and I would stay together and go next door to Ratner's Deli for breakfast after the shows, the many hours of music and drugs having finally drained us.

IT WAS on one of those gloriously warm summer Sundays at the Bethesda Fountain in 1968 that I first saw him. He was by the main drum circle, dancing like a shaman to the Afro-Cuban beat, while the crowd around him ogled—a muscular, brown-skinned, black-haired,

Roman-nosed beauty I just had to seduce. I was still in love with Richard, of course, but when this big beefy number's dark and flashing eyes met mine it was kismet. I started dancing with him and it was as if everyone else in the park went into soft focus and only he and I were in vivid 3-D.

We moved so well together, the primal eroticism was almost as good as sex. Neither of us spoke a word until the drummers took a break, at which point this dreamboat reached out his hand to me and said, "Let's go for a walk." I was so glad I'd worn my most romantic outfit that day—a vintage gypsy skirt and beaded chiffon blouse with no bra or panties underneath. He was bare-chested, wearing only turquoise jams and flip-flops. The two of us looked really hot together, I knew. And from the many eyes that were upon us as we left, I sensed that the other people there thought so too.

We walked to the Ramble, a wooded area and well-known homosexual meat rack on the opposite side of the lake from the fountain. We talked and stopped occasionally to kiss as we made our way off the paved paths and through the infamous bushes, gay men scurrying like bunnies behind them, trying not to get caught in the act—as if we cared anyway. He was Lebanese and told me to just call him Billy. I later learned he was quite well-known around the park as "Beautiful Billy."

I was in absolute heaven on that walk. I wanted those first hot kisses and caresses with Billy to last forever. But I was also dying to lie down with him, to feel him on top of me and inside of me. I thought I might have to wait until we got to a bedroom for that, but lo and behold if he didn't lead me to a certain clump of bushes and produce from their midst a small rolled-up carpet he'd obviously stashed there for just such occasions.

The freedom, daring, and danger of having sex in the middle of Central Park was a new high for me, but it also felt as natural and carefree as could be. I had years before gotten an IUD, so I had no worries about getting pregnant and this was, of course, long before HIV and AIDS.

✦

BILLY DIDN'T turn out to be a very dependable boyfriend, though. He had other girlfriends and was probably never as in love with me as I was with him. I wouldn't hear from him for weeks on end and then he'd show up at Aux Puces one night just before closing time with a plan for some wee-hours adventure. One time we walked from 55th Street all the way down to the Fulton Fish Market in lower Manhattan to watch the fish get tossed around, weighed, and iced (which reminded me of my dad's idea of entertainment when I was a kid). Another time we walked across the 59th Street Bridge, and Billy climbed up the bridge's steelwork, totally freaking me out.

Once, when Billy and I were driving home from a trip upstate, we both took off all of our clothes on a mutual dare and stayed naked the whole way, smiling and waving to the astonished people in the neighboring cars on the highway. Unfortunately, after dropping Billy off and just before returning the car to the rental place, I fell asleep at the wheel, crashed into two parked cars on Fifth Avenue, and wound up in St. Vincent's Hospital with a grossly smashed-up mouth, a broken neck, and a broken nose. Fortunately, I had put my clothes back on before it happened.

But the best date I ever had with Billy was when he showed up at my apartment early one Sunday morning to take me to church. I had long since stopped going to church, but he insisted this would be something special. When we got to the Riverside Church on the Upper West Side, overlooking the Hudson River at one of the highest elevations in Manhattan, we went immediately up to the top of the bell tower, where Billy introduced me to the carillonneur, through whom he had obviously arranged the surprise. He then led me out onto an observation deck, up a treacherous utility ladder attached to the roof of the church, and up the tower's spire.

We were almost four hundred feet in the air with nothing to hold on to but that flimsy metal ladder. Pigeons and gulls were flying around us and the wind seemed like it could blow us away. I was scared to death, but Billy kept telling me to be patient for just another few minutes. Then, suddenly, all seventy-four bells of Riverside's carillon started ringing beneath us. The sound and vibrations were unbelievable. Good thing I wasn't on acid, or I might have had the urge to fly away. Instead, I just held on for dear life and enjoyed the sensation. And, of course, I fell even more in love with the daring young Beautiful Billy.

FRANKLYN, DICK, Richard, Nilo, David Smith, Pat Ast (a funny fat girl I'd met at the Pines), and I took lots of acid trips together in 1968 at Dickie's glamorously decorated apartment—where Dickie, while tripping his brains out, would crack us up by getting fixated on his color schemes, fabric samples, floor plans, mercury glass balls, and other accoutrements of his trade. As always, the music we played was of the utmost importance. We probably wore out the vinyl on the Beatles' White Album, Big Brother and the Holding Company's *Cheap Thrills*, the Doors' *Waiting for the Sun*, and the Stones' *Beggars Banquet*. Leonard Cohen, James Taylor, and Joni Mitchell were always somewhere in the mix as well. But the album we played the most that year was Van Morrison's *Astral Weeks*. And that was mostly because of me.

Van Morrison had become my new OCD. I was more than obsessed with him; I was possessed by the power of his music. Through it, I felt as if he had somehow gained entrance to my soul and was speaking directly to me, awaiting my response. I just had to meet him, know him, tell him, show him how much his music, lyrics, and voice meant to me. But how was I ever going to do that? I wanted it to happen naturally, organically. I didn't want to scare him away or turn him off by being a fanatic. I wanted to meet him as an equal, to have someone or some situation bring us together in a way that wouldn't be awkward. But just in case that might never happen, I made up my mind that I was gonna find out how to get myself backstage at the Fillmore East.

WHILE WNEW-FM was still *our* radio station in 1968, WABC-AM, with its Top 40 format and signal that reached a hundred miles in all directions, was attracting the biggest number of listeners, especially for Cousin Brucie's long-running show. Host Bruce Morrow had been a top New York DJ since the early sixties and, along with Ed Sullivan, had cohosted the Beatles' 1965 Shea Stadium concert. Macs McAree was developing a TV show for Bruce and brought me in as an associate producer. I wound up, of course, having sex with Bruce one night after a production meeting. He was married at the time, and Macs and I went out with him and his wife, Susan, on occasion. I think she always sensed that some hanky-panky had gone on. I wore Robert Piguet's Fracas in those days, a very pungent and distinctive perfume. And Susan would always ask me about it, commenting that she could swear she'd "smelled it somewhere before."

One time we all went to a club called Cerebrum together and I almost spilled the beans. Cerebrum was a kind of pleasure dome for trippers, designed by John Storyk (who later designed Jimi Hendrix's Electric Lady Studios). There was no bar, alcohol, seating, stage, dance floor, or band at Cerebrum. Instead, it featured state-of-the-art sensory stimulation devices. You took your clothes off upon entering, donned a long, flowy caftan, and lounged around on white-carpeted platforms, where a mixture of music, sound effects, lights, smells, projections, fogs, mists, glowing orbs, and an enveloping white parachute kept you entertained. Meanwhile, sexy young nymphs massaged your feet with body cream, rubbed minted ice cubes on your lips, and encouraged you to "share in the oneness ."

It's almost impossible to be deceptive on acid (which of course Macs and I had dropped that night), and Susan started going on again about the Fracas. I was just about to blurt out that it had probably rubbed off on Bruce the night that he came to my apartment. But Macs, thank God, chimed in, describing how he always sprayed my perfume around the conference room just before our meetings, because he thought it had a psychological effect on the sponsors and network execs we were courting, and the scent must have settled in

Bruce's clothes and hair. Though we never did get Bruce's TV show off the ground, I realized at that moment what a perfect business partner Macs was for me. And through no fault of mine, Bruce and Susan wound up getting divorced a year or two later anyway.

BECAUSE OF the way he managed to get himself out and about every night in his wheelchair, Hal Fredericks became known around town as Superwheels. He and I had been friends ever since Farrell and Michael first introduced us at the Pines. One night after having dinner at Elaine's (a celebrity hangout on Manhattan's Upper East Side), Hal took me to a club called, funny enough, Wheels. Some friends of his were performing there with their band, the New York Rock & Roll Ensemble. They were accomplished young musicians from Julliard and had recently played third on the bill at the Fillmore East. They were unique in that they switched in the middle of their set from rock to classical music.

Michael Kamen played the keyboards, oboe, and English horn, sang the lead vocals, and wrote the songs. He and I hit it off from the moment that Hal introduced us. And I soon had my first really meaningful friendship with a professional musician. Michael bolstered my ego and encouraged me to follow my music biz dreams, telling me I had excellent instincts and a really good ear. And coming from him, I believed it. Because even then, when he was only around twenty years old, Michael was already considered a musician's musician. Everybody knew he had a great career ahead of him, and I envisioned us working together in some way one day. At the very least, I figured he might be able to get me backstage at the Fillmore East.

6

'69

M Y NECK and nose were already healed from the car crash, but my upper lip, which had been split open and turned into mush by the steering wheel, was still a bit numb. I had only been working at Aux Puces and on freelance productions at the time of the accident, so that meant I had no medical insurance—hence, no plastic surgery, just St. Vincent's emergency room treatment and sew-up. Somehow this wasn't all that unacceptable to me at the time. Of course, there went any future beauty contests and my trumpet embouchure. But I hadn't given much thought to either of those things since high school anyway.

On the afternoon of New Year's Eve, Nilo assembled the entire staff to decorate Aux Puces for the festive ringing in of '69. Tiny twinkle lights, so common now, were still rather new then and only available in clear and primary colors. So we hand-painted thousands of them in more striking hues—hot pink to outline the palm tree trunks, lime green for the fronds, and lavender to drape along the Moorish arches. Nilo had precooked over a hundred gourmet dinners, which would be heated up to order in what we called the "bread oven." (the first microwave any of us had ever seen—a little misting of water and a few seconds in that oven and day-old bread magically became both soft and warm). The champagne was chilling and, at $100 a head excluding drinks, the reservation list was full.

Aux Puces' waitresses normally wore sexy crocheted Clovis Ruffin jumpsuits as uniforms. But for that night Kelly O'Hara and one of the other girls squeezed, side-by-side, into one huge pink satin dress they'd found at a costume shop. And they stayed like that for the entire evening, allowing each of them only one arm free to serve. I was naked under a slinky brown-and-white-check 1930s bias-cut gown and frizzy platinum wig, my numb lips painted rusty red. David Smith wore his Stephen Burrows black-double-knit and white-leather faux-tuxedo tunic. And Richard and the boys were in their traditional French café attire. The room was ready and so were we, except for Nilo's final touch—administering a tab of blotter acid to each and every one of us. So the whole staff (except for Kelly, who didn't do drugs) was tripping by the time the first patrons arrived.

How we ever pulled that evening off, I'll never know. At 11:59 P.M., I had Lorraine Ellison's "Stay with Me Baby" on both turntables, cross dissolving them, so that her big crescendo went on and on and then climaxed exactly at the stroke of midnight, when we simultaneously switched off Aux Puces' regular lights and switched on the twinkle lights. The effect was completely theatrical and magical and took everyone's breath away. The place became a wonderland of lights. It was the most glamorous New Year's Eve I had ever known.

But, right after midnight, when everyone started coming by my booth for a New Year's kiss, things got weird. Between the acid, the numbness, and the kisses, my upper lip felt like it had grown to about five times its normal size, making me think I had morphed into a hideous cartoon character with a mouth like a duck. Traumatized, I put "In-A-Gadda-Da-Vida" on the turntable (the seventeen-minute Iron Butterfly track I used for my breaks) and went outside for some air, freezing in the tissue-paper-thin layer of silk I was wearing.

Thanks to Jay Martin's help spinning, I finished out the evening, eventually accepting that my lip was only a little bit swollen and that I was still one hundred percent human. But the *numb duck* image stuck in my mind like a metaphor for the strange, slightly off vibe that I felt in the air at the start of '69. The beautiful, consciousness-expanding, hippie-dippy, flower-power sixties were drawing to a close, and there were signs that the innocence of it all was almost over as well.

Both Martin Luther King and Robert Kennedy were dead and gone, having taken a part of our peace-and-love dream with them. Richard Nixon was the new U.S. president and there were more troops in Vietnam than ever. Lots of new drugs were going around—DMT, STP, PCP, MDA, DOM, and other combo crap made mostly from opiates, speed, and animal tranquilizers. Cocaine wasn't huge yet, but it was around. And the sight of a nitrous oxide tank was becoming as commonplace as a lava lamp in many a stoner's apartment. It was clearly the end of one era and the beginning of another, and I had reservations about the new kinds of highs people were seeking. But then again, it was the last year of the fabulous psychedelic decade that we already sensed would go down in history as the defining one of our generation. And we had to do it up right. The marking of this particular time by the yin-yang upside-down number '69 just seemed so... perfectly timed.

WORKING FULL-TIME at Aux Puces, but only freelance in my advertising career (and no longer at Bloomingdale's), I felt like I was really moving on, making room for something new to come into my life, something that stimulated me more than producing commercials. But I was lucky enough to score some really cool jobs before finally leaving the field. The first was at Altman, Stoller, Chalk, an ad agency specializing in fashion. They were just beginning to do TV advertising, and they hired me to set up a proper in-house radio/TV department. It was a great job, because they had no idea what I was doing and I could really come and go as I pleased.

One Monday morning, after an acid trip at Joel Schumacher's, I had to go in to approve an answer print of a commercial. The acid hadn't completely worn off yet and the colors were all running into each other like oozing, unset Jell-O on the screen. I got through that one by simply agreeing with everyone at the meeting that the print looked just fine. But I got fired a few weeks later for burning incense at my desk. When Mr. Altman (the president, who otherwise adored me) reprimanded me for it, I remember yelling back at him, "It's only incense! It's not dope!" I had drifted so far from the corporate mind-set that I just couldn't understand why trying to make the office smell nice could be a problem.

My favorite jobs, though, were the ones I did for McCann Erickson and Coca-Cola. They once flew me down to Key Biscayne, Florida, for three days just to represent the New York office at a commercial shoot while the Atlanta office handled the production. We stayed in a lovely hotel and my room had an adjoining door to the Atlanta art director's room. The door, of course, was locked from both sides. Before going to bed on my last night there, I unlocked the door on my side. And, just as I suspected would happen, that Georgia boy came tiptoeing into my room in the wee hours and fucked me. Oh man, I loved that kind of stuff—two almost strangers in complete darkness, not a word spoken, a one-time, secret, forbidden scene, like in a movie or a dream. The next morning at breakfast with him and the rest of the crew, we both acted as if nothing had happened. And I flew home to New York right afterward, never to see him or speak with him again.

Another time, McCann's Billy Davis, a former Motown song-writer, had created a catchy new jingle for Coke, called "It's the Real Thing," and they needed some visuals to go with it. Several of McCann's producers and art directors had tried, unsuccessfully, to create footage that looked totally unprofessional—in other words, *real*. So they hired me to go out and shoot genuine home movies that they could edit into thirty- and sixty-second presentation spots in order to sell the campaign to the clients.

I came up with the scenarios—graduation day, new puppy, new baby, first birthday, etc. And with the 8mm camera, expense account, rental car, and cases of Coke they provided, I traveled around New

England, found the locations and the families (I even used my sister Mary, her kids, and their friends for one), paid for the parties, and provided McCann with tons of shaky, out-of-focus, poorly framed, badly lit footage. It was a hit, and the new campaign got the go-ahead from Coca-Cola. Of course, typical of Madison Avenue, McCann then had professional actors, directors, and production houses redo the spots in 35mm for hundreds of thousands of dollars. Coke's "It's the Real Thing" campaign was a huge success, but the ads they used on TV never looked quite as *real* as mine.

I WAS a big Jethro Tull fan, having seen them open for Blood, Sweat & Tears at the Fillmore. One night a guy came into Aux Puces who I thought might be Ian Anderson, the group's lead singer. But I quickly realized that this guy was way too old. He had that same haunting look though—skinny, in a floor-length winter coat, with long, straggly gray hair and a matching moustache, a style that screamed eccentric artist or reclusive royal out from his cobwebby castle. He was alone and it was early in the evening, so David sat him at Nilo's table, near the DJ booth and waiter's station, where we could chat him up and make him feel welcome.

After a filet of sole Kathleen (heated up in the microwave but somehow made elegant and delicious, thanks to Nilo's culinary skills), a few glasses of wine, and some chitchat in French with Nilo, Richard, and Romy Aguirre (Nilo's South American business partner), he came over and introduced himself to me (in perfect English) as Georges Mathieu, a painter from Paris. Though, at forty-eight, he was a bit old for me, there was something really fascinating about him. His cheeks were so hollow and there was a kind of madness in his eyes. He hung out by my booth for at least an hour, talking with me between track changes. When I told him I'd never been to Europe, he suggested I visit him one day, perhaps that coming summer in the south of France. Before leaving, he wrote down an address in Saint-Tropez and asked me for mine.

A couple of weeks later, the postman delivered the most beautiful-looking letter I have ever received, from Paris, boldly scrawled with graceful flourishes by the hand of an artist for sure and containing a recent French magazine article about him. From the article and from asking around, I found out that he was known as France's greatest living painter—the only one to ever have created a giant painting right in the museum where it was hung—and he was credited with introducing Jackson Pollock to Paris. Mathieu later even redesigned the face of France's ten franc coin. In the magazine photos he wore theatrical-looking clothes—high white formal collars, a yellow silk robe, a red plaid coat with black velvet cuffs, and what looked like a gold brocade matador's suit. His Paris apartment was opulent and dramatic, with a purple velvet sofa and pink velvet drapes. And he apparently tooled around town in a mint-condition 1936 Mercedes-Benz 500K convertible.

Georges requested a photo of me, and I sent him a black-and-white one taken at Lake Minnewaska, where I'd gone for a winter weekend with Richard, Nilo, Dick, Franklyn, and a Madison Avenue friend named Joan Folger. I had no makeup on and I was tripping, so my eyes looked like I was seeing God. Then another letter came and another. There I was, corresponding with this master, this French rock star of a painter, and I was such a dummy about art. I wondered how long his apparent fascination with me would last once he realized that.

THE DANCERS from the New York City Ballet were all regulars at Aux Puces. We adored them and the way they relaxed from their highly disciplined lives by smoking cigarettes, drinking champagne, and eating the decadent chocolate gateaux at the club. At their invitation, Nilo, David Smith, Joan Folger, and I went to the premiere of Jerome Robbins's *Dances at a Gathering* at Lincoln Center's New York State Theater and to the lavish afterparty, held in theater's lobby. The dancers from Great Britain's Royal Ballet (who also hung out at Aux

Puces when they were in town) were in attendance as the guests of honor.

Michael Kamen and the New York Rock & Roll Ensemble, newly lionized by the classical crowd for being part of Leonard Bernstein's Young People's Concerts, were playing at the party. And less than twenty minutes or so into their set, my friend Joan was up at the mike singing with them. She had never done anything like that in her life. It was completely spontaneous and impromptu. But she did it so well that everyone, including the band, embraced her performance. Joan was on acid, of course.

I, meanwhile, was doing my own impromptu number—channeling Isadora Duncan by dancing around the multiple levels of balconies that encircle the upper part of the New York State Theater's lobby. In a way, I was doing it out of frustration for not being able to seduce the very handsome and famously hetero ballet dancer Edward Villella, but mostly, the 1920s peach-colored silk-chiffon dress and short bobbed wig I was wearing that evening had ignited the fantasy. The right costume, along with the right drugs, could do that for me every time. When the band played their popular cover version of Procol Harum's "A Whiter Shade of Pale," I was on the highest of the four balconies, moving with such ease and grace, I felt like I was flying. I had experienced that kind of thing once before, even without the acid, when I was a kid, ice-skating all alone in the park behind the dog-poo lot in Queens. It's as if another spirit takes over your body and you can do something so superbly for those few moments but then never ever reach that level of perfection at it again.

Having noticed me up there, David Smith suddenly appeared at the opposite end of the balcony. We danced toward each other and just as the song ended, we ran into each other's arms and embraced. We could hear the crowd below applauding the band, but when we peered over the balcony and saw everyone looking up and yelling bravo, we realized they'd been watching the whole thing and were also applauding David and me. And later that night, when we walked into Aux Puces, everyone in the place, including both ballet troupes,

gave *us* a standing ovation. I thought about how proud Miss Betty
would have been.

EVEN THOUGH I was still doing diet pills and Dr. Bishop's shots, I
was burning the candle at both ends so heavily that I'd sometimes fall
asleep at the turntables, filling Aux Puces with the amplified sound of
the needle going 'round on blank vinyl. That's when I'd have to snort
some coke—never really my drug of choice—just to keep going. On
nights when I'd had enough sleep and smoked enough pot, though,
I'd really get off, playing high-energy sets and driving the people to
dance on and on until they dropped.

It must have been on one such night that a club owner from
France came in and heard me spin, because out of the blue I received
a telegram asking if I'd like to DJ for the summer at his disco on the
French Riviera. The money was terrible, but I thought of it as a paid
vacation and a chance for some foreign adventure. As far as I've ever
known, Georges Mathieu had nothing to do with it. It was just one of
those strange, unexpected twists of fate. So without even getting any
further details on the job, I sublet my apartment to Michael Welch's
new girlfriend, Aziyade Venus, filled a couple of suitcases with hip-
huggers, boat-necks, and an amazing record collection and headed for
the Côte d'Azur.

The club was called Saint Hilaire de la Mer in Sainte-Maxime,
which was right across the bay from Saint-Tropez. My room was
upstairs over the club, as was the club cashier Denise's. It had a spectacular view of Saint-Tropez, Grimaud, Ramatuelle, and the shore-
line along the way. But, except for a bed and a chest, the room was
practically bare. I was expected to buy my own sheets, towels, hang-
ers, cups, iron, soap, toilet paper, and whatnot. I was also required to
work seven nights a week, from ten at night until five in the morning.
And they wouldn't give me a key to the place because Denise kept
the club's nightly receipts in her room and they were paranoid about
being robbed. Jacques, the owner, had a huge ego and a horribly smug

attitude. He was certainly no Nilo DePaul. And I was suddenly feeling I had made a huge mistake.

Wearing my pink Betsey Bunky Nini bikini underneath a little pink-and-white Mexican dress, I took a walk along the Sainte-Maxime beachfront toward the center of town to look for the items I needed. But I wound up meeting a hot young Frenchman at the crepe stand and hanging out with him instead. He spoke English and said that it would be better to shop for the items in Saint-Tropez, that he would take me there in his boat, and I could even water ski on the way if I liked. When we got to Saint-Tropez, he went with me to the post office to help me find the address I had for Georges Mathieu. But the handwriting was hard to decipher and nobody seemed to know where it was. I didn't have a phone number for the friends Georges was staying with there, and I really wanted to surprise him anyway. So I just bought the things I needed and water-skied my way back to Sainte-Maxime.

The next day I picked up a local guy with a little red sports car and got him to give me a ride to Saint-Tropez to once again look for Georges. He managed to figure out that the address was in an exclusive area called Les Parc. And after driving around for a while in search of it, we stopped to ask a group of people walking along the road if the house was close by. As fate would have it, Georges Mathieu was among them. I didn't even open the car door —I just climbed out over the guy's convertible and threw my arms around Georges, who was naturally in shock and also seemed a bit embarrassed in front of his friends. But I just yapped on in my exuberant American manner and made a date to meet him the next day, as I had to get back to Sainte-Maxime for my debut at Saint Hilaire that night.

People came to Saint Hilaire in sleek boats and cars from all around the Gulf of Saint-Tropez. And almost all of 'em kept asking me to play Johnny Hallyday songs—cheesy French pop that didn't mesh with my soul and funk grooves at all. None of the customers liked the music I played, though the black guys in the band I alternated sets with really dug it. The sound equipment sucked; the turntables and headphones didn't even allow for cross-dissolves. And Jacques made me pay full price for any alcoholic drinks I consumed and then complained that I drank way too many orange juices for free.

I was pretty bummed out that first night—that was, until Jean-Pierre, the sexiest of Sainte Hilaire's gorgeous young waiters, asked me to go to his place with him after work. On the way there he took me by a bakery in the center of the village. It wouldn't open for another couple of hours, but when we went to the back door, the baker sold us a couple of hot croissants that had just come out of the oven. I don't think anything has ever tasted as delicious as that first warm, flaky French croissant did on that sultry summer morning in Sainte-Maxime. It almost made having to work until 5 A.M. worth it. When I returned home to the club after my little sex romp with Jean-Pierre, Denise didn't answer the bell. She was either out of the building or asleep. Well, fuck that, I thought. I climbed the fence and walked along the precarious ledge that led to my balcony and my room. And that was how I got in and out of the building from then on.

Georges Mathieu came to pick me up at three o'clock. I thought he was going to take me to a fabulous French restaurant or to the house of his hosts in Les Parc, but instead he took me to a little café in Grimaud that was empty except for the two of us. The café owner seemed to know Georges well and spent a lot of time talking with him in French while I sat there like an idiot, wondering what the hell was going on. When Georges suggested we go to the beach, I got excited. But where he took me was by no means a beach for walking, swimming, or socializing; it was a place for sex. Well, being me and being curious about him, I figured why not. And though he was old, he was an OK lover.

I made a date with Georges for the next afternoon. But that morning after work, I went back to Jean-Pierre's again. And by the time the afternoon rolled around, I'd had enough fucking and just wanted to take one of the "bon voyage" Seconals David Smith had given me and get some sleep. And so I stood up France's greatest living painter and never saw him again. He left me a note filled with pathos, which

I've saved and I treasure along with his other letters. Had I been older, I might have been able to explain my feelings to Georges. But at the time I felt extremely hurt and kind of angry. I had hoped he was going to be my connection to French bohemian culture, not someone who only wanted me for sex. And besides, there were all of those adorable young waiters and musicians at the club who were much more to my liking for that. Obviously, art wasn't the only thing I was stupid about.

Two weeks into my stay, I gave Jacques my two-weeks' notice, but I made sure to make the most of my month on the Riviera, often being reckless in my pursuit of fun. One time I dropped acid with some French hippies I'd met at Pampelonne, my favorite Saint-Tropez beach. They were first-time trippers and none of them spoke English. Communication between us for those eight hours was hysterically funny, but had an emergency occurred or one of them freaked out or something, I, having supplied the blotter acid I'd brought from New York, could have found myself in big trouble. The *Hair* LP that I played on the battery-operated record player I'd borrowed from Denise never sounded so good, though.

The language barrier and the fact that I was so far away from home did leave me feeling rather lonely at times. So, in lieu of a friend to share my thoughts with, I began to keep a diary, of sorts. Actually, I seem to have mostly used it as a prayer book, 'cause the times when I'd go on and on for pages and pages always seemed to be when I was begging God to get me out of some mess I was in, like being down to my last bit of cash or fearing another vaginal infection (I'll spare you those). But also something inside of me just made me want to keep note of where my life was going, 'cause I fully expected it to be an ever more wondrous and adventurous journey.

July 16, 1969—*Sitting at a café across from the Cannes Railroad Station. Waiting for Joan Folger's train, arriving from Italy at 9:45 AM. Traveling light, just this hippie-dippy backpack and me. Good riddance to that fucking asshole Jacques. What a total shithead he was.*

He even had the nerve to accuse me of being an imposter, saying I was not the girl he'd heard spinning at Aux Puces. Asshole! I'm bummed I had to leave all of the records behind. But there was no way I could have taken them with me. Had my last Sainte-Maxime croissant before hitchhiking down here. Will never forget the warmth of the rising sun on my bare legs, the sparkle, smell, and color of the sea, and the cold creamy milk in the pillow-like plastic pouch on the way. No milk ever tasted so good... the milk of freedom.

July 21, 1969—Had a fabulous night watching the moon landing at Francine's house, the woman I met in Sainte-Maxime. Felt so proud to be an American. Budget's tight, but I adore Paris... the light, the smells, the graceful rounded corners of the buildings, the shop windows, and even the sound of the language that used to get me so frustrated at Saint Hilaire. I've walked for hours and hours all over the city, often losing my way, but who cares. Love sitting at the cafes, writing in my journal.

Joan and I hitchhiked around France, Spain, and Holland for much of the summer, and we certainly had some adventures. One time we had to fight off some weaselly little French guy in a black lace shirt who drove us off the main road and into the woods wanting "amour, amour." Some nights we wound up sleeping right out in the open on the side of the road or in the tents of the many German campers who had given us rides. At first, Joan, being Jewish and a bit of a princess, had some problems with our taking charity from the Germans. But we were often pretty desperate by nightfall and they were always so nice, so she soon relented.

August 7, 1969—Fucked "the guy with the biggest dick in Holland," as he's affectionately known around Amsterdam. He's the DJ at the Can Can Club, which Joan's friend owns and over which we are staying. His name is Abdul and his cock really is freakishly big. I went home with him first, and last night Joan had her turn. Neither one of us

could manage to take every inch of it. But it sure was fun trying.
Went to Paradiso... all kinds of hash for sale and kids camping out
there, tripping and sleeping all over the floor. Would like to catch a
band there one night.

Traveling with Joan made me realize I wasn't the biggest nympho
on the planet; she was, at least on that trip anyway. She fell in love
with almost every guy we met, even the Germans she complained
about. I actually grew tired of it all after a while—Joan, the sex, the
language barrier, the lack of wardrobe, the green flies that bit at the
beaches, my dirty hair, and how fat I was getting from eating so much
bread and cheese. On top of it, my money had just about run out. So
I called Dickie Decorator and he sent me three hundred dollars via
American Express for a plane ticket home.

I GOT back to New York on August 15, 1969, the first night of the
Woodstock Festival. David Smith and Nilo had already left town for
it, but Dick and Franklyn decided to go to the Pines for the weekend
instead. So they picked me up at the airport on their way out there.
I was so excited to be back in my old stomping grounds. I couldn't
wait to hit the Boatel for tea dance and the Sandpiper at midnight to
catch up on the gossip, the latest dance moves, and the whole social
scene. But something had changed while I was gone. Dick and Franklyn had both gotten pretty heavy into snorting cocaine. Some of the
other friends I used to trip with out there had moved on to mainlining
things, including the big no-no, heroin. Poppers were now stinking
up the dance floor. The gay boys were beginning to look more like
bikers and construction workers than dandies. And, tragically, Sweet
William, a graceful gazelle of a boy who worked for Stephen Burrows,
had mysteriously drowned in the swimming pool at Joel Schumacher's
house, casting a rather sad shadow over the remainder of the summer.
   The writing was on the wall. Trends that started on Fire Island
tended to spread throughout the gay community and then to the

general population. The new drugs seemed, on the one hand, to be for gaining an edge, taking control, becoming aggressive, and, on the other hand, for numbing the pain. Unlike flower children, white powder heads were very secretive and paranoid about their stashes and eventually about everything else. The airy-fairy tripping and sharing of one's jelly beans was fast becoming passé. And the Manson murders, having just occurred in L.A., signaled the end of our innocence in an even bigger way. Woodstock seemed to mark flower power's last hurrah precisely. And by year's end, with the Stones' concert at Altamont marred by four deaths, one of them a homicide, it seemed clear, without even looking at the calendar, that it truly was THE END of the sixties.

7

Charlotte Russe

A S THE seventies dawned, I was back DJing at Aux Puces a few nights a week and spending lots of time with Macs McAree writing screenplays, none of which we ever managed to sell. So I was looking for more work. At a routine Madison Avenue job interview with a preppy thirtysomething personnel director, the conversation somehow turned to psychedelics. He had never tripped and was dying to try it. And I just happened to have a few Mickey Mouse tabs in my wallet. He rented us a room at some hotel down on the West Side Highway, overlooking the Hudson River and the docks—a strange and desolate place for a hotel in those days—and I met him there later that night. There was a slowly revolving bar in the hotel's lounge and that's where we dropped the acid. He was Irish and a big drinker, so we downed a couple of cocktails while it was coming on. But when the bar stools and the moving floor got to be too much, we retired to the room.

My initial thought was that I'd have a few laughs and possibly some sex with this guy and maybe land a job. But when he started freaking out big time, I realized that the only job I was gonna get was as an eight-hour bad-trip babysitter, a job I absolutely hated. I guided him through the first hour or two, until he calmed down and accepted that he wasn't going to die there and disgrace the wife and kids he admitted to having in New Jersey. I realized the big mistake I'd made and couldn't stand to be there one more minute. So, ashamed as I am to admit it, I split, leaving the poor guy all alone in that dreary hotel room in that strange part of town, with five or six hours of his very first trip left to go. Still hallucinating and with an acid-intensified sense of panic, I called Michael Welch and Aziyade from a pay phone and managed to get a cab to their place, my heart pounding like crazy the whole time. If the guy were to do something rash, it would totally be my fault and I might never be able to live with the guilt of it. Plus, the cops would soon be on my tail. Michael and Azi soothed my nerves with some hot tea and reassuring conversation, made up the sofa for me to stay the night, and turned on WNEW-FM to keep me company when they went to bed.

John Zacherlee was WNEW's late-night DJ, and I had come to love his gentle voice and manner. As a teenager, I'd seen him hosting horror movies on TV, rising from a coffin in ghoulish monster makeup that was always more endearing than it ever was scary. Zach was someone I'd grown up with, like a hip old uncle or something. And I felt especially connected with him that night. So I telepathically sent him a few track requests, and miraculously he played them. I took that as a sign that I had to go and meet him immediately. Besides, I really needed to hear the music loud. And where better to do that in the middle of the night than at a radio station?

I wrote Michael and Azi a note, rolled a few joints, and headed down Park Avenue to the Grand Central Terminal Building where WNEW was housed. Walking there alone amid the sparkling, spiraling skyscrapers seemed exceptionally glamorous that night—a Holly Golightly Manhattan moment for sure, especially compared to the predicament I'd been in earlier that evening. I suddenly felt so cosmopolitan and so confident about how I would just walk right into the station, introduce myself to Zach, hang out with him, and spin some discs. And sure enough, when I arrived, the guard in the lobby just happened to be asleep at his desk. So I was able to sneak right

personally escorted me to a seat in the very first row. When Burton sang, "These eyes cry every night for-or you," he was looking straight at me, as if singing the words to me only. That's all it took for me to fall in love with him right then and there. Worldly wanton woman me, with all of my talk of freedom and independence—one sappy love song crooned in my direction by a genuine rock star and I melted like a little schoolgirl.

Backstage after the show, with so many girls vying for Burton's attention, I began to wonder if I was really going to be the one who would hold him tight that night. But Burton hardly ever took his eyes off of me and I wound up in his bed at the Loew's Midtown Motor Inn a short time later. We really had good sex together, Burton and me—smooth, easy, romantic, synchronistic sex. Nothing too fancy, no S&M, toys, or acrobatics—just good old-fashioned lovemaking both in body and spirit, which, despite all of my experimentations and petty perversions, has really always been my favorite kind.

Over the next couple of weeks, the Guess Who played in and around the New York area, and Burton and I made love a few more times. I thought I had found my rock and roll hero, the man of my dreams. I thought I might finally stop my promiscuous nympho behavior, get over Beautiful Billy and Richard, and have a meaningful rock star romance that would last—who knows, perhaps forever. When Burton invited me to the band's concert in Asbury Park, New Jersey, over the Labor Day weekend, I hopped a bus from the Port Authority and went down there for the night, figuring I'd take the last bus back after the show. The band was going on to Virginia Beach in their tour bus from there. Burton was cordial with me at the show, but not exactly the warm, loving guy I thought I'd come to know. Still, there didn't seem to be any other girl who had taken my place, so I just chalked it up to his artistic temperament and enjoyed the evening as best I could.

Unfortunately, I'd hung out backstage way too long and by the time I got to the terminal, the last bus for Manhattan had already left and there was no other way for me to get home. So there I was in my little white dress that barely covered my ass, with just a tiny purse containing not much more than some lip gloss, a roach clip, a bottle of Binaca, a few dollars, and my keys. And it was getting quite late and quite cold there by the ocean. I ran back to Convention Hall in desperation and found some of the band members just as they were boarding their bus. When I told them of my dilemma, they encouraged me to join them, explaining that after their two nights in the Virginia Beach area, they would be heading back up north to Boston and could drop me off somewhere near Manhattan on the way. And they swore I'd be a nice surprise for Burton when he boarded. I wasn't prepared to travel, but I really had no choice and it did sound like fun, especially if Burton's spirits would be lifted with me there.

But when Burton saw me on the bus, he seemed annoyed and rebuffed all of my attempts to be near him. My heart was broken, but this was my first time on a rock and roll tour bus and I was determined to make the most of it. I hung with the boys in the band, rolled joints for them, sang songs with them, and even took them up on a dare to give head to their sweet old country bumpkin bus driver, who said he'd never had a blow job in his life. One of the boys took the wheel, while I took the nervous old guy, already erect with anticipation, to the back of the bus and did him in all of about two seconds, right as we were crossing the Delaware Memorial Bridge. Forget about storybook romance—Burton's attitude and lack of affection had catapulted me back into my party-girl ways and I wasn't going to waste time crying over what might have been with him.

That's the only sex I had on the whole trip, though. The guys in the band let me stay in their rooms, bought me breakfast, lunch, dinner, and new panties, and generally treated me like a sister. And when we went to the beach together, I went swimming in my dress as a way to get it clean. I ignored Burton and he ignored me in favor of some local Virginia girls. And yet, during the concerts, I was still able to get off on him—and even more so on the rest of the band. Standing on the side of the stage while they played, even looking as disheveled as I must have, I felt like I truly belonged there, like I was their friend. And that was really what I wanted most out of being a groupie. At least, that's what I told myself anyway. They dropped me off on Labor

Day in some god-awful part of the Bronx, where I eventually found
the subway. And on the way home, I wrote this poem.

A Groupie Lament

Diamonds twinkle beneath my feet
On the Labor Day weekend street
Sunlight shines warm through my hair
You'd think there was no pollution there
Pimples sprout on my sleepless face
Varicose veins show the endless pace
My white dress dirty as I walk it home
But my head is up, so I'll write a poem
I'm feeling beauty in my ghetto land
'Cause I got it on with a rock and roll band
The trip was a long one; the bus was crazed
The guys and I were mostly dazed
We sang a few tunes from old rock and roll
And we hid the dope when we paid the toll
Burton ignored me, the silly fool
But the rest of the guys thought I was cool
From Asbury Park to Virginia Beach
I gave head like daybed philosophies teach
I feel good and I should and I even got a tan
On my two-day tour with a rock and roll band
You see I missed the last bus from the Jersey Shore
And a taxi driver said that there were no more
So I went back to Convention Hall
And I got on their bus and I had a ball
The motels were sterile and the food was all plastic
But at their last set on Sunday I got freaked-out spastic
I know they all love me, 'cause they told me so
As for Burton, well, I just don't know
I'm the happiest broken heart, can you understand
'Cause now I'm the friend of a rock and roll band

8

Party Favor

NANCY LEE Andrews was like a fairy-tale princess whom men went gaga over. I'd met her husband, Philip English, an Australian model, at a casting session back at Altman, Stoller, Chalk. And once Philip introduced me to Nancy, she and I became the best of friends. Nancy was a high-fashion model and into all of the latest health food trends, dietary supplements, naturopathic treatments, and spiritual practices. Neither of us was gay, but we were very attracted to each other. She gave me gifts of vintage clothes and books on metaphysics and got me to stop seeing Dr. Bishop and go instead to Dr. Soltanoff, a New Age chiropractor/nutritionist in the Village—so no more vitamin shots. I had already kicked the Preludin habit at Stephen Burrows's house in the Pines by doing nothing but eating, sleeping, and fucking this bisexual guy there named Bobby Delia for three days straight—so no more diet pills either.

Hanging out with Nancy, I was soon into raw food fasts, acupuncture, spinal adjustments, and high colonics. But since she and Philip always had the finest quality pot and psychedelics, as well as a nitrous oxide tank, I still indulged in all of those things too. Nancy never seemed to mind that Philip and I spent a lot of time in bed together. (Druggies like us often spent a lot of time hanging out in bed, without necessarily having sex.) I think that she, like most women, didn't really consider me much of a threat. I was such a notorious party girl it was obvious that I was only out for fun and had no intention of breaking up any relationships. And Nancy was well aware that we girls could have orgasm after orgasm on psychedelics without having sex anyway.

Philip had a brilliant spaced-out mind that really held me spellbound at times. And he was always cooking up some crazy scheme or adventure that I wanted to be in on. But it was Nancy who interested me the most. Maybe it was simply admiration for her strength and femininity, or perhaps it was the first real stirrings of lesbianism in me. But I must admit that knowing she hung out with Eric Clapton, Leon Russell, the Grateful Dead, and the Jefferson Airplane probably had a lot to do with it too.

DAVID TAYLOR had often come to Aux Puces with his boss, *Playboy* magazine fashion director Robert L. Green, and we soon became friends. It was David who'd introduced me to Michael Norlan, the sex machine. One night David came in all alone and quite excited, insisting that I go and audition for a play with him down on the Lower East Side. I had never known David to have any acting ambitions and I wasn't feeling them too strongly myself at the time. Plus, neither of us had any real stage experience. "But that's the whole point of this kind of theater," David said. "They call it Theatre of the Ridiculous, and they don't want overly trained actors, just people who are naturally outrageous and can be totally uninhibited on stage." Well, that's me, I thought. So a few nights later I went with him to check it out.

Climbing the well-worn staircase of the East Village loft building that housed the New York Theater Ensemble (NYTE) instantly brought me back to Betty Watson's Dancing School in Queens. The sounds, smells, and spirits inhabiting such places of theatrical endeavor are always the same. Those happy memories from childhood and the excitement of what might lie ahead propelled me up those stairs as if I had wings on my feet. Despite some of the crazy wigs and things I wore to clubs and parties, I was actually very Ali MacGraw–esque in those days, so I must have appeared very straight—David too, in his chic Italian suit—to the three-hundred-plus-pound director, Tony Ingrassia, and the colorful downtown types in his troupe. They couldn't believe we wanted to join them, but they welcomed us with open arms.

Wayne (later Jayne) County wrote the play we were doing, *World— Birth of a Nation*. He also played the dual roles of Florence Nightingale and her twin sister, Ethel. Wayne was an avid reader of *The World Tomorrow*, a magazine distributed for free by some wacky evangelist on TV. It was a mix of scientific, cultural, and political predictions with passages from the Bible thrown in—and was actually spot-on in some of its prophecies. I know *The World Tomorrow* was one of Wayne's main influences for *World*, but as for what the play was actually about, I never had a clue. All of the dialogue was made up of lines from pop songs, and it had something to do with Christopher Columbus getting castrated in a male abortion ward, perhaps in the future or in a place where time did not exist.

David played Ponce de Leon and in one scene had to take out his dick and pee in a paper cup (not sure whether that signified his discovering the Fountain of Youth or was just a urine sample for the male abortion ward). And I played Tilly Tons, an S&M necrophiliac nurse. My costume was a super-short white nurse's outfit emblazoned with little brown sausages (a waitress uniform borrowed from the fast-food chain ZumZum), with two balloons stuffed in it for big tits and a green-fur merkin on my pussy.

Whenever anyone forgot their lines (which was often), it was my job to start humping one of the dead bodies that were lying all over the stage and call out, "Where are you, Spot" to my dead dog or "I hear you, Grandfather" to my dead grandfather. I also did a scene in a black leather corset, black stockings, and boots, where I lopped off the penises (raw hot dogs) of two beautiful young brothers with a saber, while uttering shusssh-ing sounds like the ones on Tina Turner's version of the Beatles' "Come Together."

The two young brothers, Jimmy and Tommy, were barely of legal age and, except for lots of glitter, were completely naked on stage. Nudity and glitter were huge components of the Theatre of the Ridiculous. And since our audiences were made up largely of gay artistic stoners and proponents of fantasy and glamour, I could understand why both elements had such a big appeal. But those two young brothers are what had a big appeal for me. I began having threesomes with them on the very first night of rehearsals—right there in the dressing room in front of Tony and the rest of the cast—and continued having sex with them throughout the four or five month run of the play.

Tony would get furious with us if we were fucking around when we were supposed to be going over our lines (in my case, all two of 'em) or clearing out of the dressing room after the show. But Tony enjoyed watching us and he liked that we helped to raise the cast's energy level; he was always demanding "more energy!" of us. Tony also knew that no matter how disruptive or naughty I might get off-stage, I always respected him as my director and did whatever he asked of me onstage. And so it was with a mixture of chastisement, irony, devilishness, and affection that Tony christened me with my third—and admittedly very fitting—fantasy name, Party Favor.

World quickly became a kind of East Village happening, with people coming back three and four times to see it, often on acid. Other Theatre of the Ridiculous directors like Charles Ludlum and John Vaccaro came. Even Andy Warhol—the one artist I knew enough about to be impressed by—came. And they all laughed hysterically and seemed to grasp the play's deeper meaning—which Wayne said was that "if there wasn't so much male domination in the world, it would certainly be a better place ."

October 1, 1970—*Being on stage is such a high. The camaraderie, the we're-all-in-this-thing-together attitude of the NYTE is so amazing. I just wish everyone could experience this feeling. I'm sure there'd be no more wars if they could.*

Of course, we really didn't make much money doing *World*, maybe twenty or thirty dollars a weekend, if we were lucky. But each night after a rehearsal or a performance, a few of us, especially those of us with other jobs, would scrape enough together between us to go to Phebe's, an actors' hangout on the Bowery nearby, to have some food and drinks and come down from our adrenaline high. One night Tony, Wayne, Jamie Andrews (Christopher Columbus), Tony "Zee" Zanetta (Dr. Louis Pasteur/Jefferson Davis), and Leee Black Childers (our stage manager) suggested we go to Max's Kansas City instead. Amazingly, when we got there, they marched me right into the back room with them. They were Max's back-room regulars, and going there with them as an underground actress and member of their troupe allowed me to crash right through that wall of intimidation I'd felt when I'd peeked in there on previous visits with Paul McGregor.

We joined a table of other regulars who immediately made me feel welcome—Lillian Roxon, a writer for the *Sydney Morning Herald* and author of the *Rock Encyclopedia*; Danny Fields, a music journalist, record company PR man, and manager of rock stars such as Iggy Pop; Lisa Robinson, another music journalist, who later published *Rock Scene* magazine; and Larissa, a clothing designer for Miles Davis and Jimi Hendrix, dubbed "the Coco Chanel of Rock and Roll" for her thick French accent and the chic black vintage clothes she always wore. Sitting there, bathed in the womblike red florescent light, surrounded by so many friendly, creative, and accomplished showbiz people was like being accepted into a sorority—something I'd missed by not going to college. I really felt like I had made it in a big way and entered the innermost sanctum where the downtown theater and music scenes merged—where I was destined to spend many more nights, never to be intimidated by its exclusivity again.

JOHNNY WINTER moved like a lightening streak onstage. With his long white hair and superpale, superskinny body, he looked like an extension of his Flying V electric guitar. Franklyn and I went to his concert at the Fillmore but didn't manage to get backstage. So after the show, we hung out by the stage door to catch the band coming out. When they did, I gave Johnny one of my "You are beautiful" cards, but being an albino with bad eyesight, he couldn't read it. Johnny seemed to have picked up a few friends and groupies, so when his band members couldn't all fit into their limo, Johnny's bass player, Randy Jo Hobbs, got pissed off and told them he would take a cab instead—which gave me the perfect opportunity to come to his rescue. I grabbed Randy's hand and led him away from the crowd as if I knew him, and he came along with me like an obedient child. We got a taxi to the Chelsea Hotel, had some quick sex in his room, then went to a party at the house of Steve Paul (the band's manager and owner of The Scene) to watch a video of the show. I liked the way Randy treated me, especially by including me in this very intimate gathering. So when we got back to his hotel room, I showed my appreciation by doing him good.

Without elaborating here, let me just say that when it comes to sex, there are some things I have never gotten into, like bestiality, necrophilia, or pedophilia (although Butch Patrick, otherwise known as little Eddie Munster, might have been a tad bit underage when I did him). But, depending on the person, the drugs, and the occasion, I have pretty much, at one time or other, made use of every orifice and instrument of pleasure that God gave me. Anyway, little Randy Jo seemed quite satisfied and he returned my affections in kind.

We spent the whole next day in bed taking a variety of drugs (conveniently delivered by dealers living at the Chelsea) and then went to visit Johnny in his room a few floors down. Johnny's girlfriend, Carol, was there with him, looking gorgeous in a sexy black negligee, while I felt a bit leftover in my Stephen Burrows multicolored cardigan (which Johnny wanted me to give him) from the night before. Johnny was stark naked and stayed that way throughout our visit. At one point, when the late afternoon sun was illuminating the room too much for his albino eyes, he stood up on the window ledge and hung a blanket to block out the light. The blanket was pink and with the setting sunlight coming through it, it became a super Day-Glo pink, an effect enhanced no doubt by the drugs we were on. Oh man, if I had only had a camera to capture that image—Johnny in his neon white nakedness, solarized and glowing against that hot pink background. It's a rock and roll vision I'll remember forever.

They were playing the Fillmore again that night, so I rode there with them in their limo and went backstage. But Randy picked up another groupie early on and that was the end of our romance, which was actually OK with me. I had no further expectations of anything with him. I was in need of fresh clothes and grooming and he was a bit too into the hard drugs for my taste anyway. I stayed for the first show and then met Franklyn for a late dinner and told him all that had happened since I'd left him by the stage door the night before.

Oct. 5, 1970—*I don't know which is more fun, having groupie sex or sharing the details of it afterwards with Franklyn.*

ONE DAY in Central Park, when I went looking for Billy by the fountain, I locked eyes with this older, long-haired, Georges Mathieu–type guy who really gave off a dangerous vibe. He was with a bunch of people who were speaking French, and I became obsessed with him and started following him around the park. He noticed me right away but made sure to ignore me until he eventually parted with his friends and approached me. "Are you going to follow me home?" he asked. I answered yes. And that's exactly what he made me do. He walked in front of me, didn't speak to me, paid only his own way on the subway, and led me to his loft in the East Village. I trailed along like a puppy dog or like someone in a trance, knowing it was sick, but thinking of it as romance.

From the black-and-white photos on his walls, I deduced that he was either a photographer or a hunter of big game animals in Africa, though he wouldn't answer any of my queries at all. He, in fact, told me to "shut the fuck up" and only spoke to me in harsh commands like "Take off your clothes, you ugly bitch," "Don't you dare make a sound when I whip you," "You're only good for fucking up the ass,"and "Now make me some dinner, you stupid cunt." Why I stayed and put myself through the physical pain and mental abuse, I'll never know. I was just so curious about these true sadists and I wanted to see how far each of us would go. His last command—after he'd tied me up, gagged me, whipped me, sodomized me, threw the food I made him on the floor, and then forced me to clean it up—was "Now, get the hell out of here you filthy whore, and never come near this place or me again, or I'll kill you."

It was dark outside by the time I left and hard to find a cab, though I eventually did. And I know it sounds strange, but I wanted to laugh out loud when I got away from this monster with my life. I had a weird, giddy sense of satisfaction from having taken the situation so far and still survived. It all suddenly struck me as quite absurd and funny. But Mr. Big Game Hunter or whoever he was did manage to leave me hurt and scared enough to know that my S&M exploration days were pretty much over, at least with these dangerous strangers anyway.

NANCY HAD divorced Philip English and was dating Chick Casady, a roadie for Jefferson Airplane. He was the brother of Jack Casady, the band's bass player, and he seemed way too delicate and genteel to be doing roadie work. Nancy was never thought of as a groupie. She played her cards in such a way that these guys all considered her "a rock and roll lady." And I'd become her sidekick. So even though I was obviously a tart, they treated me almost as respectfully as they treated her. And it really did feel kind of nice.

Nancy turned me on to the Capitol Theater in Port Chester, New York, a great old concert hall with a much more relaxed backstage policy than the Fillmore's. We'd take the Metro North train from Grand Central (less than an hour's ride from NYC) and get out right across the street from the Capitol's stage door. Sometimes Nancy's friends ChiChi and Priscilla would join us. Being with Nancy, all we had to do was knock on the door and we'd be ushered right in. Eventually, through Nancy, I got to know the musicians, crews, and friends of the Airplane, the Dead, Leon Russell, Joe Cocker, Derek and the Dominos, Hot Tuna, the Allman Brothers, Seatrain, Little Feet, J. J. Cale, and Taj Mahal. And once the security guards at the various theaters got used to seeing me coming and going with those guys, they would pretty much let me in backstage all of the time, even at the Fillmore.

Nancy soon moved on from Chick Casady to Carl Radle, the bass player for both Leon Russell and Derek and the Dominos—and I moved on from the Airplane's roadie, Paul, and Leon Russell's roadie, Pete, to Leon's gorgeous little golden-haired drummer, Chuckie Blackwell. I'd been at the Fillmore back when Chuckie, Carl, and Leon all played on the Mad Dogs and Englishmen tour. I went crazy for that band, wanted to run away with them, even hitchhiked to a few of their out-of-town gigs but never had more than a casual relationship with any of them. But at this stage, because of Nancy, I'd come to be considered an intimate in this very special circle of friends and musicians.

Chuckie was not *exactly* bisexual, but he liked having group scenes with me and whomever he happened to be sharing his room with that night—like John Gallie (organ), Patrick Henderson (piano), Jesse Ed Davis (session guitarist), and Denny Cordell (Leon's partner in Shelter Records). I was crazy for Chuckie but not in love with him in the traditional sense. Except for the inexhaustible sex, we were very much like brother and sister. He looked out for me, always making sure I was on the guest list for the shows and any parties that followed. And he really made me laugh, both in and out of bed.

I loved all of the Tulsa Okies and the rest of the people I got to know while hanging out in Leon Russell's world—Carl, Chuck, John, Patrick, Jessie, and Denny, as well as Don Preston, Jim Gordon, Jim Keltner, Chris Stainton, Miss Emily Smith, and Claudia Lennear (thought to be the inspiration for the Rolling Stones' "Brown Sugar"). They were all so down to earth and unassuming. I, of course, worshiped Leon, a musician's musician, whose funky, soulful tunes really turned me on. And I was always hoping that one day on the road, Leon just might decide to share his room with Chuckie.

I WENT to the Gaslight a lot to catch my favorite blues singer, John Hammond. He was so gorgeous—skinny, with high cheekbones, long neck, thick lips, ample eyelids, luxurious lashes. He could have been a major pop star, but he was way too much of a blues purest for that. You wouldn't think that a privileged New York City white boy—son of famed record producer John Hammond Jr. (who signed Aretha Franklin, Bob Dylan, Leonard Cohen, and Bruce Springsteen to Columbia) and great-great-grandson of William Henry Vanderbilt— would be the one who could touch you so deeply with what was traditionally the music of poor black men, but sure enough he could. And even those old blues guys themselves would comment that John Hammond was, indeed, that good.

Bonnie Raitt often opened for John, with Denny Brown sometimes third on the bill. Luckily I liked their music too, because I sat through so many of their sets just to hear John. The Gaslight was so small, you could hang out with the artists pretty easily, as I often did, with Bonnie and Denny, but not with John. John had a bit of a stutter (though not when singing) that I found really sexy, but which, I think, made him kind of shy. And I was almost paralyzed by my own passion in his presence. His brown leather pants and blue satin shirt, his slicked-back, fifties-style hair, his long white fingers bending the notes on "Two Trains Running" or "Hoochie Coochie Man"—everything about him turned me on.

One night, when John was playing the Bitter End, a couple of blocks from the Gaslight, I went with David Smith to catch his show. David and I had the same kind of arrangement that Franklyn and I had—if I got 'im, I would go, no hurt feelings. David also loved John's music and agreed with me about John's sex appeal, so he completely understood the depth of my longings. David would have liked nothing better than to see me go off with John at the end of the evening.

I had never really come on to John before, but on that night, after his set, I just sort of snuggled up to him backstage and asked him if he had someone at home waiting for him. When he answered, "Why, no I don't" in the sexy way he did, I knew right away he was up for my affections. Oh my God, this was big for me. I never even wanted Mick Jagger or John Lennon the way I wanted John Hammond. And Van Morrison I wanted in a more cerebral way. I had a half a tab of acid in me, but this was a rush beyond all drug rushes—this was a love rush. I felt as if I was vibrating at a very high frequency and my feet weren't touching the ground. I longed to make time tick more slowly so the magnificent moments would last.

Dear David was waiting outside of the club in case I hadn't scored. And when John and I came out together, he greeted John like a fan and pretended he didn't even know me. As I walked off arm-in-arm with John into the snowy Village night, I looked back and David smiled the sweetest smile and blew me a kiss. What a lucky girl I was to have friends like David and Franklyn. I always knew that they were the ones who would stick with me forever, while the rock stars would probably just come and go.

As John and I made our way along Bleecker Street, fluffy white snowflakes collected on our dark winter coats, in our hair, and on the edge of John's guitar case. Wow, what a picture I hold in my mind of that moment—a perfect snapshot, the very essence of rock and roll romance. Even just the thought of it some forty years later still thrills me. It was mine. I had that moment. No, of course, I couldn't make it last forever, but in a way I almost have.

John lived in a loft down on lower Broadway. It was very beatnik basic, and the lighting was anything but soft. There were signs that I was in the home of a married man, including family photos and a baby's crib. I thought John would put on some groovy blues music, dim the lights, roll a joint, and serve me some old Kentucky bourbon.

But instead, he just poured me a glass of filtered water, pulled me to the bed, and started to kiss and caress me like a man who was in a kind of a hurry.

I was really nervous and embarrassed getting undressed in the brightness of that hundred-watt light bulb. I felt fat and worried that my OCD scars were showing. He, of course, looked even more amazing in the nude than he did in his leather pants and satin shirt. His skin was magnificently pale and unblemished, like a polished marble statue. And underneath it, he was nothing but muscle and bone, not an ounce of fat anywhere. Thankfully, as soon as our warm naked bodies made contact, my inhibitions were banished by the closeness. Oh, that skin! Just touching it was so unbelievably divine. But having John inside of me with his arms wrapped around me and his lips kissing mine was beyond divine.

Around 4 A.M., John told me it was time to leave because his wife would be coming home in the morning (though I think they may have actually been separated at the time). I was crushed. There was a blizzard outside and it was so desolate in that part of town. And he didn't even escort me downstairs to get me a cab, which was really rude and unkind. Luckily, two policemen picked me up and drove me to Eighth Street, where I was able to hail one. What a schizophrenic night! One minute I was wrestling and nestling in the warm arms of love and the next I was out in the cold, in more ways than one.

Oh dear diary—*I feel like such a fool. Sometimes I think I should never even go near these guys. I mean, it's one thing to be in love with them from afar, but up close it's a whole other story. I know they're only human, but I keep thinking there must be one who'll live up to the magic of his music and one who'll appreciate me. Or is it a case of groupies not being entitled to respect? Oh well, I'm glad I made love with John anyway, even though I'm so bummed out now. Anyway, I hear that gorgeous new folkie, Kris Kristofferson, will be at the Gaslight in a week or two . . . uhmm.*

9

Pop Tart

WAS JUST beginning to worry that the freelance production work
was drying up when good old McCann Erickson came through
with yet another easy little job for me. They were looking for stock
footage of oil wells for a Miller beer commercial, and, according to
their producers, there wasn't anything aesthetically pleasing enough
in New York. So they sent me out to L.A. for a couple days to see if I
could find anything there. When I arrived I watched reel after reel of
film at a stock footage house—oil rigs pumping in red sunsets, oil rigs
pumping solo, and oil rigs pumping fifty to a field. But none of them
looked attractive or exciting, at least not like I'd remembered them
looking in the James Dean movie *Giant*.

The night was still young when I got back to my hotel after that
first long, fruitless day, so I decided I'd go hitchhiking along the
Sunset Strip (something you'd never dare try today) to see what was
shaking. And when I got to the western end of the Strip, my heart
skipped a beat. Emblazoned on the marquee of L.A.'s most famous
rock club, the Whisky a Go Go, were the words "New York Rock &
Roll Ensemble." I could hardly believe my good fortune.

I hung out in front of the club for no more than fifteen minutes
when along came Michael Kamen and the boys, all smiles and happy

to see me. Michael, always the perfect gentleman, escorted me into the club and the dressing room, got me a drink, rolled me a joint, and made me feel like rock royalty. Then, after two fabulous sets and some backstage schmoozing, I went with him to his room at the Landmark, the hotel where Janis Joplin had died of a heroin overdose a few months earlier.

I was never that much of a cokehead, but Michael had some really good stuff and we wound up snorting it, smoking pot, and having sex until dawn. Michael was a fantastic lover. He really relished and adored women, in mind as much as in body, and proved it over and over with the way he made love. We'd always been just friends back in New York, where Michael had a sort of steady girlfriend named Sandra Keenan, whom I was slowly getting to know. But we were in L.A.... and New York just seemed so far away... and Michael, in typical on-the-road musician fashion, assured me everything would be OK.

We had just begun to fall asleep when I had to get up and search for oil wells for yet another day. Michael gave me some coke to take with me so I could stay awake. By 11 A.M. I had seen all of the footage available and was able to fly home earlier than planned, exhausted and empty-handed but filled with the sweet memories of my night with Michael. As a kind of guilty admission and apology to Sandra, with whom I really wanted to be friends, I wrote the following lyrics on the plane. They were the first of my lyrics ever to be set to music—in a kind of Betty Boop, soft-shoe shuffle—by Michael, of course. And Sandra, bless her heart, never seemed to hold any of it against me.

SANDRA'S SONG

My boyfriend is a rock star
And I trust him with my life
He calls me his old lady
That's something like his wife
He goes to California

Two, three times a year
I'd like to think he's loyal
But these words my head doth hear

CHORUS
They may be good at chopping wood
And carrying the load
They may be great at playing mate
But they all mess around on the road

My boyfriend's name is Michael
He's the singer with the band
He also plays piano
And he always holds my hand
He spends his evenings here
Except when he's away
I know that he's my honey
But these words my head doth say

(CHORUS)

So if you've got a lover
Who is often out of town
And if his present absence
Has got you feeling down
Well just get into your red dress
And stop your being blue
Be happy that you got him
And these words will get you through

(CHORUS)

NANCY ANDREWS introduced me to a fantastic girl named Evan
Carey who booked bands for the Cellar Door, a happening club in
Washington, D.C. Her boyfriend, Trevor Veitch, played guitar for
the folk singer/songwriter Tom Rush. Evan, Nancy, Priscilla, Nancy's
sister Jody, and I were going to a concert of his in New Jersey, so we
met up at Tom's apartment down on Eighth Street in the Village. But
when it turned out that all seven of us plus amps and guitars couldn't
fit in the one car they had, I volunteered to stay behind.

I was all hyped up for a fabulous night of live music, and then suddenly I was alone in the Village with nothing to do. I called a few
friends from a pay phone, and Michael Klenfner, record exec and former backstage doorkeeper at the Fillmore East, happened to be home
and invited me over. Well, here I go again saying I didn't do much
coke—people just kept pouring it down my nose, I guess—but Michael
had oodles of good coke and good grass too, and I inhaled a lot of both
at his place that night. We listened to records, dished about bands and
the theater (he was a big fan of the NYTE), had some laughs, and
hung out until he had to leave for an appointment. Before parting, he
reminded me that Kris Kristofferson was playing at the Gaslight.

Duh! I'd been so busy looking for work, mooning over John Hammond and Beautiful Billy, and obsessing over how I'd score with Leon
Russell that I'd completely forgotten about Kris's gig. I raced to the
club and, being kind of known there by then, was able to worm my
way in for the end of his first set. During the encore, I went into the
ladies' room and stayed there while they ushered out one crowd and
ushered in the next for the second show. That enabled me to jump
out and grab the best seat in the house, which was literally right at
Kris's feet.

All the while he was onstage, I talked to Kris with my eyes. There
was no way he could have avoided me—and it didn't seem like he
wanted to, either. He was around thirty-three or thirty-four at the
time and just beginning to be noticed by the masses. (Janis's version of his song "Me and Bobby McGee," recorded just before she
died, had not yet zoomed up the charts.) All his friends in the audi-

ence were shouting out requests and rapping back and forth with him between songs. So I had to think of something quick and clever that I could say or do in the few seconds I might get with him at the end of the show, before they surrounded him, as I knew they would. The Gaslight had little pads and pencils on the tables for your drink orders, so naturally I thought, well, I'll write him a poem.

> *Hi Kris, I'm Kathy*
> *Do you wanna be my friend?*
> *Well gee now, let's see*
> *What'll we do?*
> *Well, we'll tell each other stories*
> *And we'll make each other feel good*
> *And we'll drink some wine that's real good*
> *And we'll mellow with the moon.*

I gave him the poem as he was leaving the stage. He read it right away, then flashed his beautiful baby blues at me, smiled, and said, "You got me." Just like that: "You got me." Man, talk about approachable, receptive, and direct—that was enough to make me fall in love with him right then and there. And the best part of all was that I got him with my poetry, making me feel like it was a genuine one-artist-to-another type of thing. I got him with my mind, with my imagination. How cool was that? OK, so I was also kinda cute, but it was the poem that gave me entrée and sealed the deal in under sixty seconds.

Still, his friends wanted to party with him, so I knew it was gonna be a while before I actually got him into bed. But that made the whole thing even better. Every look and touch we had with each other over the next couple of hours—at first at the Kettle of Fish, the bar above the Gaslight where the musicians all hung out, and after that in his room at the Chelsea Hotel—held the promise and anticipation of sex. By two A.M. the entourage at the Chelsea was down to three guys, the musician Bobby Neuwirth among them, and one girl, a scruffy downtown poet named Patti Smith who I suspected may have once had a thing with Kris. It was obvious, in any case, that she certainly had a thing *for* Kris.

By three A.M., everyone had left, except for Patti. I wasn't sure what to expect and I certainly didn't want to share him with her. Thank God Kris piped up at one point and told Patti he'd take her downstairs to get her a cab. I was a little bit jealous of her in a way, because apparently she was catching a flight to London that day, something to do with a book of hers or a poetry reading there. But I figured my day would come for all of that. And there was nothing I wanted more that night than to make love with Kris.

Of all of the groupie scores I made, I think Kris Kristofferson was probably the most romantic—gentle, caring, sensual, sweet, and with plenty of stamina too. After making love, we fell asleep, his body wrapped around mine, and he kissed me every time we moved and momentarily awakened. In the morning (more like midday), we had sex again, and we talked up a storm. He even asked me to sit in the bathroom with him and talk some more while he shaved. What a darling man. He really treated me like an equal, while also making me feel like a desirable woman. If Kris had fallen in love with me, my life might have taken a whole different turn. But at least we got to have one night of bliss. Whether or not I'd ever hear from him again, I didn't know.

March 6, 1971, NYC—*Zach drove Nancy, Priscilla, ChiChi, and me up to the Capitol Theater last night to catch the first of Leon's two nights there. Carl Radle is back from the Dominos for a while, and he and Nancy are now madly in love! Freddie King was also on the bill, and Chuckie and I had some fun with him in his dressing room . . . nothing heavy, just lots of dirty talk and giggling, with them pulling down my tights to look at my ass and my pussy . . . typical rock and roll juvenile backstage behavior . . . and I loved it. Leon let us stand right on the side of the stage for his sets, and, oh man, how I get off on that Okie music! Lots of little crushes and intrigues going on . . .*

ChiChi and Pete... Priscilla and Chuckie, me and Chuckie, me and John Gallie, Chuckie and John Gallie. And good old Zach was so cool... even drove us back to the city and dropped us off at their hotel so we could party with them. Chuckie, John, Denny Cordell, and I all had sex together in Chuckie's room. Well, it was mostly me having sex with the three of them. They didn't really do anything that hardcore with each other. Priscilla was there when we were first getting into it, but she soon split. It took a lot of energy to please those three guys, but I managed, ha ha... and luckily we all got to sleep late this morning.

March 7, 1971, NYC—I slept with John Gallie last night, but we didn't have sex. John was sharing his room with Leon... yes Leon!!!... and he was afraid we might disturb him. John said that singers especially need to get their sleep, and Leon, of course, is John's boss. Lying in John's bed all night, just a few feet from Leon, was torture, but I managed to endure it. And this morning I was karmically rewarded with a whole different kind of thrill, being there when Leon called Bob Dylan to discuss a joint recording session. That was musical history in the making! And I was there! Leon's showing that kind of trust in me, to do it right in front of me like that, must mean he's accepted me as family. And that's what I've always wanted, even more than the sex, I think. It's just that life is so short and sex seems to be the quickest way of getting there.

March 11, 1971—Aux Puces is almost totally gay now... too gay for me, so I'm turning the spinning over to Jay Martin full-time. I'm so glad I got my just desserts before leaving, though... that pig, Jacques, my old boss from Saint Hilaire, came by the other night and pleaded with David to let him in. Ha ha, how pathetic! I just stood there smiling, of course, while David sternly turned him away.

❦

MAX'S HAD replaced Aux Puces as my hangout, the club I felt compelled to visit every night, whether for hours of dishing with my backroom buddies or just popping in before going home from wherever else
I'd been. The pull of the place was irresistible—and no wonder, since
so many of the people there, like Alice Cooper, Todd Rundgren, Lou
Reed, Jackson Browne, Tim Buckley, John Cale, Jane Fonda, Roger
Vadim, David Johansen, Loudon Wainwright III, and Andy Warhol,
were so intensely magnetic. The back room also played host to many
magazine writers and editors, and two of 'em, Danny Goldberg and
Ronnie Finkelstein, both of whom I was fucking, were beginning to
talk seriously about publishing my poetry in *Circus* Magazine. And, of
course, Max's always held the promise of a quickie fuck in the upstairs
phone booth with the adorable Warhol superstar Eric Emerson, or of
bumping into Andy Paley, the scrumptious lead singer of the Side-
winders, and taking him home for the night.

Meanwhile, a friend from Mad Ave. days, John Myers (a former
lover who eventually came out of the closet), hired me to help him
launch a kind of mail-order ad agency, producing generic advertising
campaigns for banks. It was a brilliant idea. Since all banks provided
pretty much the same services, all we had to do was insert each bank's
name into our prepackaged newspaper, magazine, radio, and TV ads,
guarantee them a certain geographic radius of exclusivity, and ship
them the materials. The two of us ran the whole operation from the
bedroom of John's apartment on East 66th Street. So at least I could
support myself until something came along in the field of music, TV,
writing, or acting. I wasn't that fussy about which one, as long as it
was something in showbiz. The work with John was tedious and bor-
ing, but he and I had such a close and comfortable relationship that
we always managed to squeeze in a few laughs every day. He and his
boyfriend even gave me a valuable lesson one afternoon in how to give
a good hand job.

DAVID SMITH had introduced me to an aristocratic young man
named Richard Skidmore, who worked for the anti-war activist Abbie

Hoffman. And when Richard told me that Abbie needed my services, I, of course, agreed to do whatever I could for the cause. Richard was producing audio tapes for Hoffman, which, as I understood it, would be smuggled into Vietnam and broadcast on Radio Hanoi. They had already done segments with members of the women's lib and gay lib movements, the Black Panthers, the Weather Underground, and similar organizations, and they wanted a strictly rock and roll one from me. A young guy named Dennis, who used the name Mike Rafone, played DJ, spinning tracks by musicians I'd met, and in between songs, I told stories about them, both dirty and clean. I never understood how the content of my tape could possibly match the propaganda value of the others, but Richard assured me that it would.

At the recording session, Richard told me to use a name other than my real one, because the government didn't look too favorably on these tapes. I already had three fantasy names (four, including the very short-lived Indian Summer), but Richard advised me not to use any of those, lest they be traced back to me. So on the spot I came up with Cherry Vanilla. I don't even remember where I got the inspiration for it. Maybe there was a cherry vanilla ice cream or yogurt container in the studio or something. I really didn't give it that much thought, since it was not a name I contemplated ever using again. I never met Abbie, nor did I ever find out if the tape made it over to Vietnam. And Richard Skidmore seemed to disappear from my life and David's as quickly and as magically as he'd appeared.

MY FRIEND Peter Allen had just finished his first album, and, as a favor, I wrote a very positive review of it and submitted it to *Circus* Magazine, along with some of my poems. It took courage on my part, because I didn't know if they would consider my work worthy of publication, and I was afraid of rejection. It was, after all, the first time I was really putting myself out there as a writer. Meanwhile, I was working every day with John Myers, sleeping mostly with Michael Norlan and Nancy's ex Philip English, freaking out over the Doors'

new LP, *L.A. Woman*, wondering if Kristofferson would ever call me, and hoping I'd get another chance to get close to Leon Russell.

That chance came when *Mad Dogs & Englishmen*, the documentary film about their tour, had its premiere in New York and I got to attend it with Leon and his Okie entourage—my heart racing all through it, as I was seated right next to Leon himself. Oh man, how I wanted to hold his hand, rub his leg, and make out with him in that darkened theater. But I kept my composure and contented myself with the fact that he was whispering little comments to me all during the movie. I especially appreciated him telling me during the Tulsa picnic scene, "There was a bit of mescaline in the air that day." I felt it once again confirmed his ranking of me as a trusted insider.

As we left the Zeigfeld Theater, a huge crowd of adoring fans was waiting outside to shower Leon with their affections. I felt so proud to be with him, like I had officially gained the status of *friend to the stars*, but I also recognized in that moment my own deep-down desire to *be* a star myself. I was so curious about what the rush of stardom must feel like, and I wanted to see how I would handle it. I'd gotten a bit of recognition through my DJ jobs and performances with the NYTE, but that was pretty small-time. I wanted it to be bigger and for something I'd created that was wholly my own.

Leon drove a few of us to the afterparty at some club uptown. And when he and the rest of the boys in the band learned that I had never done shots of tequila, they ordered me a triple and then another. Oh my God, it was almost like shooting speed or licking acid. I even suspected they'd slipped me some Spanish fly. But, no, it was just good old Jose Cuervo Gold and being with musicians that got me so high and so horny. After some outrageously erotic behavior on the dance floor, Chuckie, Pete, Jessie Ed Davis, and I shamelessly announced that we were going back to their hotel to party. Leon made a move to join us, but Smitty, Joe Cocker's road manager, asked him to stay a while longer. So we taxied down to the Gramercy Park Hotel without him. Damn that Smitty, I thought.

After a laugh-filled orgy in Pete's room, Chuckie and I still had energy to spare. So we left Pete and Jessie passed out in their beds and went to Chuckie's room—which he just happened to be sharing with Leon—to have yet more sex. Chuckie was a fuck machine, much like Michael Norlan, and he loved that I'd christened him "the hottest cock in rock." As the dawn light started seeping through the edges of the blinds, Leon had yet to come in. Chuckie was passed out, and I was exhausted and rubbed raw. But I still couldn't sleep, because I knew that at any minute my golden opportunity with Leon might happen.

Oh, how my heart raced when I heard the hotel room key in the door! I was bursting with sweet anticipation, more excited than a kid on Christmas morning. And there he was, Leon, my skinny Santa Claus, obviously drunk and in a mushy mood. "Is the party over?" he drawled. He was more adorable and more vulnerable than I had ever seen him.

"As long as I'm awake, honey," I cooed, "the party's never over." We made out and I gave him head, because my pussy just couldn't take any more fucking. Then we just rested and talked for a while. And those, of course, were the most fabulous moments of all. There I was, cuddled in Leon Russell's arms, talking about going swimming and riding horses at his lake house in Tulsa. Tired as I was, I could have talked with him like that forever, but the phone rang with my 8 A.M. wake-up call and instead I had to go and discuss ad campaigns with bankers all day.

Dear Diary—Things have been pretty quiet. Carl's on the road a lot and Nancy's being faithful, so we've been hanging out mostly with bands who know them both and respect their relationship. Bill Thompson is especially close with Nancy, in a strictly platonic way... I think. He manages the Jefferson Airplane and Hot Tuna and always invites us to their gigs, as well as to the Grateful Dead's. Chick Casady is still carrying a torch for Nancy, I'm sure. But he's like a wonderful big brother to us both. So no sex for me of late. Of course, there was that one wild Quaalude orgy with the Grateful Dead's road crew, the details of which are pretty hazy in my mind... maybe just as well.

Nancy called one evening and said she was hanging out with Kris Kristofferson and his piano player, Donnie Fritts, and they wanted me to meet them at the Chelsea. I was so excited because I thought it meant that Kris wanted to sleep with me again. But when I joined them at El Quijote, the Spanish restaurant in the hotel, I realized it was Nancy whom Kris was groovin' on. I tried to be upbeat and not show my disappointment and offered everyone a hit of the new windowpane acid I had just acquired. Kris had a terrible cold, so he was reluctant to take it at first. But when I assured him that acid had always cured my colds, he swallowed the tab straight away, along with the rest of us.

Kris felt better as the night rolled on, and we held court with the many people who stopped by our table. Then, we decided to catch the midnight screening of *El Topo* at the Elgin Cinema a few blocks away. The movie was filled with violent images that were at once bloody, beautiful, and bizarre. By the end of it, we were all a bit drained and Kris seemed to be burning up with a fever, so we called it a night and went our separate ways. When his symptoms were even worse the next day, Kris finally went to the doctor. Turns out he had pneumonia. I prayed Kris wouldn't hate me for giving him the acid and I never advised anyone to take it for a cold again—even though it actually had provided him with a few hours of fun and relief anyway.

I WAS spending so much time working at John Myers's, he suggested I move in with him. Since he couldn't afford to give me a raise, letting me live there rent free was his way of compensating me for helping him get the business off the ground. John's apartment was just a block and a half from Central Park, and the Madison Avenue bus, which stopped right outside of Max's, let me off on John's corner. So it was a very convenient location. And since we were both on a raw food diet at the time and having our meals together anyway, I figured why not.

A lot of my friends were also making moves around that time: Zach moved from WNEW to WPLJ, which had taken over as New

York's best rock and roll station. Nancy moved to Tulsa to set up house with Carl Radle. Nilo closed Aux Puces and moved to California to raise horses. David Smith moved on to manage a club called Tambourlaine. Paul McGregor moved his salon from 57th Street to St. Marks Place. Joel Schumacher moved to L.A. to work on Hollywood movies. Beautiful Billy moved to India with his new girlfriend. Pat Ast (all three hundred pounds of her) moved from her typist job at a Brooklyn box company to a model/salesgirl position at Halston's new boutique. And Dick and Franklyn moved into a co-op on Central Park West. But little did I realize that the most monumental move of all, one way beyond moving in with John Myers, was waiting just around the corner for me.

10

Groupie (Superstar)

FTER WE were finished dealing with the bankers for the day, John Myers and I would often invite a couple of hot guys over for dinner. Gay for him, straight for me. First, we'd all smoke lots of the great grass that Nilo was sending me from California (obviously he was raising more than horses out there). Then, while our dates watched and waited in a marijuana-intensified state of anticipation, John and I would fastidiously slice, dice, and arrange a bunch of raw, unadulterated veggies on plates as if we were creating Picassos and then serve them with water or organic apple juice. Once we'd raved over, sermonized about, and consumed the totally bland (and often gas-producing) food, we'd smoke some more pot, have a few laughs with the guys, and then lure them into our respective beds for the night.

The good-natured folkie Buzzy Linhart and the Zenned-out singer/songwriter Shawn Phillips loved it. However, jazz flutist Jeremy Steig, avant-garde pianist Paul Kilb, and actor Bengt Eklund (Britt's brother) all got a little freaked out, first by the rabbit food and our convoluted preparation of it and then by the voyeuristic setting. You see, John would have his sex romp in the bedroom and I would have mine in the living room, where I slept. But because of the shape of the apartment, we could easily see into each other's rooms through the windows when we left the shades up—which we usually did. I think John and I must have come off like some perverted nut-job of a couple in those days. But we didn't care. We looked and felt great on our strict veggie regimen, and we were laughing at ourselves just as much as anyone was laughing at us.

LEON RUSSELL played the Fillmore for four consecutive nights in May 1971. I went to all of the shows and had lots of sex with Chuckie Blackwell and the boys, but none with Leon himself. The Carpenters' version of the Leon Russell/Bonnie Bramlett song "Superstar" was all over the radio at the time, and it expressed how I was feeling. I'd loved that song ever since I'd heard Bonnie sing it on the Delaney & Bonnie tour. Bonnie, like Maxine Brown, was the kind of singer I wished I could be, but I knew I just didn't have the pipes. Her rendition of "That's What My Man Is For" is, for me, the ultimate rock and roll torch song. But it's "Superstar" that will always connect me with the passion and pathos of my longings for Leon. It paints the perfect picture of a groupie's heart. And it was originally called "Groupie (Superstar)"—a title that was soon to prove prophetic for me.

HANGING OUT in the back room at Max's, I naturally got to know a lot of Warhol people—Holly Woodlawn, Candy Darling, Jackie Curtis, Geraldine Smith, Andrea Whipps, Prindeville Ohio, Jane Forth, Donna Jordan, Cyrinda Fox, Rene Ricard, Taylor Mead, Jay and Jed Johnson, Olympio, and Ondine. And though I was often around Andy while there, I had only ever sat at his table (the big round one in the corner) with him a few times and had only been up to the Factory once—for a screening of *Flesh*, with its star, Joe Dallesandro, running the projector.

Andy and his pudgy superstar Brigid Berlin (aka Brigid Polk) used to tape-record all of their phone conversations, which were mostly

Andy saying, "And then what?" while Brigid, high on speed, incessantly yapped on about the private lives of her Manhattan socialite family. Her father, Richard Berlin, was chairman of the Hearst media empire for fifty-two years, and her mother, Muriel "Honey" Johnson, was a former debutante and a close friend of the Duke of Windsor's. Brigid and Andy also taped some colorful discussions about things like "plate jobs" and "the many different types of animal feces on the planet." Pat Hackett, Andy's secretary at the Factory, transcribed the tapes onto hundreds of typewritten pages, which Andy then turned over to Tony Ingrassia to make into a play. Tony edited them into what became *Pork*, a unique blend of Theatre of the Ridiculous and a pop-art sitcom, complete with toothpaste commercials. It was initially staged at New York's LaMaMa, its opening coinciding nicely with a Warhol art exhibition at the Whitney.

Amanda Pork, the character based on Brigid, was played by an off-Broadway actress named Cleve Roller, and many of my NYTE friends from *World* as well as my newer friends from Max's were in the production—Tony Zanetta was B. Marlowe (Andy Warhol), Jamie Andrews was Pall (Paul Morrissey), Wayne County was Vulva (Viva), Cyrinda Foxe was See Jane Run and Via Valentina was Miss Hell (composite characters), and a just-out-of-high-school Harvey Fierstein made his acting debut as Amelia (Pork's mother's maid). Leee Black Childers was, as always, Ingrassia's stage manager. I don't know why I wasn't in that production or why I never even went to see it during its brief run. I was probably too busy with my groupie life, especially since word had gotten out that the Fillmore East was soon to close forever.

An art dealer from England named Ira Gale caught a performance of *Pork* at LaMaMa and made arrangements with Andy and Tony to bring it to the Roundhouse in London for the summer, with plans to move it to the West End after that. But none of them, it seemed, were happy with Cleve Roller in the part of Amanda Pork. So when Tony suggested me for the role in the new production—reminding Andy that I was the girl with the dead dog and dead grandfather in *World*—Andy asked him to bring me up to the Factory for an audition.

I was excited beyond belief on that early June afternoon. Being recognized as an actress by Andy Warhol was huge and anointing, the chance of a lifetime. It meant that you yourself were art in some way, as precious as any of Andy's soup cans, Brillo boxes, dollar bills, or cows. But this was the lead role I was trying out for, with tons of dialogue, and I really didn't know if I could pull it off. Auditions made me nervous, and my stage experience was limited to a handful of school plays, Miss Betty's dance recitals, and *World*.

Tony coached me on a few scenes before taking me up to the Factory. But to my surprise, Andy never even asked me to do any lines from the play. Instead he enthusiastically engaged me in conversation, mostly about T V commercials and Madison Avenue and then asked me to sing my favorite hymn from Catholic school. He really caught me off guard with that request. But by the time I finished the first verse of "Dear Lady of Fatima" (off-key, but earnestly and with a rousing repeat line at the end), he joyously applauded me and gave me the part.

June 2, 1971—*Oh my God! I can hardly believe it. In just a little over a week I'll be leaving for London to STAR in Andy Warhol's first-ever play,* Pork. *I'll be living and working with my friends, collecting a proper Actor's Equity salary, and known forever as a Warhol superstar! OK, some say only the actors in Andy's movies should be called superstars. Whatever... Warhol actress, veteran, alumna, protégée... in one way or another, from this day forward, the name Andy Warhol and mine will be forever linked.*

TWO NIGHTS before I left for London, Paul McGregor cut my hair in a really severe shag. It was quite short in the front, and it made me feel so vulnerable and naked, I just wanted to cry. I was going off to face the biggest artistic challenge of my life and the loss of my long, swingy hair around my face really made me feel insecure. Of course,

Herbert Berghof would have approved of the cut, because he used to say that I hid behind my hair as if it were curtains.

Later that same night, I dropped the last tab in my acid stash and went with Priscilla to a press party for the Mark-Almond Band at the Cafe Au Go Go. At first it was all a bit surreal, because Jon Mark, the group's bass player, unhappy with the sound system, had a bit of a freak-out—cursing, swearing, and smashing his mike, amp, and guitar before walking off stage in disgust. But as the night went on, things really got interesting. John Hammond, Al Kooper, and Long John Baldry had an amazing jam session together, and the Mark-Almond Band returned to the stage and performed brilliantly. And then, at a little after-show gathering around the backstage piano, John Baldry blew my mind by reading a couple of my poems aloud. They'd been published in a local rock and roll newspaper called *Zoot*, which Mark-Almond's PR people had included in their press kits. It was the first time my poems had ever appeared in print and that was exciting in itself, but to hear Long John Baldry read them in that velvet voice of his to such a select audience of musicians and industry insiders was absolutely thrilling.

Shawn Phillips was there too, and after the poetry recitation, I went to the Fillmore with him to catch the Byrds' last set. We hung out in their dressing room, along with Elton John, Eric Anderson, and a gospel singer from Georgia named Mylon. Mylon drove me wild, and it was shameful how I came on to him when it was already understood that I was Shawn's date for the night. But he was so fuck-ing sexy, I just couldn't help it. Anyway, I later wound up with Shawn at the Gramercy Park Hotel, where I was rewarded not only with some great tantric sex (Shawn was a devoted practitioner of yoga and other spiritual disciplines), but also with witnessing the birth of two new Shawn Phillips songs.

Nights like that were what I lived for—nights that made me real-ize it was never just about the fucking. It was always about creation—inspiring it, rewarding it, being part of it, and mostly just rejoicing in the fruits of it. When Shawn wrote those two songs between our bouts of lovemaking, or I should say as part of our lovemaking, I knew there couldn't help but be some essence of me in them forever, even if nobody else ever knew about it, even if Shawn himself never gave it a thought. It was one of those moments when a groupie knows she's more than a groupie; she's a muse.

June 10, 1971—It's 10 A.M. and Shawn's been on the air since 9, doing a live concert at WPLJ-FM, while I'm at John's packing for London. We got no sleep at all last night, but I'm just bursting with energy. Shawn just did the two new songs he wrote only hours ago… and I was there… and now I'm here listening to them on the radio… how cool is that??? I'm in love with everything this morning, even this fucking haircut McGregor gave me.

OUR PLANE landed at Gatwick early on the morning of June 12, 1971, and by that evening I was stoned out of my head at a B.B. King recording session at the famous Olympic Studios in the London suburb of Barnes. Claudia Lennear had given me only one number to call in London, that of saxophonist Bobby Keys. She said that Bobby was "action central for the UK music scene." I called him late that afternoon, after Ingrassia, who'd been in London for a week already, took us on a tour of what would be our new city, our new home for a while.

Bobby instructed me in the art of mini-cabbing and I got myself out to Barnes. I went alone, because Bobby said it was a very closed session. Besides which, I liked to travel solo sometimes. It was another of those nights when I remember exactly what I was wearing—a red-and-black, jewel-printed 1950s dress with see-through black-lace insets above the tits and a flounce at the hip, black stockings, garter belt, high-heeled lace-up boots, smoky black eyeliner, and red lipstick. If Bobby had hired a rock and roll floozy from central casting, he couldn't have done better. And the reaction I got when I walked into the studio was, well, exactly what I was going for, I guess.

Bobby and his fellow horn player Jim Price were positioned on a riser behind a baffle, while B.B. and the rest of the band were clustered together in the main part of the studio. Bobby set me up with some headphones, sat me right between him and Jim, and gave me a big bag of grass and papers to roll us some joints. He also gave me a few lines of coke, which, along with the music and the rush of the moment, made me horny as hell, and I wound up giving head to both Bobby and Jim. There's a final horn section on one of the songs where Bobby is blowing his sax part almost immediately after the crescendo of my blowing him. And though the rest of the band couldn't see us behind the baffle, the engineers in the control room could hear us and were recording everything that was going down. It's all probably buried somewhere on those *B.B. King in London* masters.

Bobby came back to our sprawling Earl's Court flat with me, and I thought we would christen my new bed with a good night of sex. But after a little foreplay, Bobby decided we needed more coke and went out to the corner phone booth to call for some. I kind of knew he wasn't coming back, and it pissed me off that he was such a liar. But he left his nice big bag of grass behind, so I forgave him. And when Zee, Leee, Wayne, Via, and Eleana came home from their first evening out in London, we all got really stoned on it, and toasted to our promising new thespian lives with some cheap cognac.

DURING THE time before *Pork*'s rehearsals got into full swing, I was—except for the hours spent studying my lines—especially bad, fucking night and day with a seventeen-year-old gay-for-pay hustler named Philip. Leee had brought Philip and his friend Terry home from the Earl's Court tube station, where all of the bad boys hung out. Philip didn't charge me, of course; he and his friends only charged men for sex. But they didn't charge Leee, Zee, or Jamie either, because we were all big celebrities in their eyes.

Those Earl's Court boys always had plenty of money, both from the johns and from the photo sessions they did for a neighborhood

queen named Millie, who sold the pictures to pretty-boy nudie magazines in Europe. What I remember most about Philip, besides his
child-like persona, sexual dexterity, generosity, and devotion, was the
fact that he never wore anything twice. He really didn't have a place
of his own and he showered wherever he was, so he never cleaned any
of his clothes. Instead, he just bought new ones every day and simply
threw the used ones away. What troubled me about Philip, though,
was that I got my first-ever case of the clap from him. But that was
par for the course, I guess, and easily curable with the penicillin we
got for free from the National Health.

PORK'S REHEARSALS were grueling. The Roundhouse was big
(1,800 seats) and we didn't use mics. So, in addition to memorizing
all of the speed-freak dialogue and stage directions, I had to learn to
project my voice to the back of the house. This caused me to lose it
a lot, so a doctor provided me with a throat spray that was basically
liquid cocaine. Well, you can imagine how many of the cast members
started complaining about losing their voices after that. And Via (the
cast's biggest druggie) would drive me crazy by constantly sneaking
little spritzes of mine. It wasn't that I didn't want to share it, but I
was always very insecure that my supply might run out and I'd be left
without a voice.

To comply with Actor's Equity rules, half of *Pork*'s cast, including understudies, had to be British. A gorgeous young actress/singer/
songwriter named Dana Gillespie auditioned to be mine. She was a
former girlfriend of Bob Dylan's and she hung out with a burgeoning
UK recording artist named David Bowie, to whom she brought the
Pork script and the news of the play. Bowie proceeded to write the
song "Andy Warhol" for her, and the two of them performed it live on
David Peel's BBC radio show a few days later. (Bowie and Mick Ronson produced a version of it for Dana's 1973 album, *Weren't Born a Man*,
with Bobby Keys playing sax.) Of course, all of this was unbeknownst
to any of us in the cast. Only Ingrassia and Leee had met Dana at the

audition. And the only thing we knew about David Bowie was that Leee and Wayne remembered a photo of him in *Rolling Stone* in which he was wearing a dress.

THE ORIGINAL Hard Rock Café opened at about the same time that we arrived in London, and, as Warhol superstars, we became privileged regulars immediately, never having to wait in line to get in and always being tolerated, in spite of our boisterous celebrations, our dancing on the bar, and our sexploits in the bathrooms. I was especially tolerated, because my sexploits were often with Isaac Tigrett, who, along with Peter Morton, owned the place. The Hard Rock became our London Max's. We'd go there almost every night and be the center of attention. Seated at our table on any given evening might be the writers Felicity Clark and Joan Juliet Buck, actresses Patti D'Arbanville and Jill Haworth, actors Sal Mineo and Bud Cort, musicians Rod Stewart and Ronnie Wood, West End composer Lionel Bart, PR guru Tony Brainsby, and chanteuse Amanda Lear.

Andy's film producer Paul Morrissey had nothing to do with *Pork*, except for the fact that he kept telling Andy that I wasn't fat enough to be playing Amanda Pork, and insisting that Andy should have chosen my friend Pat Ast instead. So I ate with gusto at the Hard Rock— burgers, fries, corn on the cob, milk shakes, ice cream sundaes, and plenty of booze. I also ate all during rehearsals, because the script called for my character to consume lots of food. So I was getting a nice little belly on me. And of course Tony decided I'd be buck naked for a good portion of the play. Getting fat was fun in some ways and was obviously essential for the role, but it wasn't exactly good for my spirit or my groupie life.

July 11, 1971—*Not sure if it's the weight, the nudity, or just my insecurity about mastering this role, but I'm a little bit depressed and quite homesick for New York at the moment. Maybe it's 'cause I just heard about Jim Morrison dying in Paris. Even sent my dad a mushy poem last week. Mom wrote back, asking if I was drunk or doing drugs over here.*

LIFE AT our Earl's Court Square flat was mostly a wonderful circus. Zee, Leee, and Jamie were bringing home boys of all kinds. One of 'em, Clive (with blue hair), became our maid. Wayne was transitioning more and more publicly each day into Jayne. Via was falling down constantly from taking too many Mandies (Mandrax). Eleana, who was fucking one of the English boys in the cast, got a forgotten tampon lodged so far up in her pussy it resulted in a major medical trauma. And I had a country-rock band named Bronco living in my bedroom whenever they were in town. Friends from New York would come and stay with us, Hard Rock friends would drop by, Rod Stewart would raid our closets, and journalists would turn up to do stories.

We were interviewed and photographed for *Penthouse, Playmen, Time Out*, Italian TV, German TV, and just about every newspaper in the UK. And with the many hours of rehearsal Tony was having us put in, doing all of that press really cut into our recreational time—so we simply combined the two, not caring in the least what the journalists might see or hear while at the flat. The UK's trashiest newspaper, *The News of the World,* labeled us as "shocking" and christened our apartment "Pig Mansion." When Danae Brook came to interview us for *Rolling Stone*, I was giving head to my latest boyfriend, Nicky Kramer, right in front of her, and she and I wound up becoming the best of friends.

Except for Via, with her constant pilfering of my throat spray and the vicious tricks she sometimes played—like giving Jayne LSD and telling her it was a Mandie and giving Leee a Mandie and telling him it was penicillin—we all got along great at Pig Mansion. And we hung out a lot together outside of it as well, frequenting Granny Takes a Trip for clothes, Biba for makeup and accessories, Todd's for hair and grooming, the Troubadour for breakfast and to score drugs, Parsons for dinner, Sombrero (a.k.a. Yours and Mine) for dancing, the Marquee, Speakeasy, and Roundhouse for live music, and the Hard Rock for showing off, of course.

We were a force to be reckoned with, not only because of the Warhol banner that united us, but also because of our ability to excite the media and ignite interest from anyone tuned in to the happening scene. We were all exhibitionists and sexual outlaws, continuously flirting with scandal and stomping on social convention. And the press just ate us up. We were *the* stars of London that summer. And with the UK's ban on Warhol's *Trash* and *Flesh*, the pending possible ban on *Pork*, and the famous *Oz* magazine obscenity trials going on, we were immediately lauded by the UK's underground arts movement as fellow fighters for freedom of speech. We expected to be seen as pop in London, but we had no idea we'd also be seen as political. Our play had yet to open and we were already the most talked-about drama in town.

ALWAYS ON the hunt for new bands, Leee and I had a great scam going with the UK music scene. We would call the publicist or record company for any band we wanted to see and tell them we were Warhol people and correspondents for *Circus* and *Creem* magazines. *Circus* had just published four of my poems under the name Kathy Dorritie and my Peter Allen review under Cherry Vanilla (which I was trying out for the first time in print), and Leee had been getting his photos published in rock magazines for years. So we were able to bullshit our way into just about any gig we wanted. And, as was the music business custom back then, they'd even send a car to pick us up.

One day, while walking up the Warwick Road with Leee to get the #31 bus to the Roundhouse, we saw a most intriguing poster on a light pole. It featured a pretty long-haired blonde guy in a dress, reclining on a sofa. It was David Bowie. He was doing a gig at the Country Club in Hampstead on the outskirts of London, and Leee and I agreed immediately that we would go and see him. At the time I was in talks with *Circus* and *Creem* (both of whom loved the name

Cherry Vanilla) about doing a regular column for them. So Leee and I were actually almost legit.

The Country Club looked like someone's garage behind a suburban block of flats, small and hippie-ish, with everyone sitting on the floor. Leee, Jayne, and I boldly walked up to the woman who seemed to be running the show and introduced ourselves as Warholians, and I said I was Cherry Vanilla—the first time I'd ever done that. Initially, she seemed a bit butch—short hair, pants suit, big booming voice and demeanor—but we soon learned that she was, in fact, David's American wife, Angie, and she'd just had a baby. She welcomed us warmly, asked us to stick around after the show, and said she'd tell David we were there. She said she knew he'd be very pleased indeed. Then she scurried off to the sound and lighting booth to be the techie for the show, while we joined the fans on the floor.

Out came David, with the same long, honey-colored hair as we'd seen on the flyer, but dressed in cuffed, wide-legged, powder-blue faille trousers, a white cotton dress shirt, yellow patent-leather Mary Janes, and a big floppy hat with a feather. With him were Mick Ronson on electric guitar and Rick Wakeman (of Yes) on piano. David sat on a stool, strummed an acoustic guitar, and sang songs from his previous UK releases and from the *Hunky Dory* album he was working on at the time. When he got to "Andy Warhol," he announced to the audience that we were there and asked us to stand up and take a bow. It was the first time I was ever introduced as Cherry Vanilla, and, using the Amanda Pork character's signature gesture, I popped out a tit. That was David's first glimpse of me.

Bowie's looks and sound back then were a little too folksy for Leee and Jayne, but I loved everything about him. And I found his androgyny really appealing. In the sex area, however, I focused more on Mick Ronson, 'cause, after all, I had just met David's wife, and Ronson was single, straight, adorable, and very rock and roll. I wasn't sure about Rick Wakeman, but I could hear, amid the Donovan-like songs and Anthony Newley delivery that comprised most of the set, the seeds of something tougher and more collaborative emerging from

ABOVE LEFT: *With Lady Clauheen, not long after her abortion...* *and obviously before I learned how to style my own hair.* Hank D'Rocco

ABOVE RIGHT: *In Miss Betty's dance recital tap-dance costume,* *1953, at home in Woodside.* author's collection

RIGHT: *At Bethesda Fountain in Central Park,* *1970, in my "Groupie Lament" dress and in* *love with Beautiful Billy.* author's collection

BELOW: *A 1960s night at the Copacabana. Left to right: Bob La Tourneaux,* *Joan Folger, Frank Loverde, Dick Villany, me, Richard Thuilliette. I was in* *love with Richard but fucking Bob's boyfriend, Loverde.* author's collection

LEFT: *Robert L. Green's annual high-society party at his farm in Pennsylvania, 1970. Tripping my brains out in one of my favorite looks and hanging with some hippies.* David Taylor

BELOW: *Max's Kansas City. Left to right: Leee Black Childers, Danny Fields, me, Lisa Robinson, Henry Edwards. No makeup and a little OD'd on the suntan.* William "PoPsie" Randolph

ABOVE: *Roundhouse Theatre in London during Pork, 1971. Left to right: Julia Breck, Via Valentina, Jayne County, me— posing for Leee and posterity* Leee Black Childers

LEFT: *Photo booth at Brighton, England, during Pork. Left to right: Leee Black Childers, me, Jamie Andrews. No makeup, just acid and feeling like* **superstars.** author's collection

*Ingrassia (back row, left) and the stars of Pork on
Bond Street in London. Me, of course, baring my tits.*
© David Bailey

Onstage, Pork, 1971, with UK actors Louis Sheldon Williams and Oliver Dunbar. Leee Black Childers

In the Biba look and a heart from Franklyn Welsh, in London during Pork. Leee Black Childers

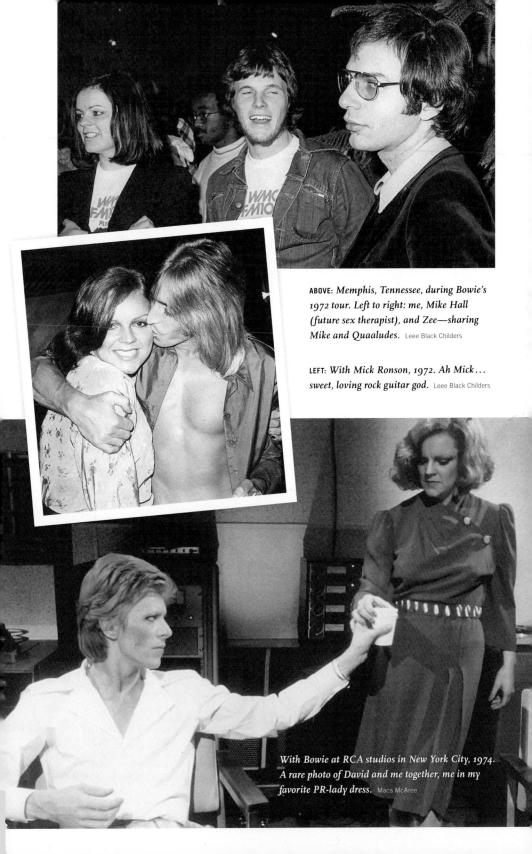

ABOVE: *Memphis, Tennessee, during Bowie's 1972 tour. Left to right: me, Mike Hall (future sex therapist), and Zee—sharing Mike and Quaaludes.* Leee Black Childers

LEFT: *With Mick Ronson, 1972. Ah Mick... sweet, loving rock guitar god.* Leee Black Childers

With Bowie at RCA studios in New York City, 1974. A rare photo of David and me together, me in my favorite PR-lady dress. Macs McAree

LEFT: *Reno Sweeney, 1974. The dress worked for nightclubbing, too.* Macs McAree

RIGHT: Wayne County at the Trucks! *1974. Making my entrance in Mrs. Ameche's emerald green 1950s dress, with silver and cerise accessories and Bob Menna in harness and mask.* Leee Black Childers

BELOW: *Max's Kansas City, 1974. Left to right: me, a Beach Boys musician, Andy Paley (we made such a cute couple), and Billy of Dino, Desi & Billy.* Leee Black Childers

In my Chelsea loft, 1974. A spur of the moment snapshot by the great Helmut Newton, who said he loved my smile and my nipples. Helmut Newton

LEFT: *At the Pink House in Water Island, 1974, in a neon red split-crotch, nipples-out stripper outfit with matching feather hat and rhinestone earrings.* Leee Black Childers

ABOVE: *Ratazzi's Restaurant, 1974, in my gold-sequined birthday suit at my first poetry reading, making a wish for my next role in the music biz.* Leee Black Childers

Reno Sweeney dressing room, 1975, with Holly Woodlawn, on the first night of my cabaret career, outdragging a drag queen in my glasses and feathers. Macs McAree

ABOVE: *Norma Kamali baby-wrap costume, 1975. It had rip-away harem pants— so great for the stage.* Chuck Fishbein

Trude Heller's, 1976, with Lance Loud, a guy who really got me. unknown

Max's Kansas City, 1976, wearing powder-blue glasses, Death to Disco button, and hugging Michael Alago, long before he became a producer and record exec. Karla Merrifield

RIGHT: With Anita Pallenberg, 1976, just after snorting Keith Richard's cocaine (see a bit of it on the end of my nose?). Steven Pines

BELOW: Robert Palmer in my dressing room at the 82 Club, 1976—got me so drunk, I went on stage practically naked. Bob Ross

On the Rocks, 1976. Go-go punky before I adopted the Lick Me T-shirt (this one says "Raspberries"). Bob Ross

ABOVE: Cover of UK's ZigZag magazine, 1977. Fierce! I loved it. author's collection

LEFT: At the studio with Ringo Starr, 1976, when he and Nancy Andrews were in love. Nancy Lee Andrews

The Roxy, UK, 1977. One of the greatest rock 'n' roll pictures of all time, with Louie's guitar and Sting in sunglasses. It was the inspiration for the ZigZag cover. Ray Stevenson

With Louie, UK, 1977. I wish I had this one in color: Louie was in a pink shirt, with lavender hair, I had scarlet hair, with turquoise net. Technicolor glamour punks!

Willie Christie

At 37 Redcliffe Square, 1977. Broke but living amid fabulous art and antiques. Ray Stevenson

BELOW: *Polaroid from UK photo session, 1977. Probably the best I ever looked. RCA had an even better one that they lost, of course.* Willie Christie

ABOVE: *RCA album cover, Bad Girl, 1978. Makeup and art direction by Franklyn Welsh.* **RIGHT:** *RCA single cover, "The Punk," 1977. Makeup and art direction by Franklyn Welsh.* Matthew Rolston

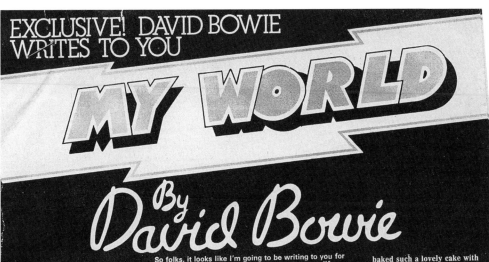

EXCLUSIVE! DAVID BOWIE WRITES TO YOU

MY WORLD

By David Bowie

Dear Mirabelle,
Aren't friends wonderful! It seems I've been away from home for so long. Tonight all my lovely friends got together and gave me just the best welcome home party ever. I always have a really great time travelling, and meet all sorts of fascinating people, also I usually manage to take a few of my favourite people along with me, but there are still people I miss, and it's really fantastic to see them all together in the same room having a good time.

It was so wonderful to see all the brightly coloured clothes and make-up . . . especially after travelling across Siberia for almost two weeks. Things are so colourless and cold in that part of the world and there just aren't any pretty things to buy even when you can afford them. The people are just like people anywhere though, and I think they got a kick out of my red hair and the Kansai clothes I was wearing. I suppose I might have come as quite a surprise to them! I would have loved to know what they were saying about it all.

Tonight at the party I wore a red and yellow satin costume. It's one of my lounging outfits, so you won't get to see it on stage. Kansai has made me so many fantastic costumes for my tours, and so has my childhood friend, Freddy, who is the other person who makes and designs clothes for me. You should have seen his girlfriend, Daniella, tonight at the party. Freddy had dyed her hair deep purple in honour of the occasion!

In Habalofusuku all the girls were running after my

So folks, it looks like I'm going to be writing to you for a while and telling you some things about my life. I never have been much good at writing letters, but now I'm going to make a big effort. So I'm sending along the first letter, which I wrote after this fantastic party . . .

platinum blond photographer. Lee, calling my name. We didn't know how to tell them he wasn't me, they seemed so determined in their mistaken identity of Lee, too determined to take a good look at him. It was really very funny at the time.

None of us have mastered the Russian language yet, though I'm making great progress in my Japanese. I was so surprised to think that

people knew about me in such a remote part of the world. I really hope to do a concert in Russia some day. I'd love to give pleasure to those people who see so little of our Western art. I hope they would like my music.

I'm supposed to be telling you about my party, but I keep getting side-tracked! So now back to the party . . . Sue Fussy, my hairdresser,

baked such a lovely cake with red and blue streaks and 'Welcome Home Aladdin-Sane' written across the top. I do love the way people enter into the spirit of the occasion! I wish you could have seen little Zowie playing with the champagne corks and flirting with beautiful Mary Hopkin. I think Zowie enjoyed the party as much as anybody — probably more if anything! We couldn't bear to see him go to bed and miss out on all the fun, so we thought he must stay up and help to celebrate. Mick Ronson from my group and my wife, Angie, did such a fabulous funky dance to an Iggy and The Stooges record. In fact, the more I think about it the more I realise that it's great to be back home. Especially if one is lucky enough to have such incredible friends.

Well, it's been a very long trip and a very long and wonderful night. Zowie's been tucked in for hours and now I must get my beauty rest. I hope you've enjoyed this little glimpse of my friends and my party and I wish there were houses big enough to invite the whole world, but since this is the closest I can come to that, I give it to you . . .

With all love,
David Bowie

"My World by David Bowie" column, ghostwritten by me for Mirabelle *magazine, 1973.* Leee Black Childers

Cherry Vanilla sticker, 1974. We stuck them in the back of many New York taxis.

Eric's of Liverpool button, 1977.
The Beatles had played here!

RIGHT: Bowie luggage sticker from U.S.
Tour I, 1972. We stuck them all over our
aluminum luggage from Biba.

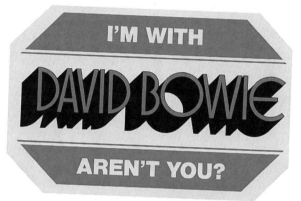

With Angie Bowie, 1975, as guests of honor at a Queen City Punks gig in Springfield, Missouri. Leee Black Childers

RCA publicity photo, 1977.
Hair and makeup by Franklyn Welsh.
Matthew Rolston

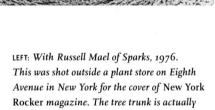

LEFT: *With Russell Mael of Sparks, 1976.*
This was shot outside a plant store on Eighth
Avenue in New York for the cover of New York
Rocker *magazine. The tree trunk is actually*
a lamppost. Leee Black Childers

At the Square Rigger in West Stockbridge, with the
Rymbo Band (Billy Elworthy on guitar), 1975. Dig
the costumes—both theirs and mine. Leee Black Childers

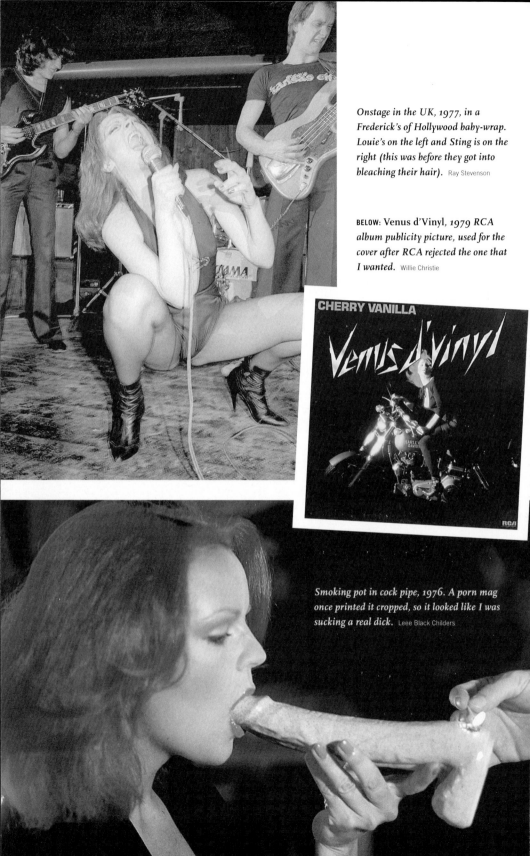

Onstage in the UK, 1977, in a Frederick's of Hollywood baby-wrap. Louie's on the left and Sting is on the right (this was before they got into bleaching their hair). Ray Stevenson

BELOW: Venus d'Vinyl, 1979 RCA album publicity picture, used for the cover after RCA rejected the one that I wanted. Willie Christie

CHERRY VANILLA

Venus d'Vinyl

Smoking pot in cock pipe, 1976. A porn mag once printed it cropped, so it looked like I was sucking a real dick. Leee Black Childers

Bowie and Ronson. If Michael Kamen was right about my musical ear, I thought, then these guys were gonna go places.

We hung out with David, Angie, and Ronno for a while after the show and, of course, invited them to the opening of *Pork*. But they were already booked for something, so they agreed to come to a later performance. No matter what Leee and Jayne initially thought about David, there was powerful electricity between all of us that night. I, for one, felt I had discovered the next big thing in music. And even though I had yet to meet my big acting challenge in *Pork*, my mind was already racing with thoughts of how I might turn the world on to Ronno and Bowie.

11

Pork

ANDY WARHOL, along with Paul Morrissey, Andy's boyfriend
Jed Johnson, and business manager Fred Hughes, came to our
last preview. They seemed very pleased with the show, though
I don't think it mattered all that much to them if it was good or not.
It had already proven to be a great publicity vehicle for Andy's simul-
taneous exhibition at the Tate Museum. The play and the cast were
being used somewhat as a marketing tool, but we were all OK with
that. The arrangement was mutually beneficial and having them
there in London with us suddenly made everything feel that much
more important. The excitement level was rising and we, of course,
were all hoping for a hit.

We had one day off, a Sunday, between the preview and opening
night. I'd had no voice at all until about ten minutes before the preview, when the doctor came and painted my throat with something
even stronger than the spray. And since I had both the play and a
news conference scheduled with Andy for the next day, I was advised
to refrain from any extraneous talking. So, after awakening around
noon to a Sunday breakfast of grapefruit juice, French toast, and coffee, guiltily prepared as recompense by Via, I spent the rest of the day
in bed, quietly cavorting with my boyfriend, Nicky Kramer.

Nicky was known around London as the King's Road Flower Child 'cause psychedelia was clearly not over yet for him. His looks made you think of a character out of an English fairy tale... *a lanky lad, with ginger hair and skin so pale.* He dressed like a court jester or the Fool in the Tarot—skinny mint-green panne velvet trousers tucked into rust suede over-the-knee boots, flowing silk shirts in pink, red, yellow, or orange, bells hanging from a leather strip around his neck, and a fresh flower often tucked behind one ear.

Nicky came off as a young aristocrat gone astray, showing signs of that kind of upbringing in the way he spoke, but—due, no doubt, to his drug intake—keeping you on tenterhooks as to whether or not he would manage to get the words out of his mouth. He was one of the few noncelebs present at the Stones' famous 1967 drug bust at Keith Richards's house and was still a bit of a mascot, it seemed, to much of rock's royalty. I just adored him, gave up all of my other London lovers for him, and, of course, asked him to be my date for opening night.

August 2, 1971—*This is it!!! Pray God I don't lose my voice.*

Pork's set was entirely white and had three main areas loosely representing the Factory, Max's Kansas City, and Amanda Pork's bedroom, all dominated by her big bed in the middle. There were no curtains; the action and lighting just moved from one area of the stage to the next, and the characters entered and exited via revolving panels at the rear. A half hour before the start of the play, just before the audience was allowed in, I took my place on the bed and stayed there completely still, as if I was sleeping, until the play began. And I was completely naked. So, as the audience members entered and sat there waiting, they were already confronted with a sight that made some of them feel rather uncomfortable.

Much like in *World, Pork* featured two beautiful young naked boys in high heels, called the Pepsodent Twins, one with his pubes powdered blue and one with his pubes powdered green. And once I woke up (a few minutes into the play), I spent a lot of time rolling around with them on the bed, before gradually putting my clothes on and moving about the set—all the while shooting "Vitameatavegamin" (Pork's *I Love Lucy*–inspired name for speed) right through my pants. Most of my scenes were either rambling convoluted one-sided rap sessions with the Andy character, played by Tony Zee, or raging quarrels with my mother character, played by Suzanne Smith. And some were quite distastefully graphic, like the one where I plopped globs of chocolate pudding onto a clear glass dish, held over the face of one of the Twins, while Vulva described the details of a plate job—a scene that caused gasps from some in the audience and led a few of 'em to walk out, especially when I proceeded to lick the spoon.

I forgot my lines a few times when talking with Andy (Zee) about Pork's three abortions and her mother's high society dinner parties, the lines all jumbled together in the script as if they were one and the same subject. But luckily I managed to hide my panic and fake my way through until I found my place again. That moment when someone would forget their lines produced such a rush of quick-thinking creativity and interconnectedness with everyone on stage, I actually loved it. Like all actors, though, I always prayed it wouldn't happen to me.

For the most part, the performance went pretty well for us all. And aside from a few hecklers shouting things like "disgusting" and "obscene"—which Jayne managed to counter with some improvised Southern-drawled zingers—the opening-night audience seemed pretty happy, laughing a lot throughout the show and showering us with bravos at the end. But then again, it was probably the hippest audience we would have for the entire run, since it was made up mostly of celebrities, journalists, family, and friends.

The afterparty was held in a wonderfully dark and cavernous space, with cathedral-high ceilings and a huge central stairway lit with a spotlight and backed by a giant mirror on its landing. Oh, the posing that went on as the party guests, all dressed in their High Street best, made their grand entrances. And we Warholians were, of course, the biggest posers of all. I wore my apricot chiffon Isadora

Duncan dress (the one I'd danced in at the ballet), with mauve suede boots, a vintage pastel-peach piano shawl (a gift from Dickie Decorator), and my huge, silver-blonde wig with kinky ringlets. Nicky wore one of his usual colorful ensembles, and we did tons of drugs, danced, drank, and made out all night, as did most of the exceptionally rowdy young crowd. Of course I'd managed to get Bronco booked to play live and they were perfect.

At one point, Nicky, Larissa, Tony Zee, Amanda Lear, a friend named Xion, and I went down to the men's room, where Andy was holding court and signing autographs. Within minutes, the Coco Chanel of Rock and Roll was in one of the stalls, sounding very much like she was giving head to some guy in there, and I was in another stall, somewhat jokingly attempting to take it from both ends at once, with Nicky at the front and Xion at the back. Andy just loved it. Watching and listening were his favorite things—especially when there was the element of our doing it, perhaps, especially for him.

We were making so much noise that the security guards heard us in the hallway and came bursting in, threatening to call the police. But the police were already there, thanks to a fight that had broken out on the street outside the place. So we all cut short our little performances and went back to the party upstairs, only to be greeted by a fifteen-foot-tall black-and-white snakeskin-patterned blow-up cock and balls being waltzed around the dance floor by members of a UK rock group called the Pink Fairies, and bottles being hurled from one of the high balconies. The blow-up phallus was great fun, but the flying bottles and crashing glass unfortunately brought the party to an end.

August 3, 1971—*After we got back to the flat last night, Nicky and I made love. Wow, it's just like after a concert, only now I'm the star and Nicky is the groupie! We stayed up all night with everyone, dishing, drinking coffee, and waiting for the morning papers to come out. At one point, Ingrassia took Nicky into my bedroom and, according to Ingrassia, gave him head and rimmed him—though I'm not sure that really happened, except in Ingrassia's mind. The reviews are*

*mostly horrid. The Financial Times says, "Pork is atrociously acted,
like almost all the American experimental theatre that has visited
us." However, they do add, "Apart from Kathy Dorritie as Amanda
Pork, the central character." One paper proclaims Geri Miller, with
her twirling silicone tits, to be the star of the show. That's the only
one that really bugs me, 'cause I just can't stand Geri Miller. I'm
not sure the English critics understand Ridiculous Theatre anyway.
I'm not even sure I understand it myself. I think the idea of it is that
what's presented on the surface is meant to be Dada and shocking,
while what's hidden behind all of the nonsense is always the same...
the pathos of the human condition. It's actually tragedy disguised as
comedy, I think.*

WE WERE into our second week and still didn't know how long we
would run or if we would move to the West End. Fabulous people
like Lindsay Anderson, Michael York, John Schlesinger, Jonathan
Gems, and David Bailey were coming to see us. But in general, ticket
sales were slowing down and our chances for long-term employment
weren't looking too good. Nicky had left for Woodstock and I was
glad. I'd gotten really pissed off at him when he sold some hash meant
for me to someone in the Moody Blues and didn't offer to pay for my
drinks one night at the Speak. I decided he was selfish and cheap—
generous with his loving, but too tight with his money for my liking.

I had a little affair with Ray Fenwick, a sweet guy and a respected
session guitarist, while secretly lusting after his friend Eddie Hardin
of the Spencer Davis Group. Leee and I got to hang out backstage at
the gigs of T-Rex, America, Humble Pie, Heads Hands & Feet, and
Brinsley Schwarz, but I didn't sleep with any of them. Actually, I'd
pretty much stopped trying, because I'd begun to feel quite ill most
of the time, something I blamed on my bad diet and the fact that
English joints contained tobacco, which always made me nauseous.
I also kept thinking I'd caught the clap again, even though the test
results were all negative.

I forgot about my maladies and got really horny, though, the night that the Bowies, Mick Ronson, Dana Gillespie, and Tony Defries (their manager) attended the play and came backstage. I was so high on the fact that these hot young musicians were hanging out in *my* dressing room for a change and that *I* was the star of the show, not them. It was like full-circle groupie satisfaction. But way beyond the ego boost was the rush of feeling fated somehow to play a role in these particular musicians' lives. I had already begun to in a way, by raving about them in letters to everyone back home.

Even though he was a lawyer and almost two years younger than I, Tony Defries came off more like an old garment center guy, complete with the big nose and the big cigar. He was shrewd, self-assured, and ready to build an entertainment empire—starting with his American launch of Bowie. Dana was a woman after my own heart—hippie, actress, singer, sex bomb, lover of musicians, and major pothead—the only one of 'em who seemed to do any drugs at all back then. And Angie was just plain fabulous—strong, smart, stylish, creative, glamorous, and very down to earth, the perfect rock star wife. Since I'd originally introduced myself to Angie as Cherry Vanilla, she naturally assumed that she should call me that, and she addressed me simply as "Vanilla"—she was probably the first person ever to do so.

After the long and lively dressing room visit, Defreis and Dana went home while the Bowies, Ronno, Leee, Zee, Jayne, and I went to Sombrero to dance and get to know each other. I was trying everything possible to seduce Ronno (hiding my real desire for David, because of Angie). But, unlike David and Angie, Mick was very shy and a little bit afraid of us—especially of me and the way I was coming on to him. So I eventually backed off. Angie made no bones about her libido or her bisexuality, and she and I wound up doing some erotic bump-and-grind routines together on the dance floor, alongside Leee and Jayne. David played it cool, hanging out in the booth with Ronno and Zee and chatting up some young guy with whom he seemed to have had, or was perhaps looking to have, a history.

Our friendship with the Bowie clan grew over the next couple of
weeks, with a few more nights out on the town together and some
casual afternoon visits to their middle-class Beckenham flat for tea
and scones. But, while David was comfortable at home and in familiar
gay discos like Sombrero, he didn't seem to take to the Hard Rock
and the way we all carried on there. We were performers offstage as
much as on, but David was rather reserved in public, and Ronno even
more so. Angie and Dana were the most outgoing of them—though
the full extent of Dana's bawdiness really only emerged inside the
Indian-tinged splendor of her South Kensington town house. We all
recognized each other as artists, but it was clear that we Americans
(including Angie) were the ones who really knew how to get ourselves
noticed.

BESIDES THE Bowie crowd, Leee, Zee, and I, the social butterflies
of *Pork*, made friends with some of the most fascinating people in
London. Danae Brook (who had interviewed us for several publications), her husband Pleasure Reilly, and a guy named Nicholas (a kind
of third partner in their marriage from what we could figure out)
lived right around the corner from us on the Old Brompton Road, in
a building that would later be home to a young pre-princess Diana
Spencer, Coleherne Court. Danae had written books on natural
childbirth and herbal medicines, and Pleasure, a former California
surfer, was a student and associate of R. D. Laing. Nicholas we knew
very little about. Pleasure had once worked for July Garland and hung
out in Rome with Sharon Tate. And he and Danae first met, funnily
enough, at the Roundhouse in the 1960s, when they, along with Tate,
Roman Polanski, and most of London's avant-garde, were frequenting
the audience-participation performances of Julian Beck and Judith
Malina's Living Theatre there.

Danae and Pleasure had two young kids and threw fabulous dinner
parties, with delicious organic food and interesting, attractive guests
like Marianne Faithfull, Chris Jagger (Mick's brother), Ossie Clark

(fashion designer), and June Bolan (Marc's wife). For the first hour or so at their gatherings, things couldn't have been more wholesome, with the kids there and everyone involved in stimulating conversations. But once the food was cleared away and the kids were put to bed, the drugs (psychedelics and Mandies for the most part, though Marianne was always on the hunt for stronger stuff) came out, the laughter and intrigues intensified, and eventually groups of three or four of us would find our way into one of the bedrooms for a little sensual satisfaction—the details of which, because of the Mandies, remain a blur to me to this day.

We'd come to London thinking we were so outrageous and wild, but we soon realized that these new friends we were making were actually way more advanced and sophisticated in their approach to sexuality than we were. The Bowies had their quaint little suburban life in Beckenham, complete with baby Zowie Bowie, yet Angie publicly boasted that she and David each had lovers of both sexes on the side. And Danae and Pleasure came off as the ideal erudite London couple, except for the fact that they had what seemed to be a threeway marriage and occasionally played host to LSD/Mandie ménage-à-whatevers. In a way it was the Living Theatre of the Ridiculous—what you saw on the surface was one thing and what was going on underneath was another. Only in this case, it was the stuff underneath that was more absurd. Or was it? Maybe that's the basic riddle of Ridiculous Theatre: what's real or theater to each of us simply depends on how we choose to see it and how we choose to play it.

THERE WAS the David Bailey photo of the *Pork* cast in English *Vogue*, showing me with my tits out on Bond Street; the full-page *Ink* magazine petition, listing our names along with people like John Lennon and Yoko Ono, in support of the *Oz* criminals; the lengthy article in *Man's World*; and the PR bash thrown by the trendy Mr. Freedom boutique. But despite the publicity we were generating, we were no longer selling out the Roundhouse and Ira Gale wasn't able to raise the money for a West End production. So on August 28, 1971, we did our last performance of Pork. All of that work and all of that momentum had suddenly come to an abrupt and heartbreaking halt.

During our one-month run at the Roundhouse, I probably turned in about six or seven great performances and one exceptional one (luckily on the night that my actor friend Hiram Keller was in the audience). Once I knew the lines so well that my mind could actually wander a bit while saying them—as often happens in everyday life—and once I'd gotten control of my voice, thanks to a voice coach named Julian Doors, I really began to think of myself as a pretty good actress. There were moments on stage when I truly inhabited the role. And that was a high like no drug or groupie conquest ever.

We were all offered the choice of either a charter-flight ticket back to New York or forty pounds sterling. While most took the flight home, Leee, Jayne, and I chose the money instead and found friends to put us up in London, while we figured out what we'd do from there. Jayne was in the middle of a romance with a straight London boy, Leee was photographing UK musicians, and I was longing for another visit to Paris, seeing as it was so close. The three of us were not yet ready for the harsh realities of survival and of being sort of nobodies in the States. We'd been celebrated superstars, the toast of the town, and living in an atmosphere that made us feel secure, and we needed time to come down and come to terms with the fact that the Warhol dream was over.

I wound up staying with Fabio Nicoli, whom I knew from the Hard Rock, at his flat on Barton Road. He was a handsome, sweet Italian guy in his thirties who had the hots for me from the moment we'd met. But it took me a while to think of him as fuckable. He actually turned out to be a dynamite lover, with one of the fattest cocks I've ever seen. And I was exceptionally horny in those days after Pork, even though I was ten or fifteen pounds overweight and still not really feeling all that well. St. Mary's Hospital reconfirmed that I didn't have the clap, but something was definitely wrong. And I knew I couldn't be pregnant, because I had an IUD.

Joan Juliet Buck and her friends were the leading young literary crowd of London. And at one of her dinner parties, I found myself extremely attracted to the writer Heathcote Williams, whose play *AC/DC* had been a hit at the Royal Court Theatre the year before. But Heathcote was known for dating models like Jean Shrimpton and he didn't seem to be attracted to me. At the same party, Joan raved on and on about a friend of Heathcote's named Jim Haynes, who she insisted I would love and with whom I could probably stay in Paris. When she called him and he said yes to the idea, I made up my mind to go the next day.

Jim Haynes was a star among the Euro-UK literati—writer, producer, publicist, creator of the London Arts Lab (where David Bowie had performed mime with Lindsay Kemp), and professor of sexual politics at the University of Paris. He issued what he called "world passports," which he encouraged everyone to present at borders and customs, and started *The Cassette Gazette*, Europe's first-ever audio magazine. He was a much sought-after guest for A-list dinner parties and he held court nightly at La Coupole, the trendiest restaurant in Paris. Jim was in his late thirties, older than I normally went for, and not in the best of shape, but I wound up having sex with him anyway—actually a ménage-à-trois with him and some girl who was also staying at his flat. It was difficult to avoid, since there was only one bed in the apartment. It was the first time I ever had sex with a woman (though I'm not completely sure about a few of the times on Mandies), and I wasn't really all that into it. But it was a new adventure and I was in France and she was French, so I told myself it was the thing to do.

I loved being in Paris again—sitting at the cafes, writing in my journal, marveling at the beauty of the buildings and the light. I also loved having a few more francs in my pocket than I'd had the last time I was there—not many, but at least enough to take the metro and have a croque-monsieur with my espresso. But I wasn't all that attracted to Jim and didn't feel comfortable at his place. Before I had time to give it much thought, though, Leee called from London saying that Heathcote Williams wanted Jayne and me to audition for the two American characters in the revival of *AC/DC* at the Royal Court. I'd only been gone for three days, but when I got back to London, Fabio, bless him, was very glad to see me.

I gave a really lousy reading at the audition and didn't expect to get the part. But surprisingly, Heathcote wanted us both, which had Jayne and me flying high. It was a supreme stroke of good luck. Leon Russell and the boys were set to be in town that November and I thought about how proud I'd be to have them come and see my show, and at the Royal Court, no less. But, after going through the application process twice with British Actors Equity, we were refused the work permits to do it. Needless to say, we came crashing down to the ground again, for the second time in a matter of weeks. Finally, there was nothing left to do but go home to New York and face the music.

October 4, 1971—*Thank God John Myers took me in again. And he even has some work I can do for pocket money. The Fillmore is gone and the Academy of Music is now the epicenter of rock in New York. Luckily I know some of the house crew, 'cause they worked at the Capitol Theater. But with Nancy living in Tulsa, I'm pretty much on my own again backstage. Hitchhiked down to Rockwell, Maryland, to catch a Leon show, only to find Chuckie with a new little groupie named Rosalind Weinberger. But, thank God, she was willing to share. Chuckie told us a great story about how Don Nix wrote his hit song "Going Down" as he was falling from a second story window onto some trash cans while stoned out on lithium. I got a ride back to New York with a trucker named Willie, who not only took me all the way to Greenwich Village, but also bought me pie and coffee at a truck stop, turned me on to the music of Jean Shepard and offered me $30 for a fuck... which, of course, I turned down. I might be a crazy-kooky-groupie-nympho-whore, but I'm certainly not a truck-stop prostitute!*

As for Max's back room post-*Pork*, the writers, actors, and drag queens who once ruled the roost were no longer the center of attention. The rockers like Todd Rundgren, Alice Cooper, Lou Reed, and Iggy Pop—their styles obviously influenced by the brutality, absurdity, cross-dressing, and glitter of Ridiculous directors John Vaccaro, Charles Ludlam, and Ingrassia—had taken over as the backroom's darlings. Warhol superstars Cyrinda Foxe and Andrea Whipps, both of them rock and roll groupies, had even replaced Edie Sedgwick and Candy Darling as the backroom's glamour girls. The focus was definitely shifting from theater to rock.

Meanwhile, right after *Pork*, while I was in Paris, the Bowies, Ronno, and Defries had gone to New York for Bowie's signing to RCA Records—something Lisa Robinson's husband, Richard Robinson (an RCA A&R man), had pushed the label's Dennis Katz into doing. Upon hitting town, they called Zee and invited him to hang out with them at the Warwick Hotel and go to the signing and dinner afterwards at the Gingerman, a dinner which the Robinsons, some industry types, and Lou Reed also attended. David still had his Veronica Lake romantic look at the time and reportedly took particular notice of Lou's short hair and urban, black-leather style. After the Gingerman, the party moved to Max's, where they ran into Danny Fields, who called Iggy to meet up with them there. So, all in one day, Bowie signed with RCA and met both Lou Reed and Iggy Pop... and apparently had a little sex thing later that night with Zee.

The next day Iggy went to the Warwick and signed a management deal with Defries, a deal contingent on the promise the Ig would go back home to Detroit for a while and clean up his act with methadone. But first, Defries summoned Zee to take Iggy shopping for a new wardrobe. Zee was totally broke after *Pork*, as we all were, and needed the little bits of cash Defries would always lay on him. He gave Zee five hundred dollars that day, the whole of which Zee spent on a pair of silver leather pants for Iggy at North Beach Leather—

pants that eventually proved well worth the price, since they became Iggy's signature look for a while. A few days later, Zee brought David, Angie, Ronno, and Defries up to the Factory to meet Andy Warhol. By that time, it seems, Zee had partaken in a three-way with David and Angie and had fallen in love with them both.

October 11, 1971—*Oh God help me. I'm pregnant. How it happened with my IUD, I don't know. And they're saying it might actually be a tubular pregnancy and a tumor. And what if the tumor is cancerous? I'm so freaked out. I just don't know what I'm gonna do. I have no medical insurance and no money. And even if I could have the baby, I'm not really sure who the father is. Though from what I can figure out, it must be Nicky Kramer. But I don't even know how to reach him now and I'm sure he doesn't want to hear about it anyway.*

No wonder I'd gained so much weight and felt so nauseous during *Pork*; I was pregnant the whole time. There was no way on earth, of course, that I could have a baby, not with the life I was living and the drugs I'd been taking. And it seemed there were some possible complications and questions anyway. I was freaked out of my mind but also thinking night and day about the amazing child Nicky and I would make. I felt like a rat in a trap, my mind going round and round in search of a solution, but there just didn't seem to be any easy way out of the incredible mess I was in.

Pat Ast took me to the clinic at New York Hospital, and after three different doctors examined me, it was decided that it was not a tubular pregnancy or a tumor but a normal ten-week pregnancy, and they said they could do an abortion (newly legal in New York) for two hundred dollars. Of course, learning that it was a *normal* pregnancy only served to intensify the guilt I was already feeling in seeking the abortion. But I thought of myself as a liberated woman and I fought to carry on with my well-known resourcefulness and practicality. I asked my brother Johnny, who had gotten quite wealthy from his advertising career, if he would lend me the money. But he refused, saying that as a Catholic he couldn't condone abortion. So my sister Mary lent it to me from her kids' bank account. Since I had cast her oldest daughter, Mary, in a Caldesene baby powder commercial when I was at Kastor Hilton, a good chunk of the money in there was thanks to me anyway. And Mary knew I'd pay it back.

Once I checked in for the abortion, I went on another roller-coaster ride of diagnosis and emotions. Whatever was going on in my belly seemed to have the doctors baffled. And with the discussion of each new possible complication, my resolve about the choice I'd made was growing weaker. I wanted so badly to be brave, but I was really in no state to have a baby and in no state to deal with a normal pregnancy, let alone a problematic one. And when I woke up from the anesthesia and asked the nurse if I'd had the abortion and she said yes, I was greatly relieved—sad, alone, and remorseful beyond belief, but also relieved.

12

Princess Charlotte Russe

TURNED TWENTY-EIGHT in October 1971, the same month that Ram Dass released his book *Remember Be Here Now*. I'd convinced myself the abortion was my only choice, but I was filled with grief and sorrow. And I was taking it out on myself with my OCD—ripping my flesh apart, bleeding and causing permanent scars. I had solved the immediate problem, but there was no escaping the emotions. I knew that Ram Dass was right, though—our focus always has to be on the *now*, not the past, no matter what we've gone through. I simply had to take responsibility for my actions, get my act together, stop crying, and move on. That's all there was to it. So I made Be Here Now my new mantra and began to once again reimagine my life.

November 18, 1971—*Praying to God for a sign... and a way to make a living.*

When T-Rex's "Bang a Gong" hit the airwaves, I clung to the floozy fun of the song, used it as my Be Here Now reminder, and started thinking about Bowie again. T-Rex's Marc Bolan was a lot like Bowie. (Marc and David, along with "Bang" producer Tony Visconti, were all good friends. Bolan played guitar on Bowie's 1970 single, "The

Prettiest Star," and Visconti played bass in an early Bowie band called the Hype.) "Bang" sounded live, uncomplicated, and blatantly cheeky. Its enormous popularity in the States and the acceptance of Marc's feather boa, eyeliner, and glitter boded well, I thought, for David. "Bang a Gong" was a huge hit and heralded a new musical genre that would soon come to be known as glam rock. And I was certain that Bowie could be glam's biggest star, even bigger than Marc.

THOUGH I'D only had a few things published in rock magazines, I was beginning to be touted around town as a mover and shaker on the music scene. Lisa Robinson was inviting me to press parties for Pink Floyd and the Kinks; Lillian Roxon, Gloria Stavers from *16* magazine, Ron Delsener, Scott Muni, Michael Klenfner, and Zach were all asking my opinion about new bands; and the now legendary rock writer/editor Lester Bangs and I were discussing the serialization of my groupie diaries in *Creem*.

Meanwhile, I was totally broke. John Myers was running out of work for me and was getting kind of antsy about my living with him. Nilo and I had struck up a deal where I sold a few ounces of his air-mailed California grass for a little commission, but I really didn't have the temperament for dealing dope and any profits I made seemed to all go up in smoke. So when Nancy Andrews came to New York to pick up some of her belongings and invited me to accompany her back to Tulsa, I jumped at the chance to get out of town and visit Leon-land.

Through a drive-away car ad in the *Village Voice*, I found a 1970 Buick that had to be delivered to its owner in San Francisco eight days later. I hadn't driven at all since the accident that smashed up my face and was totally freaked out about getting behind the wheel. So the plan was that Gene Piper (my latest model boyfriend) would come with us and share the driving with Nancy. But Gene pulled out at the last minute, leaving Nancy and me to hit the road on our own. She drove all the way from New York to Tulsa, while I manned the radio, played the tapes Zach had made us, and rolled joints from the big bag of grass that Chick Casady had given us.

Nancy and I had a real girly good time in Tulsa—thrift shops, garage sales, beers at a bar with a bowling machine (love them), fried shrimp at Pennington's Drive-In, noodles at the Rickshaw Chinese— all the while staying high on Tulsa Tops, the primo buds from Tulsa's pot crop (also the name of Leon's band). But the days I had left to get the car to San Francisco passed swiftly and soon it was time to go. Miraculously, just as I was about to pull out of Nancy's driveway, Leon's friend Miss Emily showed up with a local guy who was looking to do "a run" to the West Coast. His name was B.R. (short for Billy Ray) and the deal was that I would pay for the gas (which the car's owner was reimbursing anyway) and refrain from asking questions, and he would get the car and me to San Francisco.

B.R. didn't eat, speak, or smoke pot while driving, but he periodically snorted some white powder that I assumed to be coke or speed. And when I awoke on the morning of our short sleepover in Amarillo, I found him mainlining something at the sink in our motel room. We'd slept in separate beds and there was no fear of him coming on to me, because, for whatever reason, he seemed to detest me to the point of hardly even acknowledging my existence. But I was grateful I had him, especially around Flagstaff, Arizona, where we hit the most blinding and paralyzing snowstorm I have ever experienced. With Pink Floyd's *Meddle* blasting and my Tulsa Tops buzz, I got to enjoy the amazing whiteout in the darkness like a cinematic trip through the cosmos; but had I been alone and doing the driving, I think I would have had a heart attack.

I was so happy when we arrived in San Francisco and I was able to get B.R., the car, and whatever we'd been transporting in the trunk out of my life forever. I had made arrangements to stay at Chick Casady's charming Victorian house, and his younger brother, Michael, made me feel right at home there. After a few days, I hitchhiked up the coast to Mendocino to visit Nilo. I got my first ride from two rough looking guys in a matte black muscle car, who took me on a

detour to a winery to indulge in some free cabernet. When I realized
they were headed to a second winery, I opted out and found myself
another couple of rides, including my final one with a sweetheart of a
long-distance hauler. His truck, with its full load of giant tree trunks,
was pretty sluggish on the inclines. But I didn't mind the extra time,
because the guy himself was such a doll. Of course, by the time he let
me off in Mendocino, night had fallen.

There are moments in life when, for whatever reason, you remember everything in absolute detail. And that particular moonless
night—standing there all alone on Highway 1, where the Navarro
River meets the Pacific Ocean, in total blackness 'cept for the big
rig's fading taillights and the millions of stars in the sky—is certainly
one of 'em for me. I could hear and smell the sea below the cliffs and
feel a hint of its mist but couldn't see it. Nor could I see any of the
signposts that Nilo had told me to look for as I walked inland to find
his house. I could barely see Navarro Ridge Road itself, let alone
the sheep, horses, fences, and driveways I was supposed to be passing
along the way.

> But there in the dark and the quiet
> With the air so crisp and so clear
> I felt that divine sense of freedom
> The thing I have always held dear
> The smell of the earth replaced that of the sea
> And I thought of the good friend there waiting for me
> And the fact that I'd made it so far and for free
> I was lost but as happy as I ever could be

Of course, when I finally knocked on the door and Nilo appeared,
all smiles and brandishing a tab of acid, I was delighted to enter the
warm, welcoming atmosphere, sit by the fire, wash the acid down with
a glass of fine wine, and trip the night away with him. The side of the
house that faced the Navarro River was all glass, and with the morning's first light I got to see its heavenly view. We were perched on the

ridge high above both the river and the low-lying clouds that floated down it to the sea. And when the clouds lifted and drifted away, the sun sparkling off of the river's green and the ocean's blue water created visions of emeralds, sapphires, and diamonds so brilliant they hurt our sleepless eyes. Even without the effects of the acid, the place was psychedelic.

As always, I felt comfortable and protected around Nilo and I fell in love with Mendocino. But Christmas was coming, and we wanted to spend it with friends. Nilo needed to do a little drug run to L.A. anyway, so we drove down to the house of a guy I only ever knew as Peter Rabbit and had the best Christmas ever. Friends arrived from here and there and chipped in both the money and the labor for the most delicious organic feast. Barry dePrendergast had just produced the movie *Rainbow Bridge* (featuring Jimi Hendrix) and he showed up with a fifteen-year-old angel of a boy from Texas named Al Goulden. At midnight we all went to a screening of the film and immediately afterward Barry hired me to help him get it distributed and promoted. He also invited me to stay at his L.A. house with him, along with the film's director, Chuck Wein, and young Al, whom Barry said he had recently "adopted."

The house was on North Orange Grove Drive, in the heart of the Hollywood Hills. And right next door lived a gorgeous twenty-two-year-old aspiring actor named Don Johnson and his amazingly mature fourteen-year-old girlfriend, Melanie Griffith. Don and Melanie spent a lot of time at Barry's, especially Don—because, like me, Don found Barry, Chuck, and Al so intellectually fascinating, and because they seemed to have an endless supply of dynamite acid and grass. After a few days in the organic, vegetarian, yoga-practicing household, we all went on a lemonade fast—lemon juice, spring water, and maple syrup—in order to, as Barry put it, "purify our bodies and tune into the universe's plan for *Rainbow Bridge*." But on the ninth day of the fast, I was shocked to come home and find them all (except Melanie) shooting heroin in Barry's living room. I certainly wasn't a prude when it came to drugs, but this little incident left me confused and disillusioned about life in L.A., and I decided it was time to get back to New York and work on Barry's movie from there.

I had a connection for stolen airline tickets, which cost half the airline's regular price in those days. I got Barry to buy me one routed through Tulsa so I could stop and show *Rainbow Bridge* to Leon and the boys while they were on a little break from the road. Part of our PR plan was to get celebrity endorsements for the film, and because it featured Jimi Hendrix, an endorsement from a famous musician like Leon Russell seemed key. Plus I'd get to see my darling Chuckie there. I was pretty much over my Leon crush by then. When David Taylor (who had moved to L.A. after *World*) was also able to get a half-price ticket through my connection, he decided to join me on the journey.

Nancy and Miss Emily arranged a screening and dinner party at Leon's, complete with a baked ham, candied yams, and a pineapple/marshmallow/orange Jell-O salad—quite a heavy meal to break a lemonade fast with, but totally Tulsa and tasty. The evening turned out to be a bust, though. Leon didn't seem all that impressed with *Rainbow Bridge*, and Chuckie showed up with his very lovely Okie "wife" in tow—who couldn't have been sweeter to me. I left for New York with David the next day, without an endorsement and pretty sure I'd never allow myself to have sex with Chuckie again.

In my search for a distribution company for *Rainbow Bridge*, I met a movie biz exec named Lou Wolf, an elegant older Jewish man who took a shine to me right away. When I explained our relative lack of budget to him, Lou not only gave me off-hours use of one of his Upper East Side theaters for *Rainbow Bridge* screenings, he even covered the projectionist's fees. Lou took me out to expensive lunches and dinners and always gave me a fifty or a hundred dollar bill "for the ladies' room." And he never asked anything more of me than to have some intimate conversations over our meals together. For years after my work on *Rainbow Bridge* was finished, I continued my relationship with Lou. His "ladies' room" money saved my neck so many times. I even arranged for my sister Mary to have lunch with him once. And she got a fifty as well.

By February 1972, Bowie's *Hunky Dory* had been out for a couple of months. And though it had reached #3 on the UK charts, it only got to #93 in the States—which actually wasn't too bad considering its mishmash of styles and the lack of a single as catchy as "Bang a Gong." Plus, there were no U.S. gigs and there was little, if any, RCA marketing or PR. Meanwhile, Bowie and his band (Ronno, Trevor Bolder, and Woody Woodmansey) were already in the studio with producer Ken Scott, recording David's next album, *The Rise and Fall of Ziggy Stardust and the Spiders from Mars*, and showcasing songs from it at UK gigs and on radio and TV shows there—while Tony Defries was making trip after trip to New York to lay the groundwork for its worldwide release and a U.S. tour to promote it.

Defries had gotten in the habit of having Tony Zee around on his visits, and relying on him for info and advice about current trends, American media, logistics, and so forth. And Zee, knowing Leee and I were a bit more plugged into the music scene than he was, invited us to accompany him to a few boozy room-service dinners at Defries's Warwick Hotel suite. Pretty soon, Defries got used to all three of us being around and giving our opinions on everything from venues and promoters (Ron Delsener was my choice for New York, of course) to writers, publications, radio stations, and DJs. We weren't getting paid, but we were happy to apply our street smarts and our passion to the project. Defries made us feel that we had something to offer—our connections and a certain expertise. And his belief in us, along with the free meals and buckets of wine he provided, we (stupidly) deemed payment enough.

Pretty soon, Defries started bringing us up to RCA, introducing us simply as "friends," and letting us rave on and on about all that we wanted for Bowie, even though we had no regard whatsoever for record company protocol and no idea if what we were talking about was even close to the way things were normally done. Mostly, I think, we served as a colorful distraction, while Defries wheeled and dealed for more funding—which he eventually got, along with a commitment for the use of RCA's in-house travel department for David's tour, something RCA would later realize was a very deceptive and clever maneuver on Defries's part.

Gender-bending glam rock, also known as glitter rock, was becoming more and more popular in Manhattan, with the New York Dolls, Queen Elizabeth, Ruby and the Rednecks, and the Magic Tramps playing at Max's and the Mercer Arts Center, and emerging as the scene's local stars. But the big buzz in Max's back room was all about Bowie, even though he himself was still in London. Between the Robinsons, Danny Fields, Glenn O'Brien, Lillian Roxon, Henry Edwards, Lenny Kaye, Danny Goldberg, Steven Gaines, Ronnie Finkelstein, Lance Loud, and all of the other writers and rock pundits we'd turned on, the publicity for Bowie had risen to a level that gave credence to Defries's pushing RCA for more investment and commitment. And personally, Leee, Zee, and I were garnering much more attention for our association with Bowie than we'd ever gotten for our association with Warhol. So we played it up for all that it was worth.

WHEN NOT working for John or Barry, or hanging out with Defries, I was collaborating on the occasional screenplay with Macs McAree and hatching a plan with Philip English to sail a schooner named the *Joyette* around the Mediterranean (the cradle of civilization) in search of the meaning of life. We were planning to film the journey as we went, finding the answer in a giant Coca-Cola bottle at the mouth of the Nile—an idea that Philip and I actually pitched to McCann Erickson and Coke for possible sponsorship. Oh, and I was to be the only female on board and would be required to sexually service my five or six shipmates. Not only did this project never come to fruition, but after that meeting with McCann Erickson, they never hired me again.

February 26, 1972 —*Philip English has given up drugs completely and says I should do the same. Ha, he should see me shooting smack with*

Michael Norlan! I've done it three times so far and I threw up every time. The sex was dreamy and my sense of touch was really height-ened, both on the giving and receiving end. But heroin seems to close down some of my cosmic receptors, while pot and psychedelics open them up, and I like that better. Michael says that from the next time on, I'll never throw up again. But I think I'm going to stop it now, before it gets that easy. It's not my thing anyway. Philip's moving back to Australia and I'm not giving up all drugs just yet.

NORMAN FISHER was *the* coke connection in New York. And to know him was as much about being a member of his salon—at first in a walk-up on Madison Avenue, then later in a penthouse on Abing-don Square—as it was about scoring the dope. Lance Loud (rock writer and star of TV's very first reality show, PBS's *An American Fam-ily*) introduced me to Norman, and I finally did get pretty heavily into cocaine. In the beginning, I only went to Norman's for grass, which he kept on hand for hippie potheads like me and usually gave me for free. He considered pot a low-class, cheap commodity com-pared to coke, especially his coke, undeniably the best in New York. And because I was so indifferent to it for so long, Norman was all the more determined to teach me to appreciate it, leading him, over time, to pour thousands of dollars worth of it up my nose.

Norman loved the arts and show business and surrounded himself with emerging young artists like Richard Serra, Dickie Landry, Wil-liam Wegman, Lawrence Weiner, Sarah Charlesworth, Mary Heil-man, Keith Sonnier, Gordon Matta-Clark, Ronnie Cutrone, and Philip Glass. He showed his support for them by buying their paint-ings, sculptures, photographs, scores, and manuscripts or, in some cases, trading drugs for them. In doing so, he amassed an impressive art collection. Norman used to make me laugh and feel important with the way he'd tell everyone that I'd "been on the London stage, doing Warhol." And he was thrilled when, in March of '72, I returned to the NYTE to do Tony Ingrassia's new play, *Island*. Norman came to performance after performance, bringing friends like William Burroughs, Robert Wilson, John Cale, Maxime de la Falaise, and Lance's mom, Pat Loud.

Island was set in Fire Island, and we did it in the same tiny East 2nd Street space where we'd done *World*. The audience sat on bleachers in what would be the Atlantic Ocean, while we actors played out our scenes on the deck of an oceanfront house. The plot involved a dysfunctional family and their houseguests, including a rock band, suddenly noticing a warship off the coast and speculating about what to do about it, while also busily carrying out their weekend activities and plans. As the play progressed, the destroyer got closer and closer to shore, and the action got more and more chaotic. A luncheon scene with all fourteen of the play's characters seated around a huge picnic table, ferociously eating, drinking, passing dishes, and delivering scripted lines amid a cacophony of improvised ones, though a bitch to enact, was a prime example of Ingrassia's genius—or madness.

Leee was *Island*'s stage manager, and Zee, Jayne, Jamie Andrews, and Geri Miller were in the cast, along with David Smith's new boyfriend, Neal Peters, and Kris Kristofferson's poet friend Patti Smith. Neal gelled with the rest of us instantly, both on and offstage. But Patti, though fine in her role as a speed freak, was rather standoffish when it came to socializing. I could never tell if it was snobbery or shyness—or, in my case, maybe, just the fact that I was the one who'd scored with Kris that night at the Chelsea. But Patti brought some of her young artist friends and collaborators like Robert Mapplethorpe and Allen Lanier from Blue Öyster Cult to see the play, and we all appreciated her for that. And Norman, of course, recruited them all for his salon.

A few of us were really typecast in *Island*, especially Jayne as a transvestite revolutionary and me as "the groupie who came with the band." And Tony, once again ensuring my vulnerability, had me doing a good portion of my role in the nude. My recently divorced sister Mary brought her new boyfriend and some neighbors from Poughkeepsie down to see the play and was mortified by my lying stark naked on a chaise longue just a few feet in front of them, eating an orange and placing the peels between my legs as I delivered my lines. But in the end, her straight suburban friends seemed to love it and even came to Max's with us after the show. Jack Hofsiss (who later directed Bowie in *The Elephant Man*) tried to bring *Island* to Broadway, but that never materialized. So once again we'd put in a lot of work for a pretty short run. But at least I had given something back, in a way, to Norman.

I HUNG out at Defries's another time or two with Leee and Zee, but there was no money in it, and I had to find a way to support myself. A friend of John Myers knew an Italian prince in Caracas who needed to find a wife in a hurry. I forget if it was for American citizenship or just to keep up his pretense of being heterosexual. In any event, John suggested me for the job. And I used my old fantasy name, Charlotte Russe, until we could find out if everything was kosher with the deal—from which I stood to earn a nice little payoff and a title. Except for the Bowie clan, who addressed me as Vanilla, most of my friends were still calling me Kathy. But since I always believed in creative visualization and I kind of liked the sound of it, I started making everyone call me Princess Charlotte Russe. After a month or two, though, when the marriage scheme failed to pan out, I dropped the name forever and started thinking about using Cherry Vanilla, not just with the Bowies and in print, but for the new role I was trying to envision for my life.

May 20, 1972—*Oh God, please help. I have no money and John is hinting heavily that I should hit the road. I'm just getting my writing off the ground, but I wonder if I'll ever be able to make a living at it. I really need a miracle, God, I really do. Please make one happen, please, I beg of you.*

In summertime, if given the opportunity, I could always put aside my angst and ambitions for a chance to be at the beach. Besides which, I just had to get out of John Myers's hair for a while. So when my old friend Wally Graham invited me to be his houseguest in Bridge-hampton for the summer, I immediately took him up on the offer. I had often stayed with Wally at the Pines in the sixties, where he'd affectionately labeled me, "America's Guest," so I knew I'd feel at home with him and his ironic sense of humor in the Hamptons. And Bob La Tourneaux was also out there doing summer stock. I packed my bikini, along with Laura Nyro's *Gonna Take a Miracle*, Neil Young's *Harvest*, and Van Morrison's *Tupelo Honey*, and, with the few dollars I had to my name, took the Long Island Railroad out to what would be my new home for a while.

Wally shared the house with his boyfriend, Lauren Dunlap, who did flower paintings that were all the rage at the time. Their social circle included some very accomplished and sophisticated lesbians. And, needless to say, with Quaaludes being the drug of the moment, I wound up getting zonked out and pretty thoroughly done by a couple of 'em one day in Wally's barn. I was almost unconscious and totally on the receiving end, so there was really nothing not to like about it. Still, that episode made me realize I'd probably always be straight.

On June 10, Zee called, saying that Defries, David, Angie, and Ronno were coming to New York to see Elvis Presley at Madison Square Garden. And he invited me to join them for the show. I had never seen Elvis perform live, so I immediately accepted and took the train into town. We had incredible seats and Elvis, in his white studded jumpsuit, lit entirely by follow spots, and singing his heart out, was the personification of showbiz—totally slick, but somehow very vulnerable too. Being there for that show was one of the greatest thrills of my life.

I was also thrilled that night to see Bowie's new image. He was like a Japanese cartoon character come to life, with spiked-up, flamed-red hair, a skintight, quilted, boldly printed space suit and red leather boots with three-inch black wooden platforms. Mick Ronson's look, though not as extreme, had also been updated to complement David's. And Angie was extremely thin and much more hard-edged rock and roll and high-fashion than when I'd first met her as a new mom in London. Experiencing Elvis and being with all of them really got my music biz juices flowing again. But by the next day, they were on their way back to London and I was back in Bridgehampton.

WHILE OUT on Wally's friend Bob Henzler's yacht with a few pals one day in August, we dove off of the boat and swam to an idyllic-looking little island in Gardner's Bay. It was a long swim in, and as soon as we emerged from the water, thousands of nasty green flies started to attack and bite us everywhere. Even after we ran back into the water and—exhausted as we were—swam furiously back to the boat, the flies followed, biting us on our arms, faces, shoulders, and anywhere else that wasn't totally submerged. When we got back on deck, they were still with us, biting us everywhere they could. It was right out of a horror movie. We eventually swatted them all to death, but they had left their itchy marks on us. Within a week or so, a few of the bites on my inner thighs had swollen up into hot, red mounds, so big they rubbed together when I walked and caused incredible pain and discomfort. I should have gone to the doctor immediately, but I didn't have the money or insurance for it, and I was kind of anti-Western medicine at the time.

Just about then, Barry dePrendergast called to say that he was in Manhattan and would pay me to help him with some more *Rainbow Bridge* business and that I could stay at Jimi Hendrix's manager's Greenwich Village apartment with him. So I took him up on the offer. When Barry saw the carbuncles, as he called them, he insisted I take some homeopathic remedies and soak in very hot baths. But within days, the three mounds had multiplied to five and had gotten so big and painful that I could hardly walk at all. And one of them was erupting and spewing out puss. Barry assured me that was a good thing and that in time, they would all erupt and then heal. But I had a giant, raw, gooey crater on my thigh and as the days went on, it didn't really look like it was closing or healing at all. So that's when I called my sister Mary.

Even though I'd paid her back the abortion money, I never really liked to ask Mary for help. But when things got this desperate, she was the only one I knew who would come and rescue me. She drove down from Poughkeepsie to get me and was aghast at the sight of my legs. Turns out I had a staph infection. A few days after the doctor at the Poughkeepsie Hospital's emergency room lanced the boils, put drains in them, and gave me antibiotics, the swelling went down and I could see that the four of them he treated were going to heal much faster and leave much smaller scars than the one that had erupted with Barry's homeopathic treatment.

So there I was in Poughkeepsie, broke and afraid, with bandages covering painful, oozing wounds on my thighs. The summer was almost over, so there was no sense going back to Wally's. Barry was still quite angry with me for leaving and was wrapping up his work in New York anyway. I couldn't borrow money from my parents, who were having a hard enough time living off of my father's pension in Lake Carmel, where my mom was once again in the hospital. My sister Margaret was dirt poor, divorced, and living with her four kids in a trailer in Maine. I was too proud to ever ask my brother Johnny for another dime, and Mary made it clear that she was only willing to put me up for another couple of days. And then I got a call from Tony Zee. Once again, he was calling about Bowie. But this time it would turn out to be the call that would change my life forever.

13

Mainman

"WE NEED someone to answer the phones," Zee said. It all began as simply as that. Bowie's *Ziggy Stardust* album and tour were taking off in the UK, and Defries, whose management company there was called Mainman, was ready to establish Mainman USA (with Zee as president and Leee as vice president) and launch Bowie and the Spiders from Mars in the States. Zee had found a duplex on East 58th Street that would serve as both the Mainman office and New York residence for Defries and his girlfriend Melanie. But, aside from a table, some dishes, a couple of folding chairs, and the new phone lines, everything else necessary to turn the apartment's first floor into a functioning management office had yet to be done. And in just a few weeks time, Bowie and his entourage would be arriving, expecting their first American tour and, indeed, their whole lives to be totally organized and fabulous.

I knew right from the start that I'd be doing a lot more at Mainman than answering the phones. Of the five of us there—Defries, Zee, Leee, Melanie, and me—I was the only one with the all-around office and production skills necessary to get the practical side of the operation up and running, and quickly. So, with my usual gusto, I threw myself into the enormous task at hand—ordering filing cabinets, business machines, desks, chairs, stationery, and supplies; setting up accounts with limo services, supermarkets, restaurants, housecleaners, and dry cleaners; finding sound and lighting companies; taking dictation from Defries; typing (nobody else there knew how), banking, paying bills, making coffee; and, yes, answering the phones.

For my first few nights back in town, I stayed at John Myers's apartment. But once I knew I had a permanent job with a salary of one hundred dollars a week, my rent paid, a charge account at Max's, and limo privileges—same deal as Leee and Zee had—I moved in with my friend Hal Fredericks, where I had my own private bedroom. Mainman, with me writing the checks myself, paid Hal two hundred dollars a month—not bad for a glamorous Upper East Side penthouse within walking distance of the office. And Hal was thrilled to have me living there. I still had the drains in my legs from the carbuncles, so I wasn't bringing any guys home for sex, and I was at Mainman all day and Max's most nights, making me a pretty ideal roommate.

Things were moving fast at Mainman. But it was as if everything in my life up until that point—All Saints, Madison Avenue, my friendships with journalists, promoters, roadies, techies and DJs, and even my acid trips, where I learned how thought-forms could manifest magic—had prepared me for the role I suddenly found myself in, a role I was creating as I went along and which, with Defries's blessing, was mine to make into whatever I wanted it to be.

Zee (as road manager) and Leee (as official Mainman photographer) were traveling a lot, checking out production details, hotels, and proposed venues, and I was their anchor and expediter in New York. Their dependence on me and the responsibilities Defries was laying on me bolstered my confidence. And I relished the fact that I was so needed and so appreciated and that my training and my talents were being so fully utilized. It was a turning point in my life for sure, the moment when I'd truly come to realize my own worth. I had the *Gidget Goes Music Biz* job I'd so often dreamed of, one where I could use my imagination and experience—and even my *lack* of experience where record company and PR procedures were concerned (no rules to follow)—to Bowie's advantage and, I soon realized, to my own. I was out to prove, to myself and to the world, that my instincts were right about Bowie; and—hippie-ish though it may sound—that collective, pure-hearted passion was contagious, and when properly channeled, could conjure miracles.

To me, Bowie was like a rocket ship revving up on the launchpad, with us on the ground creating and attracting the energy necessary for its propulsion. People seemed naturally drawn to us and to the atmosphere at Mainman. There was a palpable feeling of optimism in the air. And even on days when there were setbacks, our blind faith, enthusiasm, belief in, and affection for one another never seemed to wane. It was obvious to everyone around us—most of whom had no idea how little we were earning—that Leee, Zee, and I were into Mainman for the love of it, not the paycheck. Tony Defries (unlike us) stood to make a fortune from Bowie's stardom, but the money didn't seem to be Defries's only motivation either. Clearly, we were all having fun—an illusion we thespians managed to create of course, even at times when we weren't.

To help with the workload at the office, I hired Dore Weiner, an adorable, sparkly eyed girl I knew from Max's, where she'd been the doorperson for their upstairs music scene. Dore was already friends with Iggy, Lou, and Mott the Hoople (all of whom had become involved creatively with Bowie and/or business-wise with Defries) and was willing to do just about anything to help make Mainman flourish. She had a great work ethic and a body like Dolly Parton's, both of which we all appreciated. And she loved rock and roll as much as I did. She couldn't really type, but she was good on the phones and at running errands, especially after the little hits of Norman Fisher's coke we both did here and there throughout the day—unbeknownst to Defries, of course, who had forbidden all recreational drugs at Mainman.

The days until Bowie's arrival were dwindling down and the handful of venues that were booked were not all selling out. But that didn't phase Defries. He made 90/10 deals in Bowie's favor by promising huge guarantees to the promoters, while also demanding major rock star perks in the contract riders. Bowie's record sales in the States weren't great yet—the *Ziggy Stardust* LP, released that June, only made it to #75 in the charts—and the masses still didn't know who he was. But between the continuous buzz down at Max's, an RCA press junket to the UK that summer, and the intrigue we were creating with Mainman, there was a sense within the industry that Bowie was *already* a major star and that Defries was sure to pull off his "Hollywood studio-system stable of players" and "skyscraper on Park Avenue" schemes.

Of course, we all knew that if the concert tickets didn't sell, the funds on hand at Mainman would in no way suffice to pay off the promoters. Many a day, per Defries's instructions, I'd drain the Mainman bank account almost completely, so that he and Melanie would have "cash to go away for the weekend"—though I couldn't help but suspect that it also had something to do with protecting the money from liens, should a problem arise. After a few days, we would always put the money back, sometimes depositing even more than we'd taken out—which, considering how clever, cunning, and ballsy Defries was, made me think he had some kind of secret sideline going on, by which he could multiply the dollars. He was only twenty-seven years old at the time, almost two years younger than I, but his confident, authoritative demeanor made everyone respond to him as if he were a worldly wise, professorial elder and made all of us under his tutelage feel quite protected and secure.

My duties grew daily at Mainman, especially in dealing with the members of the press, who'd begun calling about doing articles on Bowie. Of course, to make him seem more in demand than he actually was, Defries had declared David totally unavailable for interviews. There were a few select writers and publications to whom we knew we'd grant access once Bowie arrived in the States, but the rest of 'em had to be content with interviewing me. Without really knowing or even having researched that much about him, I was suddenly deemed the official spokesperson for David Bowie.

Handling the publicity was the part of the job I liked best, and what I realized I wanted to do exclusively at Mainman. I was a natural at it, and I recognized it as the most viable path to my getting out of the office and onto the road, where Leee, Zee, Bowie, the music, and musicians would be. What good was it to be in show business anyway, I thought, if I wasn't gonna be at the shows? But I knew it was still too early in the game to push for such a major redefinition of my role. I had so many responsibilities and no one to dump them on but Dore, who couldn't possibly have handled them all alone. And everyone was depending on me as Mainman's ground control. So I kept my career visualizations to myself for a while and carried on as the team player I'd always prided myself in being.

OVER THE course of a few nights out on the town, high and feeling newly self-assured, I happened to encounter three of my former groupie conquests—Jeremy Steig, John Hammond, and Bobby Keys. Usually, when I ran into musicians I knew, they were friendly and sweet. But in this case, all three of them were anything but, and collectively they really brought me down. Jeremy told me, for no apparent reason and in a most insensitive way, that the few times we'd made love had been for him "like riding a bucking bronco" and that he preferred more "feminine" girls. John did everything he could to avoid me, and Bobby refused to acknowledge that we had ever even met.

Well, fuck them, I thought—them and every other selfish, self-centered, user, loser, shit-head musician I'd ever held in such high esteem. Fuck them all! As a groupie, all I ever tried to do was give them love and show my appreciation for their music. And by then, I felt I had proven myself to be way more than a groupie anyway—not only because I'd developed my acting and writing skills and thus become a fellow artiste, but also because of the work I was doing for Bowie. When I got home to Hal's after the last encounter, I purged myself of the emotional pain, not with excessive sex or my self-destructive OCD, but with the one *constructive* thing that always seemed to work for me—writing a poem.

MEMO TO THE MUDDY-MINDED
MEMBERS OF THE MUSIC MEDIUM

Fuck you all you rock star guys
Who come to me with cocks on rise
Backroom, low-tones, hot and dirty
Late night horny, sweet and flirty
Fuck you 'cause you just don't know
This lady's head beyond the blow
Words of wisdom, goodness too
Wasted on the likes of you
Fuck you and your group select
Who call me up with cocks erect
Caring not what's on my mind
Or that I am the loving kind
Fuck you, soon you're gonna see
The righteousness of such as me
Too bad, such sad fools you are
Rejecting me, a superstar
Fuck your useless closed-up arms
Your songs of love and part-time charms
Folk and coke, enough of that
Finally seeing where you're at
Fuck your mighty attitude
Your tinsel chicks and plastic food
My simple friends are way ahead
They love me in and out of bed
Fuck you, good-bye, thanks a lot
For showing me what you have not
Suck cock love rock groupie's gone
And unlike you, she's moving on!

September 17, 1972—*They're here!*

Even though David had flown to New York for Elvis, this time the
Bowies arrived via cruise ship on account of David's fear of heights.
Within a few days, they took off in their RCA-rented tour bus for
Cleveland, for the first of eight confirmed U.S. dates. I wasn't at that
concert, nor the one after it in Memphis. But I did get to go to the
next and most important one at New York's Carnegie Hall. My DJ
buddies Zach and Scott Muni had been spinning *Ziggy* tracks and
hyping the concert for weeks on WNEW and WPLJ-FM. So the
friends, fans, and celebrities who filled the hall—including Andy
Warhol, Alice Cooper, Alan Bates, Todd Rundgren, Lee Radziwill,
Salvador Dalí, and the New York Dolls, plus writers and review-
ers from *Time, Life, Newsweek, Playboy, Rolling Stone,* UPI, and the *New
York Times*—were already quite familiar with the songs and, like me,
psyched for a night of history-making rock and roll. All Bowie and
the Spiders had to do was deliver.

And deliver they did, beyond everyone's expectations. Bowie's love
for what he was doing was so totally uplifting and infectious that
even his unlikely inclusion of Jacques Brel's "My Death" in the set
proved incapable of bringing any of us down from the high he had
us all on (and made the journalists, of course, think that he was that
much more esoteric). And Ronno was the ultimate rock guitar god.
David wasn't the most polished of performers back then—Ronno's
arrangements, licks, and back-up vocals often rescuing him from a
rough spot—and the bits of mime David did could easily have been
construed as corny. But it was exactly that vulnerability—the fact that
he went so full out for it all, tried everything, master of it or not—that
made David so appealing onstage. Even with the heavy makeup, the
Vegasy sci-fi costumes, the swishy theatrics, and the addition of jazz
pianist Mike Garson, the show came off as authentically rock and roll
and made Bowie totally desirable to men and women alike.

My night, of course, was somewhat taken up with production,
PR, and party arrangement duties, making me miss a couple of the

songs. But I still managed to see most of the concert from my coveted
front-row seat next to Angie and to join her and the whole throbbing
throng at the end, crushed up against the stage, boogying our asses
off, while bellowing the choruses of "Suffragette City" at the top of
our lungs. I still got my thrills from good music, and I still got hot
over rock stars. And though I felt I had outgrown the term, when it
came to Bowie, I knew I was still very much a groupie—'cause I was
just dying to get him into bed.

BOSTON WAS the fourth date of the tour, and Defries flew me up
there for the night to take some dictation and attend the show. He,
Melanie, and I shared the two-bedroom, twenty-fourth-floor presi-
dential suite at the downtown Howard Johnson's, while Bowie, band,
and crew were ensconced on lower floors. The concert, like the one at
Carnegie Hall, was amazing. And this time I got to catch every minute of it, without Angie around. She'd stayed behind in New York to
hang out with Cyrinda Foxe (the platinum blonde glitter It girl of the
moment, with whom she and David had obviously both been cavorting) and to enjoy the adulation of her newfound New York fans at the
Mercer Arts Center and in the backroom at Max's.

I was in my bedroom typing a contract after the show when Leee
rang up from the lobby and invited me to join him at the disco next
to the hotel, where he was partying with David and the band. I was
determined to make a good impression and become indispensable to
Defries on the road, but it was torture to have to sit there all alone
at my portable typewriter when I was so high from the rush of the
concert. So, after a bit of coaxing from Leee, I agreed to go "for just
one drink."

It was a sleazy little bar called the Other Side and the crowd looked
equally sleazy, but David and the Spiders lit up the place with their
presence. I felt so proud and privileged when I walked in and Bowie
immediately gestured for me to join them at their table and scooted
everyone over so I could sit down right next to him. But no sooner

had I settled in than Stuie, one of the band's two karate-suited body-guards (another Defries innovation, designed to boost the public's perception of Bowie's fame) insisted that we all get up and leave the club immediately. Some of the Spiders had found girls already and a few young hopefuls were hovering around David. But like obedient children, we left the girls and drinks behind and followed Stuie's orders. Seems Stuie smelled trouble, something about "queer bashing" and such. I seriously doubted there was any real threat, since the club's clientele actually seemed a lot more gay than straight. But I will always love Stuie for doing what he did that night, because it set things up perfectly for me.

At first I thought the night was over before it had even begun. Bowie, Leee, and everyone else got off of the elevator at their floors and said good night, while I continued up to the penthouse alone. Tony and Melanie were in the living room having tea and seemed pleased to see me back at such a reasonable hour. I kicked off my shoes and curled up in a big wingback chair to join them for a chat. I always enjoyed those cozy quiet moments with Defries. His intelligence and logic intrigued me. "Never assume anything and always decide your priorities," he used to tell me, "the first two lessons you must learn if you're ever going to get anything done, Vanilla." That was the best advice I've ever gotten. And I totally took it to heart.

We were just getting into a business rap when who should arrive at the door of the suite but David. But what about his fear of heights, I wondered. I mean, this *was* the twenty-fourth floor! Melanie showed him in, while I jumped up to close the drapes, so he wouldn't get dizzy from the view. The suite was very well stocked with chairs and sofas, so I was slightly taken aback—though also tickled pink, of course—when he waited for me to sit down and then squeezed himself into the wingback chair alongside me. "He's scared being way up here, Cherry," Melanie teased, "but you'll protect him, won't you?" "Of course," I offered salaciously, "right through the night if he needs it." Everyone laughed, with Defries quick to remind me that he needed his contract typed by morning. He then carried on discussing

Mainman plans with us and waxing philosophical for another forty minutes or so, hardly seeming to notice that Bowie and I were feeling each other up in the chair the whole time. I was turned on beyond belief but also insecure about the sex that would inevitably follow. I felt fat, though I really wasn't, and then there was the matter of the carbuncles. Still, Angie wasn't around and I just couldn't bear to let what might be my only chance to sleep with David pass me by.

"Come on, let's go to bed," he said, once Defries and Melanie had retired for the night. My heart was pounding so fast, but he somehow made it sound so relaxed and familiar, as if he'd said the words to me a million times before. As we entered the bedroom, I ran ahead of him to close the drapes on the floor-to-ceiling windows. "No, leave them open for a while," he implored. "It's nice to see the lights so far below." A kind of manipulation-paranoia flashed through me, but this was no time to be examining Bowie's fear of heights and wondering whether it was real or just another image-enhancing ploy concocted by Defries.

"Listen, I gotta tell ya, David," I nervously mumbled, "I'm a little bit embarrassed and I don't wanna turn you off or anything, but . . ."

"Oh Christ, you don't have a dose, do you?" he asked, as he proceeded to unbutton his pants.

"No, nothing like that . . . but . . ." By the time I'd finished telling him about the green flies and the carbuncles (which were almost all healed anyway), he was completely undressed. I wanted so much to hold that first sight of his nakedness in my mind forever. I had to force myself not to stare at the slim, pale-skinned torso, the ballet dancer legs, and the beautiful cock that was at that moment waiting for no one but me. I fixed my gaze instead on his delicate face, which still bore little traces of his Ziggy Stardust makeup. "It's just that I'm embarrassed," I confessed, "'cause I have these two big white gauze patches on the insides of my thighs. And they're not very sexy, that's all."

"Oh Vanilla," he sighed, as he came to me, put his arms around me, and pulled me close. I could feel his rock-hard readiness right through the flimsy fabric of my dress and the warmth of his breath as he kissed my cheek, my hair, my neck, and finally my lips. He was a great kisser—a sure sign in my book that he'd be a great fuck. We stood there for a while, him naked and me dressed, making out in the shadowy light. I felt so high above the world in every way. And then he sweetly whispered, "Take your clothes off, Vanilla, and let's go to bed."

"OK, but promise me you won't laugh at the bandages," I pleaded, still afraid that they might spoil the mood.

"I won't laugh at your bandages, I promise," he assured me, as he got into bed and watched me self-consciously undress. Of course, the minute he saw the bandages, he burst out laughing. And I just stood there looking down and laughing at them too, until he beckoned me, "Come 'ere."

He was a better lover than I'd even imagined—and not just in the physical sense. The sex was as dirty, rough, and aerobic as anyone could want, but it never felt like we were just having sex. It felt like we were really making love. And he acted like he didn't even notice the bandages. He was either a fabulous actor or a man whose emotions ran deep. But if it was acting, I couldn't have cared less. I was so completely enraptured with the romance of it all and he gave me the impression that he was as well. It was a totally poetic ending to a perfect rock and roll night.

Of course, "the product" (as Defries liked to call him) got to sleep late in the morning, while I had to get up early and finish typing the contract. Naturally, I was exhausted, but I was still flying high from what had happened and there was no way I was gonna neglect my Mainman duties and give Defries any reason to leave me behind the next time. He was, of course, extremely pleased when I smugly presented him with the finished contract at the breakfast table. By our third pot of tea, a sleepy-eyed Bowie ambled out of the bedroom and joined us. Not a word about what had taken place the night before was ever spoken. We just munched on our mediocre room-service croissants and got on with Mainman business, as always.

I HADN'T heard from Joel Schumacher since he'd left for Hollywood to break into the movie business, but one day he called me at Mainman to say he was in New York and wanted to take me out to dinner. I'd rushed out of Hal's that morning in a bright orange coat, blue jeans, and some orange patent-leather desert boots and was definitely looking funky, but Joel insisted we meet at the Isle of Capri on Third Avenue right after work and that how I was dressed didn't matter. After a lovely French meal and some catching up on what we both were doing, Joel walked me the few blocks home to Hal's. I told him what a lovely time I'd had and said good night. But when Joel asked, "Aren't you going to invite me upstairs?" I figured there must have been more that he wanted to tell me, maybe something he was saving as a surprise, so I invited him in.

Well, he certainly had a surprise for me all right! Joel, my good old hair-sex buddy was doing things to me that I never in my life would have imagined he'd be into. And he was actually quite good at it too. I was in a complete state of shock—delighted, of course, by this unexpected turn of events, but also a bit embarrassed that I wasn't freshly bathed and more prepared. Franklyn told me later that he'd heard Joel was seeing the same L.A. shrink as his actor friend Tony Perkins (who'd gone from gay to straight when he fell in love with Berry Berenson and wanted to have children) and that part of Joel's therapy might have been to give the hetero route a try. But after our one hot liaison at Hal's, Joel went back to being totally gay and, as far as I know, stayed that way.

Christmas, 1972—*In Tulsa at Nancy and Carl's. Came here from Memphis, after a great Mott the Hoople gig. Love those guys, so down to earth and rock and roll. Miss Emily threw a party at Leon's, but he's out in L.A., because the Tulsa cops were harassing him about drugs or something. Bobby Keys called Carl's at 3 A.M. this morning. Nancy put me on the phone to scold him for snubbing me at the Stones party in New York. Ha ha, bet Bobby never expected that!*

✦

February 1, 1973—Dore and I took Bowie to see Bruce Springsteen at Max's. He only went because he knew Biff Rose, who was headlining. But he was blown away by Bruce, as we knew he would be. They've even made plans to go into the studio together.

On RCA's recommendation, we'd used a big-time PR firm for the first Bowie tour. But they proved rather ineffective when it came to ticket sales and were way too expensive for Defries's liking. Meanwhile, in the few cities that I got to go to—in my capacity as both Defries's assistant and Mainman spokesperson—we always managed to make a big splash publicity-wise and sell out the halls. Subsequently, the success of those shows allowed us to add extra dates to the tour. So, by the start of the second U.S. tour in February 1973—after hiring a few more employees to take over the secretarial and office management aspects of my job—I was, at last, Bowie's full-time PR lady, and had almost totally morphed into Cherry Vanilla.

Soon, not just the Brits, but Leee, Zee, journalists, DJs, and everyone started calling me by the name in one form or another—Vanilla, Cherry, Ms. Vanilla, or C.V. I signed all of my correspondence and published all of my writings as Cherry Vanilla and I even registered it officially with Actors' Equity. I also began to dress up every day in my cinematically influenced sense of lady-executive attire—tailored 1940s and '50s dresses, coats, and jackets accessorized with high heels, seamed stockings, and bangle bracelets—and always with a sexy garter belt and matching bra and panties. My straight brown hair was meticulously bobbed (thanks to Franklyn) and my makeup was subtle and chic.

February 10, 1973—In Memphis. Had a little thing with the RCA promo man here, Bob Roth.

He met me at the airport
And we rapped like two execs

Our mouths were talking business
But our eyes were talking sex

The basis of my PR plan was really nothing more than to tell the world what a stud Bowie was—something to which I could personally testify. I figured contrasting that with the gayish image he already had caused the kind of mystery and controversy people liked to talk about. Radio being my favorite medium, I produced an audio tape of Bowie answering the kinds of questions they asked in teen idol magazines— like what his favorite color was and so forth—and sent it out, along with some of his more abstruse press clippings and my own bawdy ones, to DJs in the cities he'd be playing, especially those where tickets weren't selling as fast as we'd anticipated. Then I offered myself for on-air interviews, to take place a few days before each of the gigs. The eclectic nature of my press package intrigued most of them enough to take me up on my offer. And once I got on the air (often stoned out of my head on pot), the phone lines at the stations started lighting up, journalists requested more interviews with me, and the concerts always sold out.

I made a few blunders along the way, of course—like saying, while in Memphis, that Bowie was "the new Elvis" and telling a conservative newspaper in Nashville that I'd first used the name Cherry Vanilla "while making a tape for Abbie Hoffman and Radio Hanoi." But luckily, my faux pas, after initially causing some problems with pickets, protests, and show cancellations—and devastating me personally beyond belief—always wound up being the most powerful attention-getters of all. Rebels and radicals of all kinds rose up against the opposition, forced the reinstatement of the concerts, and filled the halls to overflowing. And then, when I talked about those triumphs on the radio in places like Detroit and L.A., it piqued the listeners' interest and led to successes there as well.

I was in heaven, flying from city to city promoting the shows and making detailed advance reports about each place for Leee and Zee— listing gay bars, straight bars, late-night eateries, doctors, drug stores, dry cleaners, and so on—then doubling back to join them and catch each and every Ziggy show. Defries gave me free reign to do as I pleased, and RCA provided me with whatever plane tickets, limos, and hotel rooms I needed. Plus, as a Mainman executive, like Lee and Zee, I got to sign for all of my room service and other extras at the hotels and, unlike on the first tour, didn't have to use my acting skills at checkout time.

You see, when Defries talked RCA into letting us use their in-house travel department for the first tour, RCA didn't realize that (per Defries's instructions) everyone would be charging everything they could to their hotel rooms and RCA would be picking up the tab for it all. When Leee, Zee, or I would check ourselves or anyone else out of a hotel, we would insist (as instructed) that RCA was responsible for the total bill, including everything charged to the rooms, and that we had no authority to pay the hotel directly. We always tried to do it after 5 P.M. New York time, so they couldn't get anyone on the phone about it. By the time they did, we'd be in another city and Defries would somehow appease RCA with promises of straightening it all out later. It was a bit of a scam, we knew, but without enough cash in the coffers at Mainman to cover expenses, it was the only way we could make it all work.

Of course, some of Bowie's band, crew, and entourage went way overboard with the "just sign for everything" deal, especially in the expensive restaurants, boutiques, and gift shops of the Beverly Hills Hotel. And RCA really freaked out when those bills started coming in. But the clever Mr. Defries held them at bay just long enough for us to finish the tour, raise Bowie's profile, and confirm most of the bookings for the second tour. He then, unbelievably, talked RCA into settling the bills from tour one by having them *officially* finance tour two—thereby sharing in the concert receipts and making history as the first record company ever to do so. Of course, on tour two, RCA made sure to send one of their accountants on the road with the band to keep things from getting out of hand.

Though I didn't sleep with David on the road again, both tours made for memories I'll treasure forever—frolicking in Memphis with "aspiring sex therapist" Mike Hall (who according to Zee practiced on him as well), and smoking pot with one of our police escorts there, then speeding around town on the back of his Harley at four in the morning; riding a magnificent horse named Red over honey-colored hills outside Nashville and standing right on stage with the pickers and fiddlers at the Grand Ole Opry; entertaining fourteen-year-old GTO protégées Sable Starr and Lori Lightning in my room at L.A.'s Continental Hyatt (Riot) House (where Leee managed to get my name up in big letters on the marquee); getting two cherries tattooed on my breast by the famous Lyle Tuttle; and hanging out with legendary rock and roll DJs like Rodney Bingenheimer, Scott Shannon, and Mark Parenteau all across the States.

And speaking of DJs—journalists have quoted me as saying that I gave DJs blow jobs to get Bowie's records played. I was quite flippant with my comments back then, I admit, but I doubt that I ever actually said that. If I did, it was just for its shock value and PR effect—because, technically, it wasn't quite true. I had always loved DJs and I'd had sex with a few of them, like Zach and Cousin Brucie, because they were nice guys and I wanted to be close to the music. But that was long before I ever met David Bowie. Zach genuinely liked Bowie's music from the start, and once I got Cousin Brucie to sit down and really listen to "Space Oddity," he liked it enough to play it on the all-powerful WABC-AM, which meant a great deal for an artist in those days. But there really wasn't anything quid pro quo about it. OK, maybe just a little bit in one or two cases.

March 23, 1973—*Met Bowie's boat in Vancouver today. Got him and Jeffrey upgraded. When I told David that the tiny inside cabin was probably good for his humility, he gave me the strangest look. I did a radio interview beforehand and got tons of fans and press to greet them at the dock. We toured Vancouver Island in a limo and had a lovely lunch in the hotel room I booked. And now they're on their way to Yokohama for David's sold-out first tour in Japan. The rocket ship*

has definitely lifted off and is rapidly accelerating. U.S. record sales still aren't super huge, but the publicity is and Bowie's really become a major star worldwide. I'm headed to Detroit for Iggy's gig and then to London and Paris to publicize Aladdin Sane. I've had absolutely no sex at all of late, but I'm really getting off on what I'm doing. Thank God it seems to all be working. And my second "Scoops for You" column is on the newsstands in the April issue of Creem.

14

Lilies and Lilacs

EVEN THOUGH *Ziggy Stardust* was a huge hit in the UK, RCA had a bit of a chip on its collective shoulder there. Defries had signed David, an English artist, to RCA US, not RCA UK. So the suits at RCA in London, some of whom referred to David as "that fairy in a dress," had to swallow their pride and follow the directives of Mainman and RCA US—which they seemed to greatly resent. And they also clearly resented me. (God only knows what RCA US had told them about me.) As a customary courtesy, they should have sent an RCA UK exec or A&R man to meet me at London's Heathrow Airport on my arrival. But instead, almost as an insult, they chose to send a guy low on the totem pole, an assistant from the press office with only a few months on the job, Andrew Hoy.

Andrew was young, tall, smart, cute, and gay. He absolutely *lived* for music, and he loved David Bowie's. Naturally, we bonded instantly, not only as colleagues but as friends. So, on Mainman's behalf, I decreed that all of our PR proceedings with RCA UK from that point on would be channeled through Andrew. Of course, RCA UK then began to resent Andrew as well, though there really wasn't much they could do about it. Despite their sour attitude, however, Andrew and I managed to implement a fabulous PR campaign for Bowie's *Aladdin*

Sane LP and upcoming UK tour—with me doing interviews on his behalf and getting my own face in the papers to boot.

> **April 20, 1973**—*I'm in Paris. And this time, it's first class all the way! Bowie is sailing from Japan to Russia, along with Geoffrey Mac-Cormack, Bob Musel of UPI, and Leee. They'll cross Russia on the Trans-Siberian Railway, lucky ducks, and wind up in Paris on May 3rd. Andrew and I are planning a Paris press conference. I talked Defries into having me spend a couple of weeks here doing interviews and making sure everything is properly arranged. But it's Easter time and all of Paris seems to be closing down for four or five days... as if I didn't know that, ha ha. So I got Defries to let me take a little interim vacation on the Côte d'Azur.*

✦

RICHARD THUILLIETTE and I had been writing to each other and planning our rendezvous for months. In the three years since I'd last seen him, he'd given up modeling and almost all of his worldly possessions and traveled extensively throughout India on a little bit of money he'd won in the French lottery. He'd gotten superskinny and was more spiritual and more desirable than ever. We were spending the Easter break with Richard's brother, Jean, and his gypsy wife, Christián, at their ancient stone house—without telephone, electricity, or hot water—in an area of Provence they called Barbaranque. It was mountainous and remote and my PR lady outfits didn't work there at all. Thank God I'd packed some jeans and a pair of vintage cowboy boots (gorgeous red, black, white, and gold ones that Philip English had given me in a magical Cinderella moment), which I wound up living in, along with an old wool sweater of Richard's.

The air was crisp, the sun was warm, the mistral winds were blowing, and the cherry blossoms popped against the cloudless blue sky. Hillside after hillside was covered with lavender, thigh high and in full bloom. And when Richard and I walked through it, a haze of fragrant pollen rose up all around us. It was the most intoxicating aroma, the scent of spring and the essence of romance. Blissfully, we climbed mountains together, explored caves, collected wood for the fire, visited the goat lady to buy her cheese, wrote each other poems, kissed, caressed, and slept with our bodies entwined, but, as usual, never had sex.

> The valleys were covered
> with cherry blossoms
> so white, roofing the sky
> or hiding the ground
> And I waited for you
> You came full bloom
> And so ripe too
> That the trees didn't hold their flowers
> And already took the pale green
> of the new leaves
> Fading away before you
> They will, when you leave
> Try to imitate you
> And soon, the ripeness of the fruits
> Will make the color of your energy
> Your aura
>
> Love, Richard

After four days in Barbaranque, Jean gave us a ride into Nimes, where we rented a car and drove to the medieval town of Les Baux-de-Provence. Richard had given up his worldly possessions but not his love of fine dining. And Les Baux was home to one of only five three-star Michelin guide restaurants in the world at the time, the fabulous L'Oustau de Baumanière. We were still in the same clothes we'd been wearing for days, and I felt embarrassed next to all of the well-dressed, well-groomed people at the bar in L'Oustau. But Richard's inborn

French attitude quickly surfaced and filled me with a kind of contact pride, helped along, no doubt, by our delicious champagne cocktails. And we were soon escorted to a highly coveted table beneath one of the restaurant's graceful arches.

When we'd first inquired, L'Oustau's staff told us their hotel was full for the night. But, by the time we'd finished our magnificent spring lamb and Côtes du Rhône (thank God I'd saved up enough to pay for it all) and were sipping our complimentary armagnacs, L'Oustau's chef/owner personally came by our table to let us know that they'd prepared a room for us. Good thing, since we were both way too drunk to drive.

After glorious hot showers, we fell into bed, laughing and talking about living together with Hans and making a baby. And I was feeling quite ready for that. Bowie was on his way to megastardom and the Mainman empire was growing by leaps and bounds. Defries was even talking about signing *me* as a Mainman artist, once I'd put in a little more time on the management side. And with Richard and Hans into sharing the child rearing, I figured why not be a mother. The closest we came to having sex that night, though, was when Richard gently brushed a soft pink rose, taken from our table in the restaurant, along every curve and crevice of my naked body, while I languished on the crisp white sheets, silently praying for more. (I pressed the rose in my diary and have it still.)

On what was to be our last day together, we drove down the coast to Nice, passing through Monte Carlo and Monaco, where we stopped for me to do an impromptu on-air interview at Radio Monte Carlo—thus getting Bowie some publicity and allowing me to charge some expenses to Mainman. The plan was for me to fly to Paris and Richard to fly to Milan to join Hans, who was modeling there. We would then all meet up that Christmas in Rome to make the baby (convinced we'd get into having threesomes to produce it). When we got to the Nice airport, however, Richard surprised me by agreeing to accompany me to Paris as our interpreter for the Bowie press conference, a position I'd been begging him to fill.

Our room at the Hotel George V was sumptuous and seductive, the perfect setting for sex (I hoped). Sheer white curtains blew gently at the edges of the open windows that looked out onto the courtyard and gardens below. And the furnishings were sumptuous and chic. While Richard was out renting us a stereo system and buying Edith Piaf records and hashish, I had the hotel's florist send up huge vases full of giant white lilies and light purple lilacs. The bouquets filled the room with the scent of spring and romance in much the same way that the lavender had perfumed the air in Barbaranque. (Of course, one was free and the other cost a fortune.) A New York friend, Meg Bird, who was living in Paris, stopped by with a gift of some incredibly strong grass. And after the three of us had dinner in the room and drank the minibar dry of champagne, Meg left, and Richard and I went to bed... but still no sex... same for the three or four nights that followed.

Since Richard didn't have the required wardrobe for the hotel's restaurant, we had all of our meals in our room. One evening, feeling especially decadent after bubble baths, hashish, grass, and champagne, we ordered the George V's chef's selection—a terrine of smoky paté paired with an exquisite, slightly sweet red wine. Dining in that elegant room, high as kites, in our fluffy white George V bathrobes—Piaf singing "Hymne à l'amour" and Bowie singing "Drive In Saturday," lilies and lilacs all around us—it was by far the most glamorously romantic night of my life. And, lo and behold, it was finally the ticket for getting Richard really turned on.

I'd never been aggressive with Richard before, but on that occasion as we caressed, I touched his penis—and it got hard right away. Being naked underneath our robes made the rest all so smooth and so easy. And we were soon in bed, melting into each other's bodies as if we were on acid. To finally have Richard's cock inside of me and his mouth devouring mine made the many years of waiting seem worthwhile. We were two different people that night, though, like stand-ins for the sex scene or something. There was no talk of babies or of anything else, only our moans and the music. It was Richard's first time with a woman and he seemed to be in ecstasy over the miracle of it all. But when we awoke the next morning, it was as if none of it had ever happened or had maybe only happened in a dream. Strangely, we went right back to being the way we were before—neither of us ever uttering a word about what had occurred, and both of us knowing, somehow, it would probably never happen again... for fear, perhaps, of tainting its perfection.

THE FRENCH PR plans did not go well at all. Andrew Hoy had escorted Angie and two UK journalists to Paris for the press conference, and I'd organized a couple of limos to meet their train and, later, David's train at the station. But unbeknownst to any of us, David's train pulled in two hours early. So, after taxiing to the George V on their own, the weary Trans-Siberian travelers arrived to find us all sitting in the dining room (where they'd finally accepted Richard's dressed-down style), enjoying an elegant, leisurely lunch, the limousines waiting outside. Bowie was cool, but not amused. Then, a couple of meetings I'd arranged for him fell through—Jacques Brel's movie shooting schedule prevented him from coming to dinner (the main reason Bowie had even consented to the layover in Paris) and Michel Polnareff (a French pop star I'd run into there) never called or came by to meet David as he'd said he would.

The press conference was a disaster. The French journalists didn't want to ask their questions out loud, for fear that David's answers would be used by the others there from competing publications. What totally unimaginative jerks! And there were so many things they could have inquired about—the Japanese tour, where Bowie had performed in a jeweled hot-pink jockstrap and Angie and Zee were forced to leave the country after a chair-throwing incident between the fans and the police; the new costumes by Kansai Yamamoto; the train ride across Russia; May Day in Red Square; and, of course, the lowdown on Bowie's newest character, Aladdin Sane. The silence was awful and poor Richard had absolutely nothing to interpret. The

English journalists were just as bad, figuring they'd get more exclusive moments with David on the train going home. And when one French writer finally asked, "So what do you think of French rock and roll?" and Bowie's response was something to the effect that there was no such thing because rock and roll really only worked in English, the press conference came to a final crashing halt.

When we all got back to London, sans Richard, I thought Defries was gonna kill me. Even Bowie's homecoming photo op had gotten screwed up, when the train we were on from Paris pulled into Charing Cross instead of Victoria Station as scheduled. Thank God some of the press, fans, and RCA execs who'd been waiting at Victoria learned of the station change in time to make it over to Charing Cross. But we sure pissed off a lot of people that day, including Bowie. Of course, with no cell phones back then, none of it was really anybody's fault. But, when you do PR for a star, you take your share of the blame along with the glory.

Instead of being pissed, though, Defries asked me to remain in London for the May 12 Earls Court kick-off gig of Bowie's UK tour. With eighteen thousand people in attendance, it would be the biggest indoor rock concert ever in the UK and the first time that Earl's Court was being used for such an event. The day of the concert, I thought I was gonna get fired for sure. I had talked Bowie into doing a long interview with a writer from one of the evening papers because he'd promised us front page coverage with lots of photos and praise. The band was at sound check when the paper came out, and there was only one small article and picture on page three or four. I gingerly walked up to the foot of the stage and showed it to David, feeling sure he'd be angry with me for having wasted his time. But instead, he was quick to dismiss it and told me not to worry about it. Of course, I really found it hard to not feel like crawling into a hole and disappearing. And then, about a half hour later, the newspaper's special edition came out, with Bowie pretty much dominating the whole thing. I was redeemed, and Bowie said those three little words I loved to hear, "Good job, Vanilla."

WHILE IN London, Andrew Hoy had introduced me to Lizzie Spender, a features editor at *Mirabelle*, a UK pop magazine marketed to teen and pre-teen girls. And I came up with the idea of writing a weekly column for them called "My World by David Bowie," under the pretense that it was written by Bowie himself. It was even signed "With all love, David Bowie" in his own handwriting. I dashed off the columns on planes and trains and in the back of limos as if I were David, and I sometimes depicted him hanging out in places he'd never even been. Of course, I made sure he often commented on what a fabulous person his PR lady, Cherry Vanilla, was. It was a huge hit, great publicity for David, and a chance for me to use my writing skills while also earning twenty pounds per column. Plus, I managed to get a few spiritual and moral messages across to the young girls and give them some great advice on things like makeup, hair coloring, etiquette, and travel. (A compilation of the columns, with an intro by Bowie, has since been published in book form in both Italy and France.)

WE WERE rapidly outgrowing Mainman's U.S. office, and Defries himself was ready for more upscale surroundings. So, when we got back to New York, I found him a sprawling rental house in Greenwich, Connecticut, with swimming pool and secluded grounds for $2,200 a month. And every Thursday morning, Zee, Leee, Jamie Andrews (the newest Mainman employee from our NYTE troupe), and I would limo up there and spend the day in strategy meetings with him. Defries wanted David to do an unprecedented seventy-city U.S./Canadian tour, but was finding it hard to get his 90/10 deals in all but about ten cities. Despite his star status in the media, Bowie's North American record sales were still not that huge, and promoters were not sure he could sell out arenas. Zee and I eventually convinced Defries that big stadiums were not the way to go anyway, so we shifted our focus to Bowie playing Broadway and doing movies instead, with a concert film seeming like the logical first step.

D. A. Pennebaker's *Monterey Pop* and *Don't Look Back* were among my favorite documentaries. *Monterey Pop* had screened at the Kips Bay Cinema in Manhattan for a year or two continuously at the end of the sixties, and my friends and I went to see it whenever we'd gotten to the fourth or fifth hour of an acid trip. So, at my suggestion, we hired Pennebaker to film the last concert of David's UK tour at the Hammersmith Odeon in London. And the clever Mr. Defries quickly came up with a way to finance it—by talking RCA into making it the first release on their advanced new video playback system, called Selectavision (a kind of forerunner of the DVD), which was demonstrated to Tony, Leee, Zee, and me at the RCA plant long before the general public even knew of its existence (though the film never actually made it to Selectavision until 1984).

So in July I was back in London to oversee the press for the Hammersmith show and to help organize the afterparty at the Café Royal (to which no one from RCA UK was invited, except for Andrew Hoy). At the end of the concert, just before his encore, Bowie surprised the audience by announcing from the stage that it would be the last time that he and the Spiders would ever perform live, which, of course, made everyone at the show gasp in disbelief and feel that they'd just witnessed rock and roll history—and everyone at the party feel that much more privileged and excited to be there, no matter how famous they were. Mick Jagger, Ringo Starr, Lou Reed, Jeff Beck, Lulu, Barbra Streisand, Elliot Gould, and Ryan O'Neal whooped it up with the rest of us as if it were the end of Bowie's performing career. But it was all just a clever ruse, of course, choreographed by Bowie and Defries.

Meanwhile, I'd decided to do something unique with our press releases by issuing them as numbered Mainman newsletters, thereby giving them a more artsy and collectible feel. Mainman newsletter #1 was originally intended to announce the "World's Biggest Tour Ever," the seventy-city odyssey Defries had been planning. But instead, we simply used Mainman newsletter #1 to grandly announce the cancellation of the tour that we had never announced in the first place. And we released it on July 3, the day of the Hammersmith gig, the show Bowie said was his last. It was a brilliant bit of media manipulation on Defries's part, making it seem like Bowie's dramatic and unexpected retirement was the reason why the "World's Biggest Tour Ever" had been cancelled and not because we couldn't pull it off.

THE SUMMER of 1973 was a busy one. Along with promoting Bowie, Ronson, Iggy Pop, and Mott the Hoople, Mainman was preparing to launch and/or expand the careers of Wayne County, Tony Ingrassia, Dana Gillespie, Freddi Burretti, Daniella, Kansai, the Flower Travellin' Band, Annette Peacock, and Jipp Jones (aka Angie Bowie). David and Ronno were at the Château d'Hérouville in France recording David's covers album, *Pin Ups*, and Mick's first solo album, *Slaughter on 10th Avenue*. Leee was there with them and we hired Meg Bird from Paris as their production assistant. Meanwhile, Zee had found a spacious loft on 18th Street and was renovating it to be the new Mainman office. And Defries kept coming up with the money, somehow, to keep it all going.

One morning, out of the blue, Barry dePrendergast's then seventeen-year-old "adoptee," Al Goulden showed up at Hal's door and declared that he had come to New York to live with me. Al was so cunning, young, and beautiful that both Hal and I welcomed him immediately with open arms. Like Richard, Al was a virgin where females were concerned, but in no time he became my lover. We spent the weekends at a low-key Fire Island community a mile or two east of the Pines, called Water Island, where I shared the rent on a pink beachfront house with Macs McAree and a few other friends. Gene Piper was staying at the house next door and I was still having sex with him as well.

Al turned out to be a total hooker, taking advantage of my generosity and that of my friends. I appreciated the fact that he'd gotten me back into yoga and vegetarianism, and I still wanted to fuck him, but I just didn't want him living with me anymore and neither did Hal. I was tired of paying for everything (our Mainman salaries had increased, but not by much), and I thought it was time for him to fend for himself. He was really good at silk-screening, so I arranged for him to earn a little money by making Mainman monogrammed scarves, which we used as promotional gifts for friends and business associates. He then sweet talked both John Myers and Paul McGregor into letting him stay with them, cleverly ensuring himself places both in town and at the beach.

In October, when my friend Paul Jasmin—who'd painted David's portrait for the Bowie fan club booklet and once tried unsuccessfully to fix me up with Richard Gere—fell in love with a California woodsman and decided to move to the guy's cabin in the redwoods, I paid him eight hundred dollars key money and took over his psychedelic sex pad of an apartment in Chelsea. Finally, I had a hip, spacious place of my own, where I could be creative and entertain my lovers in style. Besides Al and Gene, I had a couple of new ones—Bob Menna, the most handsome male model/bad boy in New York, and Jody Burns, a deliciously nerdy holographer. (I'd hired them both for a video of the Astronettes—a Bowie-produced group starring his backup singer, Ava Cherry—Jody for his expertise with lasers, and Bob as Ava's on-screen leading man.) I never did get to Rome to make a baby. Richard was tromping around in the mountains of Afghanistan, and our magnificent tryst in Paris seemed to have fulfilled all of my romantic longings for him.

By this time, I had delegated most of my Mainman PR duties to Dore, Cliff Jahr, and Meg Bird (who had just moved back to New York), and was exclusively writing and producing commercials and music videos, not only for the Astronettes but also for the new albums by Bowie, Ronson, and Dana Gillespie. I hired Macs McAree to direct and coproduce the shoots, and I did all of the voice-overs myself (which both earned me money in SAG and AFTRA fees and provided me with health insurance). I was really in my element at this stage of the game and thrilled with my VP position as the head of Mainman's new audio/visual division, Mainman Productions. Besides Macs, I had a wonderful secretary named Peggy and an assistant named Daryl Peck, who was also the houseboy at my new Chelsea apartment. And because Defries never really liked the 18th Street location for Mainman, he let my staff and me have it for our office, while he, Zee, and a host of new Mainman employees moved to an uptown Park Avenue space.

With our Madison Avenue and underground movie backgrounds, Macs and I knew how to produce things professionally yet inexpensively. I tried to convince Defries that we should record everything that we possibly could, because it would all be valuable one day and because we were doing it so cheaply at the time. For Ronno's "Slaughter on Tenth Avenue" shoot, Macs and I wrote a scenario based on Mick's idea for the song and got around fifty of our friends to be in it for free. Bob Menna played a gun-wielding pimp and Susie Fussey (Mick's real-life girlfriend and Bowie's hairdresser) played the beautiful bar girl Mick tries to rescue from a life of prostitution, while I played the evil jealous whore who gets her killed. We rented the equipment, hired the crew, lit the whole corner of 10th Avenue and 48th Street, supplied everyone with drinks and food, provided a limo for Mick and Susie, and delivered sixty-, thirty-, and ten-second album commercials, plus a full-length music video on 16mm film blown up to 35mm for a total of three thousand dollars. Of course, RCA UK contended that the commercials had suffered "film shrinkage" and couldn't be used on British TV. But that, I surmised, was just an excuse not to spend money on the airtime to run them.

When my friend Tony Carr dyed my hair a shocking shade of red, it marked the final step in my total transformation into Cherry Vanilla. I just knew I'd at last found my ultimate persona. I pumped up my wardrobe at a neighborhood vintage shop called Early Halloween and wore photoshoot-worthy makeup (learned from Franklyn) from morning 'til night. And to feel extra sexy, I started going around without panties—until Defries scolded me about it one day when it became all too obvious at an RCA meeting. I was almost thirty. I had a certain style, a hot career, a cool apartment, the freedom to express myself both sexually and artistically and the experience to handle it all. I was having the time of my life.

The Midnight Special was a televised weekly variety show featuring live performances by prominent musical acts. It aired on NBC and was the only show of its kind at the time. Michael Lippman, a lawyer from Creative Artists Agency (who represented Bowie, Ronno, and Dana) helped Defries score not just a spot on the show for David, but an entire ninety-minute broadcast for him to make into whatever he wanted. Bowie created a campy cabaret-type show, starring himself, Marianne Faithfull (dressed as a nun), the Troggs, Carmen, the Astronettes, and Amanda Lear. He called it *The 1980 Floor Show* (though I'd already christened it *The Midnight Special Special*, which is what we called it around Mainman). It was shot over three nights at the Marquee Club in London and I was sent over there to keep an eye on the camera crew and make sure they were capturing David's best angles. I then flew to L.A. to sit in on the editing sessions at the NBC Studios in Burbank.

As usual, I was trying to lose a few pounds, so early each morning, before getting ready for NBC, I would swim some laps in the pool at the Beverly Wilshire Hotel where I was staying. One morning I decided to try the special spa treatment there—which turned out to be special all right! I was washed, oiled, encased in a rubber suit, heated, iced, exfoliated, moisturized, and massaged by a master. But I was also given something I thought only guys ever got with a massage, "a happy ending." Charlie, the old Swedish masseur, seemed quite accustomed to massaging the inside as well as the outside of a body. Cocooned in terry-cloth pillows, with cucumbers on my eyelids, I didn't say a word or respond in any way. When he tried to put his old Swedish penis in me, however, I protested. I could hardly believe what had happened and I just loved that I could charge it to my room, especially since Mainman was paying.

My friend Paul Jabara, whom I'd known since he was in *Hair* (he later wrote Donna Summer's big hit "Last Dance"), was also staying at the Beverly Wilshire at the time, and he got all excited when I told him what had happened. The next morning when I went down for my swim, instead of being the first person at the pool/spa area, Jabara had already signed in and was getting his treatment. But when we met up later that day, he told me that his special had been nothing like mine and that Charlie's complete services seemed to be reserved for ladies only. I never went back for another session, because knowing what was coming would have taken away the element of surprise, which was what made it all so exciting in the first place. And besides, there were other major intrigues at that hotel, namely Warren Beatty.

Warren lived in the Beverly Wilshire's penthouse, and I was determined to meet him. On my first day at the hotel I sent him a dozen red roses, with a card signed simply Cherry Vanilla. On the second day I sent him a single red rose, accompanied by a poem about an imaginary character named, what else, Beverly Wilshire. On the third day, which turned out to be Halloween, I sent him a pair of Frederick's of Hollywood split-crotch panties, stuffed inside a Tampax super box and wrapped in the dust jacket of John Lilly's *Center of the Cyclone*, with a note saying only "trick or treat." Meg Bird had flown out to assist me for a few days and together we hurried to straighten up the suite and ourselves, because I just knew that the Halloween package would stir Warren's curiosity enough for him to come knocking at our door.

Sure enough, within minutes, Warren was there at the door, accompanied by none other than the great Joni Mitchell, whom he was dating at the time. Meg was amazed that I had actually pulled this off. I was wearing a long 1940s tiger-lily print hostess gown with nothing underneath. And the big beautiful Warren Beatty immediately grabbed me, lifted me up and gleefully spun me around. Then he and Joni made themselves at home on the sofa. Warren seemed to be looking around for a TV camera and refused any drugs, while Joni fearlessly did a few lines of coke with Meg and me. They were both really down-to-earth and fun. And Warren paid me the biggest compliment of my life, telling me that, until the Halloween gift, which had arrived while Joni was there with him, he'd thought the roses and the poem were from her. Wow, and it wasn't even one of my better poems.

Angie was in L.A. around this time doing *The Tonight Show* to promote *The Midnight Special Special* and launch her modeling career as Jipp Jones. Franklyn did her makeup and she looked stunning, both at the rehearsal, wearing hot-pink toreadors with a chartreuse top, and on the show, wearing her mother's lavender chiffon dress from the fifties. Except for one time when she got pissed at me for leaking to the press news of Bowie's affair with June Millington (of the female rock group Fanny), Angie and I got along great. I'll always remember the knowing, sisterly looks we gave each other when Burt Sugarman, the *Midnight Special*'s executive producer, showed us both, in such a clichéd Hollywood mogul manner, the bedroom that conveniently adjoined his office. We laughed about it over margaritas at Alice's Restaurant on the Malibu Pier, where she also confessed to a mad love affair she was having out there, but never revealed with whom.

I saw a lot of old friends in L.A. Nancy Andrews was working for record exec Lou Adler and got us all VIP treatment at the Troubador, the Rainbow, and the Roxy. John Schlessinger and his boyfriend Michael Childers were taking me to dinners and talking about casting me in John's upcoming film, *Day of the Locusts*. Don Johnson, who was broke at the time, kept asking to borrow my limo to go to the bank. Barry dePrendergast still served up the best drugs in town. And Franklyn Welsh (who'd by then become totally bicoastal) and I even drove up the coast to Guerneyville to visit Paul Jasmin and his lumberjack lover, stopping overnight at the ravishingly rustic Big Sur Inn.

But meeting Joel Schumacher for lunch one afternoon at the Columbia Pictures/Warner Bros. lot in Burbank was surely the most memorable of my Hollywood reunions. This was when he was still doing costumes, before he became a famous director. I felt like Rita Hayworth in her prime arriving in my limo and being waved through those studio gates. I thought we were having lunch in the commissary, which had always sounded so glamorous to me. So when Joel came out of his office with some sandwiches in a brown paper bag, I was kind of disappointed. But after climbing through a maze of sets and scenery with him, we somehow magically wound up on the set of Shangri-la, the mythical city from the movie *Lost Horizon*. There we were, two kids from Queens, sitting on the steps of a place that had ignited some of our earliest dreams, dreams that were at last coming true for us both.

EVERYTHING WAS going splendidly at the start of 1974. Macs and I had produced TV commercials for Bowie's *Changes* and *Diamond Dogs* LPs (using a subliminal image of Guy Peellaert's original *Diamond Dogs* cover art, complete with dog dick, which RCA, of course, made us remove), recorded radio commercials for Christmas and Valentine's Day promotions (when Mr. Blackwell named David to his Worst Dressed Female List, I even made a radio campaign out of *that*), budgeted, scripted, and storyboarded the filming of *Wayne County at the Trucks!* and came up with an idea for *Faaaaabulous!*, a feature-length docudrama starring the whole Mainman family. But when our five-camera shoot of Mick Ronson's first solo concert, at the Rainbow in London, did not go well—not because of us, but because Mick was nervous—Defries decided to pull our editing budget and put the footage into storage. He did the same with the Wayne County concert footage once we got it in the can—which was doubly disappointing, because I'd made a spectacular entrance in it, arriving on the back of a Ryder truck, wearing the emerald green cocktail dress Mrs. Ameche had worn to her husband's 1955 *Silk Stockings* premiere on Broadway, with Bob Menna, in a black leather S&M harness and mask, as my date.

March 29, 1974—*Today Defries told me that he's closing down Mainman Productions. He thinks I'm getting carried away, spending too much money, planning too many shoots . . . and just as we were about to rent the house in the Hamptons for the summer to make* Faaaaabulous! *I think Tony's making a big mistake, 'cause even if it came out awful, I just know it would be a cult classic and make its money back one day. I'm not quite sure what this all means yet. I can't go back to doing PR. There's no challenge for me there now. And without a "me" on the staff, would I want to be a Mainman artiste?*

15

Fame

B ACK AROUND the time of *The Midnight Special Special* the cracks in Bowie and Defries's relationship had first begun to show. And by the Spring of 1974, you could cut the tension with a knife. While David had been on tour and living in England, Angie had been making trip after trip to New York, working on her Jipp Jones venture and on her friend Dana Gillespie's career—which Angie could see was not getting the attention it needed from Mainman. Defries had recently rented the Bowies a rock star–worthy house in London, but up until then, they'd been living in the same fourteen-pound-a-month Beckenham flat where we'd first met them in *Pork* days. So when Angie saw Defries with his Greenwich, Connecticut, estate and pied-à-terre penthouse on East 55th Street, his Cadillac, chauffeur, Park Avenue office, extensive staff, roster of artists, and schedule of projects in development—all seemingly funded by Bowie's earnings—it was only natural that she tell her husband about it.

Also, David and Mick Jagger had been friends for quite a while, and were palling around more than ever. Mick was well-versed in economics, so they would likely have discussed the financial ins and outs of the music business including, perhaps, the insanity of David's *50/50 after expenses* contract with Defries—which, of course, gave David zero control over the ever-increasing income he was generating worldwide for Mainman.

Whatever had eroded their trust in Defries, the Bowies were clearly no longer happy with him and the whole Mainman operation. Defries temporarily quelled their anger by ensconcing them in a two-bedroom suite at New York's swank Sherry-Netherland Hotel, where they managed to run up around twenty-thousand dollars' worth of room service charges in a month. The Bowie-Defries affiliation continued out of necessity for a while, but it was clear to everyone around them that their whole Elvis-and-Colonel-Tom-Parker dynamic was disintegrating. As was the Bowies' marriage, it seemed.

David liked my apartment on 20th Street, and he also liked Norman Fisher's coke. He'd recently acquired an insatiable appetite for it, and I had, of course, hooked him up. And since my days were winding down at Mainman, I guess David felt comfortable getting high with me and opening up about anything and everything that was on his mind. He spent many an evening, often an all-nighter, sitting in one of my canary-yellow enameled wicker chairs, doing lines, drinking milk (he never ate at all during this period), and telling me one crazy story after another—Defries and Adolf Hitler were buddies... Lou Reed was the devil... he himself was from another planet and was being held prisoner on earth—going on and on about power, symbols, communication, music, the occult, Aleister Crowley, and Merlin the Magician. I never did any of David's coke (and, what's more, he never offered). I just sat there, smoked my pot, sipped my Café Bustelo, and got totally into his rap. This was probably the period when I was most in love with him.

Sometimes David would busy himself with my record collection—Duke Ellington's *Live at Newport* and the Ohio Players' *Skin Tight* were among his favorite LPs. And occasionally he and I would have sex in my mirrored, mosquito-netted, dichromatic-lit, pink-satin bedroom, taking everything a bit further than we had that first time in Boston, and utilizing the many new sex toys I'd since acquired. One time, after I'd arranged for him to shop privately at the new Yves Saint

Laurent boutique on Madison Avenue and get the most fabulous black wool overcoat, he came up the five flights of stairs to my apartment, fucked me without ever taking off the coat, and then left immediately to hang out with Mick Jagger. Bowie liked my bedroom so much he even brought Claudia Lennear and Jean Millington (the other sister from Fanny) there for sex on occasion. I didn't participate, but I got off on how much he appreciated the setting.

Springtime '74—*Took Bowie to Margo Sappington's ballet,* Rodin, Mis en Vie, *at the Harkness last night—sticking my neck out, 'cause he really wanted to go to the Apollo instead. Michael Kamen did the music and David loved it, as I knew he would. I think what really impressed David, though, was the fact that Rudolf Nureyev was there. The air around them when those two passed within inches of each other in the bar area at intermission was electrified beyond belief! David and Michael clicked instantly. And after I left them there with the ballerinas, they went back to Michael and Sandra's and stayed up all night making music. As of this morning, Michael is David's musical director for the* Diamond Dogs *tour, and he's bringing Earl Slick and David Sanborn on board. Michael told me he had no idea where his next gig was coming from after the ballet, and he thanked me profusely.*

ONCE MACS and I tied up loose ends at Mainman Productions, Defries offered me a Mainman artist contract that would grant him complete ownership of my writings—past, present, and future. I was feeling pretty desperate but knew enough not to go for that. Instead, I talked him into giving Macs and me two thousand dollars, no strings attached, to launch our own company, Vanilla Productions, which would make commercials and videos for other rock and roll artists. We set it up in my apartment and retained our devoted secretary, Peggy. (I had fired Daryl during the Ronson Rainbow shoot in London, when he accused me of spending too much time at the hairdresser's.)

Only problem was that most record companies in the United States weren't using radio and TV ads, and MTV had yet to be invented. Vanilla Productions was a little bit ahead of its time and was soon out of business. Peggy found another job, but Macs was determined to stay on as my partner, no matter what I wanted to do next.

> **June 14, 1974** —*Oh God, I have to think of something fast to pay the bills. The only thing left for me to do in show business is to be the artist myself. And maybe it's time. Of course, without a Mainman and money behind me, it just seems impossible.*

I had once given out about thirty Xeroxed copies of a collection of excerpts from my diaries. I called it *Pop Tart*, and it was a hit with my friends. So I decided a book—a professionally produced, signed, numbered, tit-printed, limited-edition book of my poetry, with pictures—was the vehicle I needed for my next step. And since the cover was going to be a photographic reproduction of one of the classic compositions books I always carried around with me, I simply worked that into the title, calling it *Pop Tart Compositions*. Macs art directed it and found a printer who was willing to wait a few months for his money, while I organized a pitch letter and a list of potential buyers for the 250 hardcover copies at $25 each and 500 softcover copies at $6 each. The response was immediate, with checks arriving daily. (Michael Kamen ordered six hardcovers.) But those little bits of cash tended to go out as fast as they came in, so we were always on the lookout for freelance work to hold us over until I got my next big idea.

I almost landed a weekly on-camera rock and roll gossip columnist spot on *Speakeasy*, a TV show J. Walter Thompson was putting together with *Woodstock/Monterey Pop* MC Chip Monck. I was writing my own lines for it in the form of poetry and providing my own props and set—a red-satin, heart-shaped candy-box bed that some artist friend of Macs's had made me, complete with giant brown satin chocolates for pillows. The show itself got produced, but my proposed segment didn't, for fear, they said, of its being too risqué for TV.

Macs and I would each occasionally score a writing job—industrial and educational films for him, rock and erotic magazines for me. But they weren't really that lucrative, and they took up a lot of our time. We were working our asses off, but we were just barely making the bills, and we still had the printer to pay. Some days, just holding on to our dignity and keeping a roof over our heads seemed impossible. But we both knew that we belonged in showbiz, and it was that belief and attitude that got us through—that and a little help from our friends.

Neither Macs nor I had a credit card, but luckily, an exotic, aspiring stage director named Daisy Dowleh, whom we'd befriended at Water Island the previous summer, was waitressing at a theater district restaurant called McHale's Gaiety Café. She arranged for us to run a tab there and then pay it off from time to time when we got a chunk of cash. We had the same deal with the girls at the Chelsea Charcuterie for takeout and with Joyce at Early Halloween for our clothes. So thanks to them and their trust in us, even on days when we were flat broke, Macs and I always managed to eat well and look good.

ANGIE BOWIE loved going on and on in her over-the-top way about the art of sucking pussy, making poetic comparisons to eating a ripe juicy fig and such. She knew it wasn't my thing and she kind of taunted me with it, but all in good fun. So one stoned-out evening when both she and Franklyn were hanging out with me on the big platform bed that served as my living room sofa, I decided to shut her up once and for all by pulling down her panties and giving her head. Franklyn couldn't believe what he was witnessing. And we were all laughing so hard, I probably didn't do a very good job. It was way more funny than it was erotic and it didn't make me wanna go lezzie, but I loved that we could all be so crazy, free, and playful with our sexuality. And I just figured, hell, if I was only gonna suck one pussy in my life, it might as well be Angie Bowie's.

EVEN THOUGH Macs and I were struggling to pay the bills, we still managed to spend much of the summer of 1974 at Water Island. Macs had a one-sixth share in a pink house that year, and I went along as "America's Guest." Water Island had no electricity in those days, hence no stores, restaurants, or discos—which was fine by me, 'cause I was well over the whole disco scene by then. And the emerging new genre called "disco music"—except maybe for the first Barry White and Love Unlimited LPs—just wasn't my cup of tea.

Fans of popular music were splitting into two distinct camps at that time. You were either "rock" or you were "disco." Most gay guys I knew went the disco route and embraced the whole lifestyle it encompassed— dancing at the Loft, the Limelight, Ones, and Le Jardin; pumping iron and wearing moustaches, beards, shaved heads, and nipple rings; sniffing poppers, snorting coke, and squirting something called Spray up their noses on the dance floor ("Spray" was distributed by a Manhattan doctor in nasal spray bottles at $90 a pop and was probably an early form of Ecstasy). Meanwhile, I was still drawn, as always, to the skinny-straight-boys-in-tight-pants-and-black-eyeliner-playing-live-smoking-pot-and-doing-speed world of rock and roll.

Eventually it felt like I was living in a whole different realm from my gay friends. When I was out on Fire Island, I started spending less and less of my Saturday nights walking down to the gay, disco-drenched environs of the Pines and more of 'em content to stay in the quiet, unplugged community of Water Island. I got my music fixes there via my state-of-the-art, battery-powered, pre-iPod, pre-Walkman headphones radio, and both Gene Piper and Bob Menna were nearby for sex. (Although Bob had fallen in love with a beautiful German model that summer and, when not hopping over to Europe to be with her, was trying his best to be faithful.)

I was still writing the weekly "My World" columns for *Mirabelle*, so even though Bowie had never set foot on the island, I portrayed him to *Mirabelle*'s eleven- and twelve-year-old readers as doing all of the things I was actually doing—sitting on the deck of the pink house, marveling at the stars and the full moon in Aquarius; listening to a

Long Island station playing Schubert's Ninth Symphony on head-phones during a huge lightning storm; indulging in a bit too much Mouton Cadet rouge; channeling Rudolf Nureyev while dancing at the edge of the ocean; lying in bed by the open windows, letting the sea breezes and moonlight wash over his naked body while the rhythm of the waves lulled him to sleep. Man, there was so much sex and stoner stuff going on between the lines in those columns; I can't believe I ever got away with it.

Macs and I took one last stab at doing outside work before con-centrating solely on me. We bid on TV commercials for Club Med and *Soul Train*, put together a possible movie deal with Paul McGregor, and tried to sell *Ice Pop*, a skating show for television that I'd written to showcase Peter Allen's third album, *Continental American*. Angie was in the process of dissolving her ties with Mainman, so we also made a valiant attempt at doing her PR and getting her signed to the Zoli Modeling Agency as Jipp Jones, high-fashion model.

We knew Zoli from Water Island. His agency was really hot at the time, representing Brooke Shields, Hiram Keller, Bebe Buell, Verushka, and most of our Water Island friends, including Bob Menna. So it seemed like it was gonna be a breeze to get Ms. Jones signed and working. But when we brought Angie up to Zoli's office, besides specifying that she be booked only for the most select jobs and at an especially high daily rate (which was all fine with Zoli), she also insisted that she have final editorial approval of all of the magazine layouts and ads in which she appeared. This was something that nei-ther Zoli nor any agency could guarantee to their models back then, so the meeting was over—and so, unfortunately, was our professional relationship with Angie. But we all remained friends and she subse-quently did a few major photo spreads for the British tabloids with photographer Terry O'Neill, where she got the creative control she sought. We couldn't blame her for wanting it; she'd been trained by Mainman, after all.

I STILL hung out with the Mainman clique a lot, despite the fact that I no longer worked there and that it was at times a bit tense—Defries telling me not to trust David; David telling me Defries was pure evil; Leee and Jayne pissed that Leee had been fired and Jayne's career had been pretty much shelved; Ingrassia realizing, after a disastrous attempt at designing the *Diamond Dogs* shows, that he and Bowie could never work together; and Zee, so disenchanted with what Mainman had become, drowning his sorrows in alcohol, drugs, and excessive sex.

One night, however, despite the dissatisfaction and dysfunctionality, they all got together and threw a little party in a suite at the Plaza Hotel. Bowie, Mick Jagger, and Bette Midler showed up, but for some reason—white powder no doubt—immediately barricaded themselves in one of the suite's walk-in closets. I'm not sure who invited him, but at one point Rudolf Nureyev appeared and wanted, of course, to meet Bowie, Bette, and Mick. But no matter how much we knocked on the door and coaxed and pleaded, they just wouldn't come out of the closet, and Nureyev soon left the party. It was all quite awkward and embarrassing. And poor Rudolf must have felt very hurt, or maybe just jealous that he wasn't in there with them.

THOUGH MY future and Macs's was uncertain, I had definitely gained an air of confidence and developed a style that made people take notice of me wherever I went. My hair—thanks to a Leonard's of London concoction obtained for me by Bowie's makeup artist, Pierre La Roche, who was staying with me while trying to get his green card—had evolved from flaming red to neon fuchsia. I hardly ever left the house without a full face of Vegas showgirl makeup. And I'd go out in the middle of the day wearing stretch satin toreador pants (only available from Frederick's of Hollywood back then), leopard-skin springolators (also from Frederick's), a gold lame trench coat (Early Halloween), and killer eyeglasses with frames from the 1950s that my optometrist found stored in his basement. The teenage boys in the neighborhood used to follow me down the street with whistles and catcalls and would ring my bell at all hours asking if they could come upstairs—something I was smart enough, thank God, never to allow.

Franklyn had started doing the hair and makeup for *Oui* magazine's fashion shoots, working with world-renowned photographer Helmut Newton. One night he arranged for the three of us to go out to dinner together, and when Helmut came by to pick us up, he asked me to get into my scarlet satin robe and do a little five-minute impromptu photo shoot with him. Using only a point-and-shoot camera and the available light in my bedroom, he took fantastic, studio-quality black-and-white photos of me, both alone and with Franklyn. I knew I wasn't as gorgeous as the models Helmut was used to shooting, but I was becoming more and more confident about whatever it was I had that made me attractive to people. And being photographed by a connoisseur of beauty and sexiness like Helmut Newton really helped bolster my belief in myself. But, of course, like most women, I was still insecure about not being perfect.

Perfect or not, when I walked into an early rehearsal for *Fame*, the new Ingrassia play (a rather callous and unusual take on the life of Marilyn Monroe) that Mainman was producing, I felt the hushed, stunned reaction, everyone's attention on me. It was then that I knew I'd perfected my persona and polished my aura enough to be ready for the stage again myself. For a moment, I wondered why *I* wasn't playing Tony's *Marilyn*. But I immediately realized that I didn't need to be reading other people's lines anyway. I had lines and poems of my own to bring to life. And that's when I knew what my next move would be—a live poetry reading, something I'd never attempted before. And I'd do it at a party for my upcoming thirty-first birthday. No one would have to pay and they'd all get free drinks and birthday cake, so I'd be pretty much guaranteed a sympathetic audience for my debut. And I could autograph and sell my books afterward to cover expenses.

✦

NANCY ANDREWS had been living on her own in L.A. ever since her breakup with Carl Radle. I think the amount of coke, booze, smack, MDA, or whatever it was he was doing while in the Dominos just got to be too much for her to handle. Not to mention, Carl and Eric Clapton had such a seemingly impenetrable bond that anybody, even beautiful, psychedelic Nancy, the love of Carl's life, could easily have felt a bit left out around them. But by the fall of 1974, after a brief period of working with her sister Jody as Mainman's West Coast publicists, Nancy was blissfully cohabitating and running around the world with her new steady boyfriend, ex-Beatle Ringo Starr.

Nancy and Ringo were very close with John Lennon and his girl-friend May Pang while they were all living in L.A. But John and May had left for New York that October to work on Lennon's album *Rock & Roll*. John would turn thirty-three on October 9 and Nancy and Ringo wanted to give him a unique birthday gift—something Ringo had apparently managed to do for his friend and fellow Beatle throughout their relationship.

John and May were staying in an apartment on East 53rd Street. Nancy had a pretty good idea of their routine, so she asked if I would arrange for a mariachi band to be waiting outside of their building, singing and playing "Happy Birthday" as they left for the studio that day. I was in a bit of a dither at the time, dealing with the amoebas I'd somehow contracted—the drugs I was taking making me even sicker than the organisms they were meant to kill. But, of course, I couldn't say no to Nancy and Ringo. So, after trying a few talent agencies to no avail, I started calling Mexican restaurants all around town until I found an available mariachi band. Ringo had authorized me to pay them a decent fee and everything was set to go.

But when I arrived at John and May's building the next day, there were no mariachis. I must have spent twenty minutes in a phone booth frantically trying to find them. Finally, one of them informed me that their leader had gotten mugged the night before on his way home from the restaurant and was in the hospital. It sounded like a story to me, but what could I do? I realized it was hopeless even before I saw John and May emerge from the building, walk right past me in the phone booth, and hail a taxi. I felt terrible, but Nancy and Ringo were very understanding and promised we would try again the next year.

October 16, 1974—*my thirty-first birthday and a monumental day in my life. Today I am doing my very first poetry reading as Cherry Vanilla. And I hope it works.*

For the event, Franklyn and I had found some vintage gold-sequined fabric in the garment center and Tina Bossidy, his editor/ stylist at *Oui*, got a seamstress to make it into a skintight kind of female Elvis bodysuit for me. Franklyn, as always, did my hair and makeup to perfection. I planned to read poems from *Compositions* and some specialty stuff I'd written for the occasion. I even wrote a part for Kelly O'Hara to play, though I really didn't give her much to say. David Smith (from Aux Puces) was the master of ceremonies, and it was produced, of course, by Macs McAree—who, for whatever reason, had just changed his name to Max Rippough, Max with an x and the last name pronounced like *rip-oh*, though everyone saw it as *rip-off.*

We staged the reading as an invitation-only private party upstairs at Ratazzi's, on West 48th Street, a restaurant Max and I had been frequenting since our advertising days. The place was packed with around a hundred and fifty friends and coworkers from all of my previous professions. (Bowie was on tour and couldn't be there.) And they all seemed genuinely delighted with the show, laughing and applauding throughout it, congratulating me and buying my book at the end. What I knew right away from that performance —flimsy and Dada as it may have been—was that I had an act that was exclusively mine, something I could do to make money and at the same time promote whatever products I decided to create.

DESPITE NEW York's financial crisis in 1974, most people I knew were still out on the town almost every night. And, besides rock and disco, New York had a pretty healthy cabaret scene going on—from GG Barnum's and the Gilded Grape for lip-synched drag-queen shows to the Duplex and the Grand Finale for torch songs and snappy patter performed by actual recording artists, Broadway moonlighters, and veterans of the cabaret circuit itself. But the most elegant, exciting, eclectic and expensive cabaret of them all was Reno Sweeney.

To dine and catch a show at Reno's in those days had the same cachet as being at the Copa in the fifties, and to play it was to have made it in the cabaret world. Phillip Locascio, Reno's maitre d', took a liking to me right away, and David Smith just happened to be Reno's bartender. So that meant tab-signing privileges for Max and me and an instant connection to Reno's owner Lewis Friedman. I remember getting really dressed up to go there, drinking champagne and feeling so la-di-da chic, while enjoying the likes of Peter Allen, Brenda Bergman, Linda Hopkins, Genya Ravan, Phoebe Snow, Ellen Greene, the Manhattan Transfer, Quentin Crisp, and more. I was often taken there by my hair colorist, Tony Carr, and the fashion illustrator Robert Richards, who thankfully always picked up the check. And I was instrumental in getting Dana Gillespie a gig there. But, naturally, quietly, I was also eyeing the place for my own act.

THE AUTUMN of 1974 held the promise of some major triumphs for our friends in New York's theatrical world. *Sgt. Pepper's Lonely Hearts Club Band on the Road* was set to open at the Beacon, with Leee working for its producer Robert Stigwood; and Ingrassia's *Fame* was opening first at the Truck & Warehouse Theater downtown and then at the John Golden Theater on Broadway. And Max and I were, of course, invited to all of the premieres. Unfortunately, however, *Sgt. Pepper* ran for only sixty-six performances, and *Fame* opened and closed on its first night on Broadway.

But though the theater stuff wasn't working out so well for the people we knew, rock and roll sure seemed to be. The Ramones had been together and performing for a few months and were gaining a devoted following. Patti Smith had released her first single, "Piss Factory," to much acclaim, and Debbie Harry (everybody's favorite waitress at Max's Kansas City) was fronting a much talked-about new band called Blondie. The New York Dolls had led the way in attaining success in the music biz, and it looked like many more in the downtown crowd were on track to do the same.

NOT LONG before Christmas 1974, I landed my first-ever professional cabaret gig, as Holly Woodlawn's opening act at Reno Sweeney. Lewis Friedman seemed to love my poems and stories at the audition but asked if I had some songs that I could do as well. I wasn't prepared for that at all, but good old Max, acting as my manager, piped up quickly, saying that we had a composer and a few songs in the works. So, as soon as Lewis told me I was hired, Max and I went into intense production mode. And by my opening night on January 7, 1975, I had background music for my poems and three original songs in my act, written and performed with my piano player, David Schaefer, a talented young musician Max had found who, at seventeen, should not have even been in a bar.

Since I was quite aware that I wasn't the greatest of singers, the very first song I wrote and performed with David I called "Luna Tuna." It told the story of someone who sincerely wishes they could sing, but can't—which I felt would ring true with a lot of people in the audience. The chorus went "Carry a tune, carry a tune, I would sing like a loon if only I could carry a tune." I purposely sang it more and more off-key as I went, and had everyone cracking up by the end. And that was, of course, music to my ears and gave me the courage to deliver the other two tunes, "Hard to Be Soft When You're Hard" (the title kinda says it all) and "Wise and Wicked Woman," the theme song for my show. Max and I produced and distributed strips of "Wise and Wicked Woman" trading stamps, featuring a beautiful Robert Richards drawing of me, that could be saved as a memento of the show or used to get a discount on my book.

My five-night engagement at Reno's went extremely well. I was thrilled with the $750 I was being paid for the run, and my reviews were really fantastic. Danny Fields said in the *Soho Weekly News* that I was "One of the best new acts to debut in New York in many many months" and that my material was "a breakthrough for club performers of all sexes." Of course, Danny was a buddy from the backroom at Max's, but he certainly wasn't one to pander. All of my friends came to see me, and Angie Bowie sent a telegram from London to wish me good luck. On closing night, Bowie and Mick Jagger popped in together to catch my last show. (Holly Woodlawn states in her biography that they came to see *her*, without even mentioning me, but... well, let's just say that they came to see us both.)

David and Mick arrived in the middle of Holly's early show, took a banquette at the back of the room, and asked me to sit between them for the rest of her act. David Smith immediately sent over a bottle of champagne. I was wearing a black Frederick's of Hollywood backless, wet-look jumpsuit, and the feel of those two on either side of me, right up against my bare skin—not to mention the thought of the enviable position I was in—got me so excited I wanted to scream out loud with delight and hold on to the moment forever.

When I took the stage for the late show and could see the two of them sitting there together, looking like they were totally enjoying themselves, I felt positively high (naturally, I was anyway) and superblessed. They left right after my set, stopping by the dressing room to give hugs and kudos to both Holly and me. My act was a bit ditzy, I confess, but my comedy timing seemed to come naturally and the audiences just ate it up. Despite the fact that Max and I were essentially broke, life couldn't have been sweeter. And Mick and David showing up really put the icing on the cake.

16

The Bard of the Hard

WITHIN A few months, I'd become a popular cabaret entertainer, writing and directing my own shows, building quite a following, and getting a staggering amount of press—in *People, Women's Wear, Oui, Variety, Michael's Thing, Village Voice, After Dark, Daily News, GQ, In the Know, Genesis, Gallery, Hit Parader, Soho Weekly News, Circus, Creem, Rock Scene,* and more. I was playing little clubs all around Manhattan, including a return to Reno Sweeney in the headliner spot. And I even did a week in Chicago at the Man's Country bathhouse, where David Schaefer wore a bathrobe over his stage clothes (a wink to the towel-only crowd), and I made my entrance in an airline stewardess getup, singing, "Hi fairies, I wanna fly with you"—which, thank God, was taken in the right spirit. While out there, I appeared on *Kup's Show* and was profiled in the *Chicago Tribune* by a brilliant young writer named Bruce Vilanch.

The three Vanilla/Schaefer songs I had from my Reno's debut and a few of my classic poems, like "Groupie Lament" and "Memo," I did in every show. But I also wrote new songs, poems, and patter for every engagement—most of it stuff I could never use again, because it was either too time/location specific or just not worthy of repeating. When I'd do it fresh, it would all work somehow. But when I'd go back and read it to myself a week later, I'd wonder how on earth I'd ever gotten away with it. Of course, I always felt that performing was mostly about making a connection with the audience via the cosmic forces anyway—the words and music only there as rhythmic conjurors of the spirits and faux focal points. Or maybe I just saw it all through Theatre of the Ridiculous eyes. At any rate, a big part of it, I believed, was magic. And I just loved being up there and wielding the wand.

I used a lot of props in my act, most notably my favorite vibrator from the Pleasure Chest, an electronic clit machine I called Eddie (short for Con Edison and in remembrance of Eddie Rock). I did a kind of QVC commercial for Eddie, pitching him by way of a poem containing lots of double entendres. I even dressed him up in red sequins for my Valentine's Day show. I also did a little Mad Ave.– type of jingle while fondling a Hungry Man frozen dinner box: "I ate a hungry man tonight, a tender piece of chicken / I got my oven nice and hot and felt my heartbeat quicken / I have a hearty appetite and since I felt the price was right / I ate a Hungry Man tonight / and Swanson made it good."

Not all of my material was done for laughs, though. There were some poems I did solely for the sound and the cadence of the words and for the way they could conjure a feeling, without necessarily being understood intellectually, even by me—especially ones that had come to me in streams of consciousness, like "Go Down on the Sound" and "Street Symphony." And in between the poems, songs, and other bits, I did a lot of little one-liners—like my Mae West–inspired tribute to Dharma and Zen entitled "This Takes Care of the Maharishi."

> *Radiance consists of sleeping enough nights alone to keep*
> *some cream on your face*
> *and enough nights with a man to keep a smile on your face.*

I was writing like a maniac, not only new material for my shows, but also magazine articles for *Penthouse* and *Viva*, radio commercials for Steve Lawrence's *Picture Newspaper*, and a proposal for a TV show I called *Cherry's Jubilee*. There were always press kits, invitations, letters, posters, flyers—all with my tagline, "A production so pure, it must be Vanilla"—and books to get out and telephone calls to be made. But no matter how hard I worked, there was never enough money to cover expenses and never enough time to get everything done. And the only sex I was having was with Eddie.

Luckily, Max and I had some freelance helpers (unpaid, except for petty cash and dinners): Michael Smyth, a friend from Mad Ave. days; Man Parrish, a sixteen-year-old beauty who years later would have the disco hit "Hip Hop Be Bop"; Daisy Dowleh, my backstage dresser (who was loyal to me even after I, shamefully, once punched her in the face, on an out-of-control adrenaline rush, for screwing up a quick change into a Norma Kamali backless, assless wedding dress); Zee and Dore, who were winding down their tenures at Mainman; and David Smith, Neal Peters, and Leee, who made sure my name and picture always stayed in the papers. Their belief in me made me feel like *I* was the rocket ship this time, even without Defries's money or clout. I knew I was no David Bowie, but I was blasting off for somewhere nonetheless.

WHEN BOWIE split with Defries at the beginning of 1975, he and his girlfriend Ava Cherry moved into an apartment right down the block from me on 20th Street. I only stopped by a couple of times: once for a cup of tea and a delightful little game David liked to play—you named your favorite colors from the different stages of your life and he'd play you the corresponding tracks from Ken Nordine's album *Colors*—and once to leave a note under his door, thanking him for some records he'd lent me and telling him that I would always be his groupie. It felt like we were teenagers growing up in the same neighborhood. It was lovely, but it didn't last long. By spring he was living at Michael Lippman's house in Los Angeles, preparing for his role in the Nicolas Roeg film *The Man Who Fell to Earth* and getting a little too far out there on the combination of cocaine and Southern California.

After not hearing from him for a month or two, I was excited when David finally called. I thought for sure it was gonna be about making a record with me, something we'd been talking about for a while. But when I heard how freaked out he was, I instinctively reverted to my subservient role with him and patiently listened. He proceeded to tell me that a hex meant for him had been placed on Lippman's house and that a powerful black-magic force was pulling him deeper and deeper into a web of pure evil—something to do with a group of L.A. girls trying to have a "devil baby" with him. He said he desperately needed "a white witch to undo the spell." Of course, my first thought was, well, maybe if you stopped having sex with them—duh! But I held my tongue and gave him the number for Walli Elmlark, New York's most celebrated witch at the time, who just happened to be a fan of mine—though I'm not really sure just how white her magic actually was. I never knew what came of all of that, but the spell apparently got reversed and turned into good luck or something, because, as far as I know, no devil baby was ever conceived, and by that summer David had his first #1 hit in the States—"Fame."

ONE DAY, while being interviewed at WQIV-FM, New York's first and only quadrophonic radio station, I was introduced to their star newsman, Gabriel Sanders. I, like all of my friends, was already in love with Gabriel's voice and his intelligent reporting. But when I met him in the flesh—so blond, blue-eyed, and good looking—I was completely enraptured. I was over Gene, Jody, Bob, and Al by then, and ready for a steady, grown-up romance. And I decided it would be with Gabriel. He seemed pretty taken with me too, so I invited him to my next show. It was great to be able to do that, even more effective than my "You are beautiful" cards.

A week or two later, Gabriel came to the show, and I took him home afterward to make love. I was floating on air for the next few weeks. Forget about rock stars, I thought, these super–socially con-scious, brainy types are where it's at. The sex was great time after time, and I'd started thinking of him as my new boyfriend. And then one night he came to a show with another cute guy from WQIV in tow—and introduced him to me as his longtime lover. I never had the slightest suspicion that Gabriel was gay and finding out kind of blew all of my fairy-tale plans—though I figured as long as it was OK with his boyfriend that Gabriel keep fucking me, then nothing had actually changed. But when Gabriel and I went to Water Island a few weekends later, the sex just wasn't working anymore. So I was back to jerking off with Eddie.

EVERYONE WAS always commenting on how unique my nightclub act was. Only problem was that it was a wee bit too unique. I could fill little clubs in New York and Chicago and maybe L.A. and San Francisco, but my shtick was never gonna fly in the rest of the country. And if and when Bowie did make a record with me, how were we ever going to categorize it and sell it? I'd always heard about people who had written just one hit song and lived off of it, or at least supplemented their incomes with it, for the rest of their lives—maybe not big posh Hollywood lives, but they at least had that little bit of security. I figured that would suit me just fine. But I knew that "Luna Tuna," "Hungry Man Swanson," and the like were never gonna make the hit parade. I also began to question if comedy was all I really wanted to be doing anyway. I was already making novelty music, so I thought, why not go ahead and make real music—the kind I loved, rock and roll.

David Schaefer wrote and played my little ditties for fun and some cash, but he was a serious student of classical music and not at all into rock. So I turned to my friend Michael Kamen. Michael was busy with the latest phase of his own career, composing soundtracks for movies. But when I read him the lyrics I'd written for a rock song, he instantly came up with a riff and a melody for me. The words were my way of exorcising the disappointment I felt over Bowie's seemingly forgotten offer to make a record with me. Instead of using his name, I used the name his Ziggy Stardust hairdo had always brought to mind for me, "Little Red Rooster." Michael cut out a few superfluous lines from the choruses, and just like that, I had my first rock and roll song. All I needed then was a whole lot more of 'em.

As if on cue, Nancy Andrews called to tell me that Leon Russell's piano player, Patrick Henderson—whom I knew from the tours and from Tulsa—was looking for a lyricist with whom he could write. Within days, I scraped together enough money to fly (on stolen tickets) out to Oklahoma. Carl Radle was on the road, and he graciously lent Patrick and me his house and at-home studio for a week, so we could live and work there together. Leon was also on the road and Miss Emily let us use the grand piano in Leon's royal-blue-floor-to-ceiling-shag-carpeted studio as well. Patrick was really quick at coming up with music for my poems. And before the week was out, I had a sizable repertoire of songs, including "Groupie Lament," which he'd turned into a tender, touching ballad. All I needed to do was to learn how to sing them and get a band together to play them.

I don't know how we managed to do it, but by the summer of 1975, Patrick was living with Max and thanks to Mick Ronson we'd found some excellent musicians—Gary Ferraro (bass), Hilly Michaels (drums), and Billy Elworthy (guitar)—to play with Patrick and form what I called the Rymbo Band (a tongue-in-cheek reference to rimming), with our absurdly titled theme song, "Disco Rymbo." We also found a super-cool roadie named Tom Morrongiello to handle all of the technical stuff. Tom and Gary lived locally, Hilly and Billy moved in with me on 20th Street, and we worked out the songs together in about a week. I could have used a lot more practice, but we couldn't afford it, since auditions and rehearsals ate up hundreds of dollars in studio time and the tab Daisy set up for us at McHale's was growing huge from having to feed everybody. I dreamed of a place outside of the Manhattan media spotlight where I could play my first few gigs with the band and not have the expenses outweigh the income.

Even though I'd fired Daryl Peck from Mainman Productions, he and I remained friends. Daryl had always introduced me to fabulous people, like Italian filmmaker Franco Rossellini, whom I adored, and Italian actor Guido Mannari, whom I fucked, of course. (My last gift to Kelly O'Hara, before she left New York to join some cult that didn't allow her to associate with anyone who was gay or did drugs, was fixing her up with Guido for a night of torrid sex.) So when Daryl said he had some friends up in western Massachusetts, whom he knew would adore me and could probably help, I figured why not.

Gordon Rose and Jon Rick were longtime lovers and business partners who owned a restaurant, bar, hotel, and recording studio in the heart of the Berkshires and were willing to book us if we'd work for food, drinks, drugs, transportation, and accommodations. They sounded like my kind of guys. It wasn't easy getting the boys to work for nothing, but it was summertime and everyone was up for getting out of the city and spending a week in the mountains. And so that's where I made my debut as a rock star—at the Square Rigger in West Stockbridge, Massachusetts. OK, it was a little motorcycle bar in the middle of nowhere, but I sure enough acted like a rock star. And Gordon, Jon, and everyone else there treated me like one as well.

A whole entourage of friends came up from the city (Gordon and Jon feeding and housing them all), and Leee was like my personal paparazzo. I brought my own #54 Special Lavender gels for the lights, had three costume changes per show (thanks to Tina and Franklyn), and used Daisy as my dresser and personal assistant. (I never punched her or anyone again, thank God, no matter how crazy the adrenaline made me.) Gordon and Jon supplied a limo that shuttled us back and forth between their club at one end of town and their hotel at the other, a distance of about two city blocks—though we usually wound up walking in front of it while it followed us down the street. I did interviews with the local media, and we packed the place every night.

At this point, I still had a lot of poetry and comedy in the act and the boys in the band all wore matching outfits, which they hated—black tank tops and white cotton knickers adorned with a print of red roses and male models' faces (Tina had gotten them for free from some fashion event and they were actually quite fabulous). And I insisted they deliver some lines I'd written for them, which they also hated. They wanted to be known only for their musical prowess, while I was still developing mine and was relying on the comedy to camouflage the fact that I wasn't exactly hitting every note.

The neighboring town of Stockbridge had a famous mental institution called the Austen Riggs Center, where Judy Garland and James Taylor had each spent time, and where the local rich kids went to get over alcohol, drugs, and depression. Most Riggs patients were allowed to go out at night, so the Square Rigger was often filled with heavily medicated crazies. One night, while I was doing a mock TV commercial—in which Eva Braun was singing the praises of Adolf's Meat Tenderizer to her lover, Adolf Hitler—one of the Riggs patients (who failed to catch the Nazi put-downs in the lyrics) got so incensed by the Hitler mask I alternately donned with the Eva one, he threw a heavy glass ashtray at it. The impact made me see stars, but luckily the mask was thick and rigid enough to keep the ashtray from breaking my nose (again) or worse. I retired that little skit immediately and stayed away from heavy subject matter after that.

Keeping the band happy was a major hassle times four, and I could already see what I was getting myself into. But I had chosen that road and the rewards were so high when they came that they were quickly addicting. For a few minutes here and there in every show, provided the technical stuff was all working, the five of us would become one and soar. (The rush of making music with a band, when it all goes right, truly *is* like taking off in a rocket.) And feeling the bass vibrations through the floorboards and the drums right behind me drove me well beyond the limits of my normal energy. But I still had so much to learn, improve, and perfect; it was all a bit daunting. It was also up to me to keep the whole operation going. Another advantage—a *huge* advantage—of having a band was, of course, Billy Elworthy. Billy was fragile, pale, and blond, like a Christmas tree angel. He played great lead guitar, practically lived on Kit Kat bars, and was very satisfying in bed.

✦

October 10, 1975—*Didn't do John Lennon's birthday thing this year, because he got the best gift of all . . . a baby boy for him and Yoko!*

By my thirty-second birthday, the Rymbo Band was over. They had gone on strike the afternoon of a scheduled gig at Trude Heller's (the Greenwich Village club), demanding $600 per night between the four of them, even though I was only getting $600 for all of us for the week. The show was sold out and I had to scramble to get some substitute musicians with only a couple hours' notice. Michael Kamen came to the rescue. He put my roadie, Tom Morrongiello (a skilled musician and the only one who knew all of the songs), on guitar, Ian Hunter (my friend from Mott the Hoople) on bass, Gui Andrisano (from the *Diamond Dogs* tour) on backup vocals, and himself on piano. The room was packed, and I was smoking pot and drinking Southern Comfort to soothe both my throat and my nerves. Lance Loud, with his band, the Mumps, was my opening act and while they were on, my new band studied my lead sheets in the dressing room. Michael said he was sure that one or more of the drummers he'd called would eventually arrive, but when none had actually made it by show time, we went on without one.

I could be so easily thrown as it was, by anything that changed how I was used to hearing things—a strange piano, a different monitor mix, a new guitar solo, the sound of the room, the overtones, the harmonics—and there I was fronting a band that was as alien to me as my songs were to most of them. I felt really lost in space, and I know it must have all come off as truly bizarre. Morrongiello was calling out the chords to Ian and Michael, while Gui was joining me on the hooks and choruses with amazing gusto, though not necessarily the right lyrics. Sal Celli, a drummer with the New York City Ballet, showed up by about our third song, introduced himself to us and the audience, and proceeded to set up his drums and join in while we carried on as if nothing unusual was happening. It was utter chaos, sheer improvisation, truly living theater—and the audience just loved it. Some even said it was the best show I'd ever done.

The Rymbo Band came back the next night and finished out the week for sustenance pay, but despite Mick Ronson urging them to stick with me, things soon fell apart permanently. Billy and Hilly left to play with Michael Bolton, and Gary didn't want to play without them, so he quit too. And since I knew from Ronno that Patrick was the one who'd instigated the revolt, I decided to make a clean sweep of it and let him go as well.

Thankfully, Morrongiello stayed on as my guitar player and musical director, but it meant starting the whole audition and rehearsal process all over again. I had a few bookings lined up at Max's Kansas City and the Square Rigger, and even one out in L.A., but I knew the fees I was getting would never cover a whole new round of rehearsal studios and other expenses. *Compositions* sales had slowed to a trickle, and Vanilla Paper, Inc., the corporation we formed to publish it, had gone bankrupt. Max and I weren't personally liable, but even so, we were hoping to pay off the printer—something I felt awful about not having done already. As always, though, with money or without, we managed somehow to pull off the impossible.

Since the new band all came from Staten Island, I called them the Staten Island Band and started writing new songs with them and doing less and less comedy in the act. They were all really great musicians but, just like the Rymbo Band, keeping them happy was a constant struggle. They knew I'd be the one who'd probably get a record deal, not the band as a whole, but all of them wanted their own solo careers as frontmen anyway. (None of them had the personality, stamina, or ingenuity to pull it off, though.) My plan was to turn them all into songwriters, make a record with them, pay them their union fees and royalties, and let them keep all of their future publishing and recording rights—my inevitable hit record serving to let us all do what we wanted after that. Getting them to write songs, however, wasn't easy. Unlike with Michael or Patrick, I had to practically drag the songs out of them, their reluctance to believe in their own melodies matched only by their reluctance to sing backup vocals with any degree of enthusiasm.

That moment when two creative people first present each other with their contributions to an artistic collaboration can be so intimidating. I was as shy about showing my lyrics to musicians for the first time as they were about playing their melodies for me. But any ego-driven angst I was willing to put myself through always proved worth it when a song came together and I heard it for the very first time. Tom Morrongiello was particularly reticent about writing with me, yet we wrote some beautiful songs together, including a gorgeous ballad called "Keeps on Snowing," which he sang so touchingly in my shows. (I used to give each band member a featured spot).

Tom, like the rest of them, could be difficult in other ways too. At the last minute, on the day we were all leaving to drive across country in his van to play Studio One in L.A., Tom decided that his sixteen-year-old sister had to come along with us. Not only were there already six of us with our luggage and equipment in the van, but his sister was also one more mouth to feed *and* a minor we would be transporting across state lines. I really had no choice in the matter, though—without both Tom and his van there was just no way we could do the show. We bombed at Studio One, where they were more into disco divas than rockers and where I was really off my game the whole night. But we had a wonderful time visiting Nilo on his ranch up north. One of his horses and one of his goats gave birth while we were there, and the pot and LSD flowed as usual (probably my last full-blown acid trip).

On the way home from the West Coast, we stopped for a few days in Tulsa, where my Okie friends had booked us a gig and secured us a house for our stay. The Staten Island Band was quite happy for a change, both because Leon Russell came to the show and because they all managed to hook-up with sexy Tulsa girls—except for Tom, whom I'd been sleeping with for a while. But when, for some reason, he wouldn't make love with me that night, I went nuts, stole the keys to his van (which he never let anyone drive), and went cruising around Tulsa. I hadn't driven in years and had never driven a van, so naturally Tom was worried and a bit pissed-off. When we got back east and it came time for our third gig in the Berkshires (we'd recorded the Vanilla/ Morrongiello song "Shake Your Ashes" for the *Max's Kansas City* compilation LP during our second), Tom simply refused to go and I had to get yet another guitarist.

And that's the way it went, over and over, time and time again. I'd just get a new band together and get used to singing with them when one or more of 'em would become contrary or leave for a better-paying or more prestigious gig. I was like a casting agent for rock musicians. I had a reputation for choosing great ones, so established artists would often come to a show and make them an offer they couldn't refuse. Even my music biz godfather, Michael Kamen, sometimes hipped my boys to other opportunities, which really hurt. It got to a point where I just started billing myself as Cherry Vanilla and This Week's Band. It was disheartening, exhausting, and expensive. But, at the same time, my singing was improving and the buzz about me was constantly growing. Getting a record contract (even without Bowie) really began to seem like an attainable dream. I just had to keep it all together for a little while longer.

BY AUTUMN 1975, I'd become (with whatever band I had going) a regular headliner at Max's Kansas City, Trude Heller's, the 82 Club (the same tranny bar where I'd spent my seventeenth birthday with Gil), and the Square Rigger (which Gordon and John had since expanded, providing space for bigger crowds, and a special dressing room where I could make my costume changes). I'd also done a bunch of one-nighters all around the New York area. At the Ice Palace in Cherry Grove, when I did my "Billie the Cop" poem for a second encore, Billie, the gorgeous strawberry-blond Suffolk County policeman for whom I had written it, and his handsome partner, Julio, walked right up to the front of the stage (unplanned and in their uniforms), put me in handcuffs, and carried me off—to the howls and applause of the Fire Island crowd. The three of us then went by water taxi to the Pines and had sex in their room at the Boatel until dawn—the interlude forever etched in my memory as a Tom of Finland drawing.

My publicity was still going strong. I even got myself on the nightly TV news shows when I put my ass- and hand-print in a block of pink cement outside of Trude Heller's. I had convinced Trude to start a wall of fame there and let me be the first to leave my mark. Trude was a notorious Village dyke who had taken a special liking to me. Lenny Bruce had played her club and Marilyn Monroe had hung out there. Trude told me I was like a combination of them both. I was flattered, of course, and I even accepted an invitation to spend a weekend at her house in the Pines. My friends all warned me she would rape me, but she did no such thing. Only problem was that I woke up on my first morning there with a case of hepatitis B and had to return to the city immediately and be hospitalized (luckily, I still had my SAG medical insurance from doing the Bowie voice-overs). Trude kind of soured on me after that, as if I'd ruined her weekend on purpose. She still booked me at the club, but she soon lost interest in the wall of fame or any of my other publicity ideas. (The three-hundred-pound block of cement with my ass-print hung on chains outside of her club for years, until it was stolen by my friends Lenny Prussack and David Loehr, with the help of their neighbors from a scrap metal yard, a blowtorch, and a crane.)

Bowie showed up with Norman Fisher at a Trude's gig one night and heard "Little Red Rooster" for the first time. He seemed to find the song amusing, and we talked once again about making a record. But then, like always, there was no follow-through. So I made a couple of demos with other producers but was never happy with either the results or the deal. They always wanted me to sign away all of my future publishing, and I knew that wouldn't be a smart move. Genya Ravan, whom I adored, was hot to produce me, and she brought some record execs around to see me, but they were not as impressed with me as she seemed to be. That rejection combined with the fact that I often went hoarse from the screaming I was doing (in most clubs, the monitors sucked and I could never really hear myself) prompted me to start studying voice with Keith Davis, who had coached both Judy Garland and Peter Allen. Thanks to Keith, I finally learned how to use my voice and protect it, even when I was screaming and shouting the fiercest of my rock and roll songs.

In between rock gigs, Tony Zee and I put together a little cabaret show called *Snacks*, featuring myself, Jayne County, my latest keyboard player Kasim Sultan, and some modern dancer friends of Zee's. It was a weird, eclectic mix of song, dance, and skits, directed by Zee and MC'd by me. Ray Davies of the Kinks came to see it and offered to help us develop it into something bigger. Ray had experimented with theatrics in his own concerts and thought we had the seeds of something special with *Snacks*. But we were just doing it for fun and a little bit of cash. Jayne and I were already too into our rock and roll careers, and Kasim (who had a voice like Paul McCartney's) was getting offers to make his own records at the time. Besides, Jayne, Zee, and I had already committed to a limited run of the Jackie Curtis play *Vain Victory* for Tony Ingrassia.

DEBBIE HARRY also appeared in *Vain Victory*, and the rest of Blondie's members supplied the play's musical score. Debbie was much friendlier as a fellow actress than Patti Smith had been, and the boys in her band were nice as well. I'm sure they did their share of bitching and moaning like all musicians, but they seemed so enthusiastic and so obviously devoted to Debbie. Patti also appeared to have that same kind loyalty and backing from her musicians. Knowing I never had it from mine really brought me down. I yearned for a band that would believe in me. I didn't mind them using me as a stepping stone. In a way I was doing the same to them (though I was also orchestrating and financing the whole endeavor). I just needed them to hang in there with me long enough to get a record deal. Then I'd be able to pay them enough to make them feel important and stick with me for a while. It was such a catch-22—I needed the deal to keep the musicians, but I needed to keep the musicians to get the deal.

By Christmas 1975, I was so stressed out, I just broke down and lost faith in it all—my abilities and creative visualizations, the magic, rock and roll, showbiz, even Max. I was behind in the rent, the phone was about to be shut off, there was nothing in the fridge, my roots needed doing, I'd picked at my face and was afraid to be seen, and my holiday spirit was nowhere to be found. But God bless Norman Fisher; he managed to change all that in an instant with the best gift ever—a real live seven-foot-tall Christmas tree, delivered to my fifth-floor walk-up, already in a stand, adorned with lights and tinsel and ready to be plugged in. Along with it, he sent a gaily wrapped box containing a Halston black-cashmere hoodie (the first of its kind), an ounce of grass, and the money for the rent. By New Year's Eve— when I guest bartended for a tea dance at the notorious gay leather bar the Eagle's Nest—I had stopped feeling sorry for myself, regained my determination, and resolved to get back in the rock and roll arena and once again fight for my life.

17

The Punk

B Y THE start of 1976, thanks to Michael Kamen, Patrick Henderson, Kasim Sultan, Hilly Michaels, and Thomas Morrongiello, my songbook contained "Tulsa," "White Chocolate," "Madison Avenue," "Tricks of the Trade," "Stuck in the Studio," "Publicity," "Breathe," "Foxy Bitch," and more. And as with my acting, DJing, PRing, ice skating, and Isadora Duncan dancing, there were nights on stage that were truly magical, with nary a bum note from me. But there were also some when I'd sing horribly off-key or miss my cues to come in. There was even a time or two when the band started playing one song and I started singing another. I had only ever done my shows stoned, which helped lessen my inhibitions and enhance my improvisations, but didn't make for great consistency. As out there and unpredictable as I was, however, the clubs were booking me, the audiences were embracing me, and the music biz honchos were circling around.

Morrongiello was back in the band and, despite the Tulsa van incident, was still fucking me—although less and less ever since I'd told him that I loved him. Tony Zee was staying in my guest room while he decompressed from Mainman and figured out what the next stage of his life was gonna be. I always thought that if Zee had been straight, he would have made the perfect husband for me. We had a similar take on life—a little wry at times, perhaps, but always with a curious fascination for our fortunate fates. And Zee was as devoted a friend to me as Max, so it was good to have him staying at the flat.

February 5, 1976—*On TWA flight 840, heading home from L.A. Loved being with Franklyn. Great haircut, as always. Peter Hugar photographed me lying by a pool, all dressed and with boots on. Went to a party up in Benedict Canyon for the relaunch of Sonny and Cher's TV show. Weird idea, now that she's married to Gregg Allman. Some guy slipped me a Quaalude and I got completely out of it, chasing Richard Perry into closets to kiss him and patting all of the Osmonds on their asses. Oh God . . . at one point, I think I mounted Joel Schumacher around the waist and fondled Charlotte Rampling's breasts, while telling her I wasn't a lesbian, but that I loved her. She was so fucking cool and groovy about it; made me love her that much more. Paul Jabara gave the featured toast. Strange moment. After wishing good luck to Sonny and Cher, he added, "And may the Arabs and the Jews all find a way to get along with each other!" Peter Brown called yesterday, inviting me over to have sex with Johnny Wyoming, while Peter took pictures. Well, fuck that, Peter! How about a record contract or a part in one of your new movies?*

February 26, 1976—*Did CBC Live in Halifax and stopped in Montreal, so I could catch Bowie's show. Spent hours with him after but didn't have sex. He played me some great new Iggy Pop tracks and his own new electronic stuff. It's funny, kind of primitive and childlike . . . a couple of versions of "Waiting for the Man" and something he called "Bubbles." I'm sure it'll get more sophisticated as he goes, but right now it sounds kind of hokey. We finally talked about my album. David doesn't want me to do rock and roll. He says we can record in Switzerland and I should be "The Electric Beatnik," doing poetry with his synthesizer stuff. I figure I can do that and still do rock and roll as well. Why not?*

February 27, 1976—David flew me from Montreal to Toronto yesterday, but I never got to see him after the gig, and I had to fly home early this morning. Now what? The Bowie roller-coaster continues. I'm doing Tomorrow *with Tom Snyder next week. Network TV! Whoopee!!*

March 9, 1976—I'm in Detroit. Just did The Lou Gordon Show *on WKBD-TV, and Will Geer, Grandpa from* The Waltons, *was on with me. Sexy old guy. I think he's gay, but we flirted anyway. He made some buns and gave me a couple during the show. I held them up and said, "I've got Will Geer's buns in my hands on TV," and I got a big laugh. God, I love doing TV talk shows. Maybe I should have one of my own.*

AT THE end of March, when Bowie's *Station to Station* tour hit New York, Norman Fisher threw him the most lavish and exclusive soirée. The whole top of Norman's mantelpiece was completely covered, like a snowy Christmas landscape, with the finest cocaine. And we all cut little paths through it with straws. It was the most decadent and generous display of refreshments I had ever seen offered by a host in my life. Naturally, I was happy to encounter David there and to have the chance to talk with him again. But when I approached him in my usual adoring manner, he uttered something abrasive sounding in German and quickly turned and walked away. I just stood there for a moment, hurt and in a state of dismay. Whatever it was that he'd said to me and whatever it was that had changed since Montreal, I pretty much got the message from his demeanor that my Electric Beatnik album was kaput. And I wound up drowning my sorrows in a night of sex with Rolling Stones percussionist Rocky Dzidzornu.

AS SPRING rolled into summer, I was really getting weary. It was a constant struggle to make ends meet, I hadn't heard from Bowie, and my musicians were driving me crazy with their constant kvetching.

They could never understand why I was always the one being photographed and interviewed and not them, why we weren't making any money, or why I had to fly to California for my haircuts. I was picking at my face profusely and having to pile on the makeup to hide the sores. Tom had stopped fucking me. I wasn't hot for any of the other boys in the band and I didn't have time for anyone outside of it. And even Eddie had gone and died on me, having suffered some kind of electrical overload one night and nearly setting my pussy on fire.

And yet, in some ways, everything was developing nicely. We were playing lots of gigs. My publicity was nonstop. And thanks to David Leong, I had the hottest new white stretch satin bodysuit with built-in push-up bra and a clear plastic bomber jacket with dime-sized rhinestones that reflected the stage lights like lasers. Plus, I had some fun new songs in the set, especially one I'd written with Tom called "Purgatory." When I did it at the 82 Club, I wore a long white dress that I'd burned around the bottom and Max rigged some crude silk-like flames to rise up all around me during the choruses. I had the couture, the craftiness, and the creativity, but it was all such a struggle—and I still didn't have *the* song yet, the one that could be my big hit.

IN OCTOBER, Nancy and Ringo called to arrange for John Lennon's birthday surprise. And this time they made sure that there was no one to depend on showing up for it but me. Nancy had seen me do a poem I called "The Story" at some oil man's party in Tulsa. It was my version of how Romeo and Juliet really died, and she thought it would be perfect for John—who was living at the Dakota with Yoko and their baby son, Sean. Nancy had set everything up secretly with Yoko. So when Max and I knocked on their apartment door and John answered and saw us standing there with the bar stool we'd brought with us, he was naturally a little taken aback. But Yoko soon appeared, ushered us into their foyer, and informed John of what was going on.

Realizing it would involve a performance, John took great pains in placing the stool right underneath the foyer's central lighting fixture and adjusting the light to shine directly on me. He then excused him-self for a minute and came back with his cassette tape recorder, into which he announced, "Birthday gift from Ringo and Nancy, 1976." There was one other guy there with them, to whom we were never introduced. Max and the three of them sat on the floor while I per-formed the poem, playing both Romeo and Juliet, switching voices and positions on the stool and air-humping to simulate sex. Yoko was busting a gut laughing from the start, but John just sat in stunned silence, not quite sure what to make of it all.

THE STORY

Look tither my darling
there's a light in the sky
Oh Romeo, Romeo
turn here your eye
It looks like a comet
or a bright burning sun

> *Oh tell me fair Juliet*
> *what have you done*
> *Nay, I've lost my hard-on*
> *You've spoilt the fun*

But Romeo sweetheart
I beg you to see
this little blue spaceman
who stands over me

> *Oh Juliet baby*
> *what didest thou eat*
> *that giveth thee visions*
> *so crazy my sweet*
> *Alas, I do love how you*
> *tickle my feet*

Oh Romeo, Romeo
thy body is hot
But look at the size
of the organ he's got

      Hey Juliet honey
      now cut out the crap
      You treatest me like
      I had just caught the clap
      Oh alright Julie
      I'll lookest about
      'Tis soft
      so I might just as well
      pull it out
      Well bloody blue babies
      now hearest me shout

      Oh tellest me cock man
      what is it thou craves
      To make the fair Juliet
      and me slaves

Oh Romeo, feel
his blue skin is so hot
I do thinkest maybe
I like him a lot
Oh Romeo why don't you
go sleep on the cot

      Juliet, Juliet
      what dost thou mean
      Cannot your fair eyes
      recognizeth a queen
      It's me that he wants
      so why don't you split
      It's me that he wants

and not your old clit
But first giveth here
a good dose of your spit

Oh Romeo, Romeo
where hast thou gone
The spaceman has killed you
with his great big hard-on
I guesseth there is now
no reason to try
I might as well open
my legs to this guy
and go for a ride
on that cock in the sky

Oh Romeo, Romeo
this is insane
He getethsts me off
on pleasure and pain
Oh hereest I cometh
to join you in sleep
I've hadeth enough
of this spacey blue creep
Our story's a secret
for the whole world to keep
And though they should laugheth
there's many will weep.

John had gotten more and more into the poem as it went on and, at the end, they all gave me a standing ovation. We stood around talking for a while afterward, and I was really surprised to learn that John already knew who I was. He said that he and Yoko had seen me a few months before on *The Tomorrow Show* and that they loved what I had to say—and they especially loved the poem that I'd read, "Rare Birds." I was in heaven at that moment. John and Yoko watched *me* on TV!

And they liked me! And what meant even more to me, of course, was the fact that they liked my poetry.

As we were leaving, John asked us to wait for a minute, because he had something he wanted to give me. He was gone quite a while, and my curiosity was in overdrive. He eventually came back to the foyer clutching a bottle of twelve-year-old whiskey, with a drink or two already missing from it. "Here, for the way home," he said, as if we were about to go trekking across the moors on a chilly Irish night. It was the most touching and sincere gesture, like something a country cousin or a good neighbor might do. And for months afterward, I took great pleasure in serving my friends shots from "John Lennon's Bottle" and telling them the tale of how I got it.

> *On a blue horizon*
> *When the world was young*
> *Rare birds filled the morning sky*
> *Their songs on air were sung*
> *Now they're gone forever*
> *Sometimes I wonder why*
> *And then a song comes on the air*
> *We're rare birds, you and I*

I WAS booked to play at Gordon and Jon's for the Halloween weekend and, except for my bass player, Jay Nap, I didn't have any musicians. Morrongiello had left me for some projects with Earl Slick and David Johansen; Kasim was playing with Todd Rundgren; and my drummer, Frankie LaRocca, was having a hernia operation. I had less than a week to replace them, rehearse, and get everyone up to West Stockbridge. I'd already found a keyboard player named Zecca Esquibel, a bisexual Brazilian who had never played rock but was classically trained and had developed his chops with some major funk bands (and still wore the platform shoes and backless Lurex jumpsuits to prove it). Luckily, Manny Mancuso, a drummer for the Flushing, Queens, band Chords Melody, had asked to audition and said he'd bring along Chords guitarist Louie Lepore. So once again I rented a rehearsal room and prayed that it would all work out.

The minute I met Louie Lepore, with his Capodimonte-like beauty and his streetwise Queensy attitude, I was over-the-moon horny for him. And when he plugged in and played his guitar, I wanted to fuck him right then and there. He and Manny gelled instantly with Zecca and Jay. And by the end of the three-hour session, I had my new band—and, I hoped, my new boyfriend. When Louie said he was living with his parents, too far out in New Jersey to make all of the Manhattan rehearsals, I invited him to stay with me—specifying that he'd have his own private bedroom (Zee having long since gotten an apartment). All during the audition, Louie had seemed rather shy. So when he flashed his long-lashed John Hammond–like eyes at me and boldly replied, "Why can't I sleep in your bed with you?" I could have died! I fell madly in love with him on the spot, and moved him in to live with me that night.

When Louie saw my loft, he was already quite obviously impressed, but when he read the card on the bird-of-paradise arrangement signed "With love and thanks, Nancy and Ringo" and got to drink from "John Lennon's Bottle," he just couldn't contain his excitement. And I loved that about him. He was as much a groupie as I was—or at least the same kind of starstruck romantic when it came to rock and roll. It made him all the more sexy to me. Neither of us felt the need to act cool about it. It was so much more of a turn-on to be honest and admit that we all yearned to get up close and personal, in one way or another, with our idols—and most especially with rock gods like the Beatles.

Louie was just about perfect in my eyes—twenty-one, hot, talented, lean, and clean—with a big nose and baby-soft cheeks that he'd never yet shaved. He was a fabulous cook and was always, always up and ready for sex—and usually the one to instigate it. Even before we got to Stockbridge, I'd decided I'd be completely faithful to him. It was easy, because from the moment I met him, I truly lost all desire for anyone else. I probably would have been monogamous with many a previous boyfriend, too, if they had cared about me enough to demand it, the way that Louie did from the start.

In his old-world Italian-ness, Louie was possessive and a bit para-noid, always thinking I had eyes for other guys. I'd fought for years to keep those kinds of bourgeois thoughts out of my life and love affairs. But, like the young Irish-Catholic girl I once was, I found myself flat-tered by Louie's little jealousies and suspicions and captivated by his macho 1950s attitude. And I became quite possessive and fixated on his faithfulness myself. It might not have been very feminist of me, but it was making me feel very feminine and I liked it.

HAVING GORDON, Jon, and West Stockbridge in my life was miraculous. Not only did I get to breathe the clean mountain air and enjoy a little respite from picking up the check, but I also got to play in a place where I was pretty much universally loved—except by the town's selectmen, who'd once shut me down on obscenity charges—and where I could try out new musicians and new material without the fear of falling on my face in the big city. And being there with Louie was so romantic and something of a rock and roll rebirth for both my psyche and my resolve. Having my own bands had pretty much demystified the whole musician thing for me. A few months earlier, I probably would have dumped them all if Bowie had called; but Louie reignited the fire in me, and renewed my desire to fulfill the *band, boyfriend, and hit record* dream.

Max and the rest of my entourage were always happy in the Berk-shires, because most of them managed to get laid there. They also got to snort the excellent cocaine that Gordon and Jon were serv-ing up by the bucketful. Seems a former chef of theirs owed them a huge amount of money and, as a way to pay them back, gave them his enormous stash of what was probably the purest coke I ever had in my life—even purer then Norman Fisher's. It looked like clumpy brown sugar until you took a razor blade to it. The more you chopped it, the more the brown clumps disappeared, leaving nothing but the whitest, fluffiest, finest cocaine. And if you left it out for a while and the humidity got to it, it somehow pulled itself back into the little brown clumps again. It was just one of the many fabulous perks of the Berks for which I was eternally grateful.

November 29, 1976—Played four nights at Richie Alexander's new place, On the Rocks. A guy from London named Miles Copeland came in and said if we want to play in the UK, he can book us a tour. Jay got so drunk, he fell of the stage. Miles seemed to love it, but I certainly didn't. Couldn't get too mad at Jay though . . . since I myself got so drunk that time at the 82 with Robert Palmer, I fell asleep on stage during Morrongiello's number.

A fresh breeze seemed to be blowing in the music world in the late seventies. A lot of new bands besides us were coming up, all with a similar stripped-down garagey sound and urban image. But instead of feeling like we were in competition with each other, it felt—to me anyway—like we were all taking part in one giant piece of theater together. It was a movement or an uprising of sorts, by which we got to rebel against something—namely disco and over-produced rock. OK, we weren't battling segregation or protesting the war in Vietnam, but we had something we could stand for nonetheless. *Creem* magazine had christened this new wave of raw, bare-bones music "punk rock" when the Ramones first came on the scene in 1974. And by '76 the name and the style had definitely caught on. There was even a magazine called, simply, *Punk*.

We New Yorkers embraced the whole idea of punk as the latest rock and roll pose, with a wink and a nod to the triviality of our little rebellion. Jimi LaLumia, a writer, record retailer, and loyal fan of mine, even launched a "Death to Disco" button- and bumper-sticker campaign—adding humor, credence, and a slogan to the movement.

But in the UK, where punk was exploding, it was doing so with a real class-struggle message and a heavy political bent. Of course, the fact that they were taking it so seriously over there created a huge sense of intrigue among those of us who had always revered and romanticized the land of Merseybeat and Carnaby Street. And most New York bands I knew yearned to go over and play there, mine included.

Of course, I came on in such a cheeky American way—personal freedom being my only possible political stance—I wasn't sure I'd go down so well in the UK's punk scene, which was touted in the press as being anarchistic and pseudonihilistic and didn't really sound like that much *fun* to me. But then again, I hadn't gotten signed yet, and I kept thinking about how, when you got publicity in London, the press was pretty much national, whereas my write-ups in New York were mostly local, which left me the whole rest of the United States to conquer. I was also thinking about Andrew Hoy. He'd long since become an A&R man at RCA UK and, as such, had the power to sign new acts to the label.

Fashion-wise, I didn't really go for punk at first. I still wanted to be pretty and glam, no matter how unattractive everyone else was making themselves. The pins through the cheeks I found especially ugly. For my early rock shows, I'd worn mostly dress-up costumes left over from my cabaret days—Norma Kamali's baby-wrap with rip-away pants, Stephen Sprouse's sequined tap shorts and leotard, a white dress shirt of Bowie's with Franklyn's mother's fringed 1950s capris, David Leong's bodysuits, the gold birthday number, a traditional Chinese dress with thigh-high zippered slits designed by Franklyn, and an array of cheap finds from thrift shops and Frederick's of Hollywood. But the more I evolved as a rocker, the more I favored performing in simple dressed-down things, like T-shirts, shorts, and vintage sweaters. I still wore high-fashion makeup, and my hair, though bleached and dyed the color of maraschino cherries, was amazingly healthy and shiny. But as my music started moving more and more towards punk, so, it seemed, did my outfits. The shorts I wore most often were made of metallic gold leather and went so far up my crack, it's a wonder they didn't disappear. And my favorite T-shirt was one Neal Peters had given me, emblazoned with the phrase "Lick Me." Saying "lick me" was like saying "fuck you," and I thought that was pretty punky. But what's more, that "Lick Me" shirt was like *The Red Shoes* for me; when I put it on, I became a punk rocker. Of course, since the girl in *The Red Shoes* becomes enslaved both by the shoes and her ambitions, I was aware of the danger as well as the magic of that shirt.

December 2, 1976—Played Lafayette High School in Brooklyn tonight. First "punk rockers" to ever play there. Did the new song I wrote with Zecca, "I Know How to Hook." Everyone thinks it's about prostitution, but it's really about how we all hook our way, in one sense or another, through every day... and also about how everyone always says I write great hooks. And I got to use that name Penthouse *magazine called me, "The Bard of the Hard."*

THE BERKSHIRES were like a New England greeting card scene at Christmas—the twinkle lights, the snow, the warm, cozy fires. And being there with Louie—except for when we couldn't get my lethal red hair dye (Tony Carr had taught Louie how to do my roots) out of the brand new fiberglass bathtub at Gordon and Jon's hotel—was divine. I was more deeply in love than I had ever been, the band was really sounding tight, and my OCD was non-existent. I even got to play Mrs. Santa Claus in the West Stockbridge Christmas Parade, wearing my gold sequined jumpsuit and a borrowed white fox coat, and riding down Main Street in an antique sleigh pulled by one of Jon Rick's horses. And the Square Rigger was, as always, packed every night.

I'd had to coax the music out of Louie, but we eventually managed to write some killer songs that I really loved singing, especially "Hard as a Rock" and "So 1950s," my lyrics for both inspired by Louie, of course. The absolute best thing about Christmas 1976, though, was that I knew, finally and for sure, that I had *the hit song*... the best one

I had written with anyone… the one I'd been praying for… the one that just couldn't miss—"The Punk."

The term "punk" wasn't new to me. Back in the 1950s, we had always called a certain kind of bad boy "a punk." But I always knew that most of them were really just sweet kids with a bit of excess anger and energy that they needed to vent. And the boys in the punk bands seemed no different to me than those basically harmless punks of my youth. So I wrote the lyrics that I felt summed up the whole punk-rock scene, and Louie matched them with the perfect melody. There was no question in my mind at that point; I was gonna get a record deal and my first hit single was gonna be "The Punk."

Black leather jacket and his cycle slut
Big sunglasses and a new haircut
Studs all up and down his faded jeans
Says he's from the city, but he comes from Queens
Hot pink guitar and his Fender amp
He walks on the stage like he was a champ
Sings his songs about the latest craze
Says I'm gonna take ya through another phase

CHORUS
Hello he says like a beefy hunk
Well I'm a little angry and a little drunk
Enough he says with all this disco funk (junk)
I wanna rock and roll, I wanna be a punk
I wanna rock and roll, I wanna be a punk

White skin crying for the golden sun
He ain't James Dean, but still he has his fun
He lives for music and he wants it live
Says I'm not gonna stand for all that disco jive
Worn-out sneakers and lucky charm

Tattooed tiger on his playing arm
Gets you hot, 'cause he's a horny guy
Says I'm up in the lights, so you can watch me die

LEEE WAS in London managing Johnny Thunders and the Heart-breakers, who were on tour with the Sex Pistols, the band that seemed to personify the UK punk attitude. For weeks, Leee had been calling me, raving about how incredibly exciting the scene was and insisting that I get myself over there "to be a part of rock and roll history." I kept thinking about going but always wound up deciding against it. For one thing, I wouldn't have my devoted fans, a healthy percentage of whom were gay and had followed my journey from theater to cabaret to rock. I knew the crowds abroad would be different and probably more specifically punk. And besides, I'd yet to hear a "Bang a Gong" or a "Let It Be" or anything powerful enough to make me wanna pack up and leave.

And then one night, as I was walking toward the back room at Max's, I heard a ferocious musical assault coming out of the speakers, and I stopped dead in my tracks to listen to it. It was "Anarchy in the UK" by the Sex Pistols, and it was all I needed to hear. It had an energy I just couldn't resist, and I decided right then and there that I was going to London. I'd have Max arrange a tour through Miles Copeland, and I'd sell everything I owned to get us all over there. I had my cowriter, lead guitarist, musical director, hair-colorist, pussy-trimmer, and lover all in one with Louie. I had Max, a band, an agent, and my dear friend Andrew Hoy. And I had some notoriety from my Warhol and Bowie days to get the press and the gigs.

January 8, 1977—*Had my going-away sale today. It was a madhouse here. Hundreds of people came, and they robbed me blind. There were so many, it was solid body to body, like the Fillmore East used to be. And all kinds of drugs were going round. I sold things for practi-*

cally nothing and people stuffed a lot into their pockets, especially the smaller items, like my jewelry. Sad to lose the 14k-gold LOVE ring and ingenious roach clip with macramé tassel that Nilo gave me and my favorite little picture of the girl on a swing. Barely raised enough money to cover the bills and get us all one-way tickets, even though it's only Max, Louie, Zecca, and me going. Manny quit the band right after our New Year's Eve gig at On the Rocks, because I was writing pretty much exclusively with Lou. And Jay can't to go to London, because of his other gig with the Boyfriends. Miles likes it this way, anyway. Seems his younger brother is a drummer and has a three-piece band, with no publicity hooks to get bookings. So he figures that they can be my opening act and then his brother and the bass player can also play with Louie, Zecca, and me. We can travel in one van and share the equipment. And I'm to pay them ten pounds each per gig. Miles says they're really good musicians and they call themselves the Police. A terrible name for a band, if ya ask me.

18

Bad Girl

I T WAS February in London. And I'd forgotten how bleak it could be. Max had flown over a few days ahead of Zecca, Louie, and me and booked us into a real fleabag of a hotel—one room for the four of us, communal toilet and tub—no glacéed fruits or fresh-squeezed orange juice like at the Inn on the Park, no limo waiting outside. We went to the Roxy on our first night in town and caught a set by the Damned. The place seemed like a big firetrap to me—a dank, low-ceilinged basement with a steep staircase at its entrance, packed to the gills with "punters" smoking "fags." But the buzz there, the electrifying energy of the Roxy's young no-future crowd, really did feel, as Leee had said, history-making.

The Roxy was to punk what Reno Sweeney was to cabaret, and I would soon be playing there with my lead-guitarist boyfriend by my side. It was all so rock and roll perfect as to almost be a cliché, even, I suppose, down to the starving-artist sleaziness of it all. I was so in love and feeling so brave that everything seemed exciting and romantic. Though from the publicity I'd gotten on my arrival—mostly good, but with a couple of papers already putting me down for things like my name, age, hair, groupie past, and even my manicured nails—I could tell that conquering the UK and getting the almighty record deal wasn't gonna be a piece of cake.

WE MET the Police at a cold, damp rehearsal space and got down to business right away—Miles Copeland's brother, Stewart, playing drums and a guy named Sting playing bass. They had a guitarist named Henry Padovani at the time, but he wasn't needed in my band and would have cost me another ten pounds per night. They were professional and cooperative, though I sensed a bit of condescension, or maybe just a little embarrassment, when they had to sing the "cock-a-doodle-do" choruses of "Little Red Rooster." And there was definitely some rivalry going on between them and Louie and Zecca. I was quite insecure and praying they'd all just accept each other and make it sound, as much as possible, like what I was used to—and fast, 'cause we were playing our first UK gig in a couple of days. The Police were, as Miles had claimed, excellent musicians, but that didn't stop Louie and Zecca from bitching about them, especially about Stewart, whose tempos they both complained wavered.

March 1, 1977—*We played our first gig at Alexander's in Wales tonight, and both my set and the Police's went over great. They had a baby grand piano there, and I think Stewart and Sting were surprised at how I slinked and snaked all over it and really let loose on stage. I can't believe I'm actually singing my own rock and roll songs with a dynamite band in a foreign land. It's all so surreal and dreamy.*

March 2, 1977—*Been living on potato chips and beer. I really miss pot. Had a little hash, but the tobacco always makes me feel so sick. The Police get high on over-the-counter uppers and downers called Benylin and dodos. Thank God they're not into smack like lots of the punk bands over here seem to be. We listened to Bowie, Boz Scaggs, and Steve Reich in the van. Everybody is getting along. I like Henry*

Padovani the best. He's got those ugly-beautiful looks, like a French movie star.

March 3, 1977—*Played the Roxy tonight. Gave my all and went down "a bomb," which means good, I'm told. What a rush! There's so much excitement about punk over here. Every band playing it, or anything close, can't help but feel ultraimportant... like the eyes of the world are upon us. Besides us, Miles books the Sex Pistols, the Clash, Generation X, Chelsea, the Cortinas, Sham 69, and practically everyone who's over here from New York... and promotes us all as "new wave," in order to, as he says, "broaden the parameters of punk." But I like being called punk. It makes me feel more rebellious and tough. And I love the challenge of the punk audience. I could do without the "approving" (??) projectiles of spit, though. We're going on the road for a few dates with the Heartbreakers, so I'll get to spend a little time with Leee. Jayne's over here too. She played the Roxy last night and was outrageous. She has real tits now from the hormones and she let me feel them.*

WHENEVER WE went on the road, Sting's wife, Frances, packed him a week's worth of sandwiches and fruit in a box so he wouldn't have to spend money on fish and chips and gyros like the rest of us. Frances was a sweetheart. I believe she and Sting had met when they were both in a Christmas pageant, with Frances playing Mary and Sting playing Joseph. They had a newborn baby son named Joe, and I got to hold him sometimes at their flat while the guys were loading the van. Because I liked Frances—and Stewart's and Henry's girlfriends as well—I tried to avoid keeping track of any groupie activity I might have observed going down. But, due to the fact that we didn't make enough money for hotel rooms and we had to ask people we met in each club if they would put us up for the night, I imagine it must have been hard for those guys to avoid certain compromising situations. At least Louie and I had each other, and we made love anywhere and any time we could, often in the dressing room or the van, when nobody was around.

> **March 10, 1977**—*Played Eric's, right across the street from where the Cavern Club was, where the Beatles had played! Wasn't ready for Johnny Thunders shooting blood from his needle onto the hotel room walls. We had rooms as well, a luxury. Louie ("Maurice" when he's coloring my hair) did my roots and I did his. His hair is lavender now and Zecca's is turquoise. We're Technicolor punks! The UK hotels chintz on the heat and hot water during the afternoons, so we froze with the bleach on our heads. We wrote a great new song about being here though, called "Liverpool."*

THERE WERE a couple of journalists at the *New Musical Express*—also known as the *NME* or, to some, "the enemy"—who really ripped me to shreds. But aside from them and one or two others, the rest of the media, including the fanzines, were mostly singing my praises—or, at the worst, poking fun at my Vegas-y image. Since I always liked going against the grain and agitating the naysayers, I'd started wearing some of my old glitter/glam outfits again—in the midst of the most punk-centric scene on the planet. And for a London club we played called the Nashville, I even wore a real girly, frilly flower-printed dress, with some Scottish folk-dancing shoes I'd found at a thrift shop. When I did get punked out and wear the *Lick Me* shirt, I abandoned the gold shorts and just wore it with some ankle boots and black underpants.

I guess I equated being a punk with being ballsy and different. And I was—but not only in my looks. There really weren't any other blatantly sexual, satirical women like me in the punk-rock scene at the time, especially in the New York contingent. Debbie Harry was more the teenage-dream type—the gorgeous, streetwise girl next door—and Patti Smith came off kinda like a guy and seemed to take herself pretty seriously. Of course, Madonna hadn't emerged yet and would do so in the disco world, not in rock—and certainly not in punk rock.

While my music was real rock, it was, at the same time, a bit of a send-up of rock and especially, I guess, of punk rock. It must have seemed pretty oddball to many of the young, self-styled UK anarchists, but there was no way I could be anything but me. True, I wasn't a raging whore in real life anymore (except with Louie), but I still stood for sexual freedom and still loved being both slutty and funny on stage.

March 15, 1977—Played Dingwalls in London. Dave Robinson from Stiff Records came backstage and said I was great. I remember sleeping with him back in '71 at Brinsley Schwarz's house, and he was very tender and sweet. He says we'll have lunch next week and talk. I hope he means about a record deal.

Playing gigs, traveling, and sleeping on floors was exhausting. Everywhere we went it was chilly and wet, and the heater in the rickety old van Miles had lent us didn't work, so we were always cold and always getting sick. Thank God Louie had his grandfather's heavy wool overcoat and I had my Early Halloween royal blue beaver (the collar of which I'd trimmed with an ostrich–feather boa in the exact same color blue). We got antibiotics for free from the National Health, but I had reached a point where they just didn't seem to help anymore. It was like I had a permanent flu ever since arriving in the UK. And I just couldn't seem to shake it.

March 16, 1977—Melody Maker asked me to write a piece for them. Not much money, but good publicity… as if I'm not getting enough already, ha ha. It's going to be about a day spent in bed with Louie… what else!

The money I was making was barely enough to cover the cost of the Police and the petrol we were burning or the occasional hotel room on the road, let alone the rent for a London apartment. But thanks to Norman Fisher, we were soon living in the most beautiful parlor-floor Victorian flat, just a block or two from the beloved Pig Mansion. It looked out onto a gothic church at the front and a row of lovely gardens at the back and had two bedrooms, one for Louie and me and one for Max. Zecca slept in the living room on a yellow silk sofa next to a black marble fireplace and under a chandelier that had once belonged to Oscar Wilde.

The flat, at 37 Redcliffe Square, was owned by Mario Amaya, an art critic from New York who'd been wounded along with Andy Warhol in the Valerie Solanas shooting back in 1968. It was filled with important pieces by Warhol, Robert Rauschenberg, and Yoko Ono, along with valuable antiques and a fabulous collection of books. Mario, whom I'd only met in passing, was a charter member of Norman's salon and, as director of the Chrysler Museum of Art, was living in what he called "No-fuck, Virginia" at the time. I agreed to pay him forty-three pounds a week until I got a record deal, at which point I would pay him triple that amount, retroactive from the time we moved in. And because of Norman, Mario trusted me. The flat had no central heating, so we froze our asses off and had to deal with both a bit of black mold and a problematic paraffin heater. But it was home sweet home, and we were grateful to have it.

The funds from my New York apartment sale had long since run out and between gigs we were borrowing five pounds a day from Miles Copeland—something else I would pay back when I got signed—out of which we managed to squeeze enough for Max's cigarettes, daily tube fare to Miles's office, and dinner for the four of us each night. Brussels sprouts, at eleven pence a bag, were our mainstay, along with potatoes, aglio e olio, and eggs. And sometimes we'd bake a tiny canned ham and split two beers between us. The rest of our meals were mostly tea and toast—which was pretty much all I could keep down anyway.

March 18, 1977—*Oh God, no! This can't be happening. Not now, God. Oh please, God, not now. I'm pregnant.*

For a woman who's in no position to bring a child into the world, having one in your womb has got to be the worst, most soul-wrenching thing that can ever, ever happen. The whole bottom falls out of your life, and every thought, plan, hope, and dream you have is suddenly eclipsed by the heaviness and the urgency of the situation at hand. And there's no getting away from it, not even for a second. It's there inside of you, with a heart that's already beating. And in its primordial struggle to survive, the tiny entity is changing your hormones and manipulating all of your emotions. Your will and your reasoning helplessly fall prey to your inescapable, natural maternal instincts. You want the child. But you know there's just no way in hell that you can have it. And that was, once again, the situation I was in.

I was dead broke, with people counting on me for their survival and with outstanding debts that depended on a record deal for me to pay them. Andrew Hoy had hinted that RCA was interested in signing me and a guy from CBS Records was buzzing 'round, but I still didn't have a firm offer. And what record company was ever gonna sign a pregnant punk rocker selling sex and irony? And if I didn't get signed, then what? Being a welfare mother would be a fate worse than death for a woman like me. Louie made it clear that he would have nothing to do with the baby. And I felt guilty for even laying the crisis on him. I didn't get pregnant on purpose. It was the last thing I needed in my life. I was on birth control pills at the time, but I must have missed one somewhere in the mayhem of our moving from the States. At any rate, it was my responsibility and I had fucked up.

I was exhausted from crying and vomiting and going over and over in my mind what options I might have. There were moments when I was ready to just plunge ahead and have the baby, come hell or high water. But I needed Louie to want the baby too—and he didn't. He pleaded with me not to have it, saying he was just too young and that it would ruin his life. He said he would hate me forever and he would leave me. And besides all of those emotional considerations, there was the ever-present matter of survival. Where would I be if he left me—a pregnant punk-rocker trying to get a record deal without a cowriter, musical director, and guitarist? I had put Louie in a position where he was irreplaceable. And I'd put myself in a position where I had to have another abortion.

I didn't hate Louie for not wanting the baby; I understood. It wasn't inside of his body, so he could never know the depth of what I was feeling. I forgave him. And I tried to forgive myself. I reasoned that the soul destined to manifest in that baby would find another being through which to come into the world, and that, as my mother would say, everything happens for the best. But I had seen the bond that exists between mother and child—even my sister Mary, I knew, would put her kids before me in a crunch—and I worried that I might never have that, that I might always be out there on my own. But assuring myself first place in someone's life was no reason to have a baby, not if I couldn't take care of it. Everyone always thought of me as being so strong, even though I really wasn't—at least not in that instance. And I still had to deal with the fact that abortions didn't come easy on the National Health; there had to be a medical reason for one. But after a long consultation with a nun and a doctor at St. Mary's Hospital, it was decided that I was mentally and emotionally incapable of coping with a child, and a "pregnancy termination" was granted. And when they did it, the procedure once again proved difficult for the doctors, though they weren't exactly sure why.

March 25, 1977—*I should be in Amsterdam now, playing at the Paradiso, but I'm at home recuperating, and the Police are there with Jayne instead. I'm so embarrassed 'cause Jayne said they announced from the stage last night that I canceled my dates because I had an abortion. Not that I'm ashamed of it. But I'm not exactly proud of it either. And I would have preferred that it remained somewhat private. Ha, I guess I'm pipe dreaming to think you can retain your privacy while at the same time seeking fame. Speaking of which, I'm not so sure how much of that I really want anymore. I think I've already had enough of it to know that fame isn't exactly all that it's cracked up to be.*

BY APRIL, I was back doing gigs with the Police. And, in my need to lash out in some way, I wrote (with Louie) my punkiest song ever, "No More Canaries." It was based on a report I'd heard on the radio saying that a virus had wiped out all of the canaries, leaving only yellow parakeets (or budgerigars, as the Brits called them), a report that later turned out to be false. The lyrics were metaphorical, commenting, on the one hand, on the possible demise of our whole species and, on the other, taking to task the hypocrisy of UK punk bands like the Sex Pistols and the Clash for putting down the corporate world in their songs while at the same time signing record deals for hundreds of thousands of pounds with major labels. Even the anarchists wanted to be stars, even if it meant joining the very system they were railing against. "Canaries" was our fastest, hardest song ever, and I loved performing it 'cause it really helped to exorcise my pain. And instead of further increasing my animosity or derision towards the UK punks, it made me feel for the first time a genuine kinship with them. We were all posers of sorts. In one way or another, we were all caught up in the same conundrum.

> **April 3, 1977**—*Played the Nashville again tonight. CBS and RCA both wooing me. Things are good with Louie, though the dream may be forever tainted.*

THERE WERE moments on the road with the Police I remember as clearly as that starry night on Highway 1 in Mendocino. One was the time we all came within an inch of dying when Sting fell asleep at the wheel. And one was the time we stopped at a quaint, cozy roadside café for tea and scones with clotted cream and jam—so deliciously comforting on a cold, rainy day. But my favorite time was when we drove down south to play Plymouth and Penzance and we stopped off at Stonehenge. We had to go miles out of our way to get there. And though it was almost evening when we arrived, I was astonished that there was no one else around but us—no guards, no tourists, no ticket office, and no concession stands. I remember how silent we all were and how long we stood there in the piercing cold wind. I remember Louie's arms around me, keeping me warm, and how I wished that the others all had someone special there to hold as well.

Of course, our little excursion to Stonehenge made us late for the Plymouth gig, and the boys had to set up with the club already full of people while I did a quick change and makeup job in the no-mirror, no-light, no-privacy dressing room. We blew a speaker in the sound system on our first number, so we had to turn the stage monitors toward the audience and use them as our only amplification. But we actually did one of our best shows ever there. At least that's what everyone said; we could barely hear ourselves and couldn't tell. After the gig, we all went home with a guy named Baggins—"as in Bilbo Baggins from *The Hobbit*," he said—who was putting us up at his sheep farm for the night.

It was really dark when we arrived at Baggins's farm, so we couldn't see much, and it was so cold in his old stone farmhouse that we all slept with our coats on and wool scarves wrapped around our heads. Louie and I got the only available bed, with a sharp-as-a-nail spring sticking up right in the middle of the mattress, but at least we didn't have to sleep on the floor like everyone else. Despite the humble accommodations, however, we all slept like rocks in the countryside quietness. And in the morning we woke to the sound of a hundred sheep baaing and a sumptuous breakfast of French toast, bacon, and coffee, lovingly prepared by Max and Baggins and served next to a roaring fire.

I liked the Police—even though I sometimes found Stewart's sense of humor a little sophomoric and snarky—and I was happy that we were helping each other out. But I had no idea at the time that, whenever Stewart and Sting got Louie alone, they were trying to persuade him to leave me and join their band instead. Thank God Louie was man enough in that regard to do right by me, especially with the fragile state I was in. But it wasn't only a moral choice for Louie. The Police were still pretty three-chord punky in those days and hadn't yet developed their signature reggae-rock sound. Louie would be locked into a group situation with them and unable to pursue his own career, at least not until well after the Police took off anyway—and whether or not they ever would was still quite uncertain. What I was offering Louie was the chance to write and play with me while also going after his own record deal. Of course, in hindsight, Louie probably wishes he'd taken them up on their offer.

LOUIE AND I had begun to go out on the town again when we were back in London. We were already a well-known rock and roll couple and were always welcomed at the clubs free of charge. There were a few cool people on the scene who I always enjoyed bumping into— Soo Catwoman, Jon Savage, Mark P, Gene October, and the adorable Billy Idol, who always managed to grab my ass when Louie wasn't looking. And though I never found myself lusting after any of the punk-rock musicians, I did feel the old spark of sexual desire one night when I was introduced to Phil Lynott of Thin Lizzy. His black gypsy looks and lilting Irish brogue were so appealing that, for the first time since I'd met Louie, I found myself entertaining a little momentary fantasy about another man. But I quickly put it out of my mind, and I lavished all my love on Lou when we got home.

In the daytime, we'd often walk down to the King's Road, where our contemporaries liked to cruise and gather. We'd spend hours browsing the shops —especially Malcolm McLaren and Vivienne Westwood's Seditionaries—ogling the fashions and dreaming of the day when we could afford to buy them. We ran into Debbie Harry, Johnny Thunders, and some other Max's Kansas City alumni there one afternoon but declined their invitation to go to someone's flat and "do some dope," which I knew meant heroin. I wasn't about to indulge in drugs the way I once had, and I wasn't about to cheat on Louie, but I was beginning to let myself feel the fun and fascination of the rock and roll world once again and to enjoy the special place that I'd carved out for myself within it.

April 10, 1977—*Norman Fisher died yesterday. I had no idea his cancer was progressing so fast. And to think how he took care of me right to the end, making sure I had a roof over my head and believing in all of my dreams.*

It was my third time playing the Nashville, and it was packed. Andrew Hoy was there with the RCA bigwigs, and they, along with the journalists and punters, seemed primed for a memorable night. I had risen to the top of the punk-rock/new-wave scene. Like me or not—and the NME still didn't—I was a star. CBS had already lent me six hundred pounds just to think about signing with them. But I was really hoping to sign with RCA—even though I had such a dubious history with them. Elvis and Bowie were on RCA, and Andrew would be there as both my A&R man and my producer. He'd previously produced only one overlooked single and a couple of demos, but I liked what I heard in the tracks. They were gritty, live-sounding, authentic rock and roll and were somehow big without being overproduced. And that's what I wanted—no massive studio tricks, just honest, straightforward rock. (Though, to tell the truth, I might have used a little Auto-Tune had it been available then.) Plus, Andrew's boyfriend, Ian Stuart Lane, was a fabulous singer and always able to give me both confidence and frank critiques about my own vocals.

As I sat in the Nashville's dressing room that night, nervously waiting to go on, I couldn't help but think how far my love of music had taken me—right up to the point of playing the biggest music-biz role of them all, that of the rock star. I was, of course, excited beyond belief. But at the same time, I was acutely aware of the box I'd put myself in. The band thing was actually a burden and not at all conducive to the freedom and independence I'd always claimed was my ultimate goal. And I wondered if it was really true love with Louie or if I'd just convinced myself it was because he simply fit the bill. And what would happen if and when I got the hit? Would I then feel compelled to keep it all going, squeezing myself into skimpy costumes, getting face-lifts and tummy tucks and re-creating "The Punk" in one form or other for the rest of my life? Would I buy a little cottage in Woodstock, make Louie into the rock star, and have his babies? Or would I get back to being that weirdo loner kid I once was, enjoying my solitude, without the need for an audience or a man?

I brushed all of those thoughts aside, of course, as I took to the stage—determined to remember my lyrics, try my best to sing on key, and enjoy the glorious be-here-nowness of it all. Louie and I had just written a country tune, the one I'd decided (at the height of punkdom) would be the title song of my album and serve as my faux manifesto. I was well aware that, of all of the roles I had played in my life, of all of the things I had ever been or ever would be, people would probably always choose to call me a groupie. It's simply human nature to go for the term that implies the greatest measure of sex and sleaze—even though the passion of the groupie is probably the purest, holiest thing in all of rock and roll. So to show 'em how little they knew, I thought I'd give 'em yet another put-down name to call me. It was one my father had given me so many years before—and probably the one that made me so determined to succeed.

BAD GIRL

Hey you little angel standing there
Shining like your long brown curly hair
Careful now don't give your love for free
Or you may turn out a bad girl like me
I'm just a bad girl, Mama told me I would cry
I'm just a bad girl, that's why

Hey what's all this fuss about my name
When I'm just tryin' to make you glad you came

And how more honest can one woman be
Than a great big grown-up bad girl like me
I'm just a bad girl, Mama told me I would cry
I'm just a bad girl, that's why

(LOUIE)
No you won't cry no more with me
I'll make you feel so good and I'll kiss you sweetly
I'll sing you songs they'll never understand
I'll be a good boy, I'll be your man
Oh oh, I'll be your man

I'm just a bad girl, Mama told me I would cry
I'm just a bad girl, that's why
Yes, I'm a bad girl, makin' love and gettin' high
I'm just a bad girl, that's why.

Epilogue

So I did get the RCA contract—and the limos, ass kissing, aggravation, and frustration that came along with it. By the second album, I was blatantly defying them, recording mostly love songs and even a hymn instead of the hard rockin' stuff that they wanted but probably wouldn't have promoted anyway. I never did have the hit. And after RCA, I just walked away from the whole idea of it. Louie and I moved back to Manhattan, where he joined Zecca's new band and cheated on me with the female lead singer. When we split, I met and married a beautiful twenty-one-year-old German boy. But that soon ended in a divorce, after which I vowed to never again share my life with a man. I was better off on my own.

I reinvented myself constantly over the years, eventually realizing that there was one thing that I could do totally on my own that made me happy and could pay the bills: write. Words were for free and were always good to me. And I didn't need musicians and all of the rest to make them mine. So I wrote magazine articles, bios, press releases, ads, proposals, commercials, whatever I could to earn a living. I also had a lot of odd jobs, including taking bets on the horses and Jai alai, establishing and running one of America's first phone-sex agencies, searching undercover for missing children, ironing sheets for a textiles showroom, and working as both a landscaper and a Lancome makeup artist. In addition, I produced an all-girls variety concert series in New York, did an Ingrassia play in Berlin, and played a couple of reunion gigs with the Bad Girl band for old times' sake.

A lot of my old friends passed on—many in that first big wave of AIDS—but a few are still alive and still close to my heart. And the second half of my life has been filled with as many incredible characters, artists, and celebrities as the first half, most of whom have proven to be both genuine and loyal, especially Tim Burton, Rufus Wainwright, and Dito Montiel. Plus, I've had the pleasure of working on projects with the likes of Chet Baker, Roger Waters, Marianne Faithfull, Betsey Johnson, Norma Kamali, Lauren Hutton, Frank Morgan, Stephen Sprouse, Steven Meisel, Bruce Weber, John Kelly, Diane Pernet, Flea, Ronnie Spector, and more.

In 1985, I got arrested at Le Parker Meridien hotel under suspicion of being a hooker. I was, of course, nothing of the sort—didn't even look like one at the time and was actually at a business meeting regarding Isabella Rossellini and other famous models, for whom I was making connections in the acting field. I sued the hotel, and they settled out of court. But it was little compensation for having been carted off in handcuffs and forced to spend the night in a New York City jail cell. I did, however, manage to get Isabella a part in a play that summer at the Berkshire Theatre Festival, where I'd served as publicity director the year before. I also set her up with Marc Shaiman, who helped her learn to sing "Blue Velvet" for her role in the David Lynch film.

About twenty years ago, I lost everything, including my mind for a while. Penniless and in the depths of depression, with my OCD raging, I suddenly found myself homeless. It was a lesson in humility and compassion, which, thanks to Jon Rick, hard work, and Prozac, was soon over. Fifteen years ago, I drove across the country from the Berkshires to Hollywood where I established Europa Entertainment, Inc., the U.S. office for the composer Vangelis, whom I'd met in 1977 when we were both on RCA. And I continue to run it to this day. My friendship and association with Vangelis has been the greatest blessing of my life, because he's living proof that a man can have as much integrity about his humanity as he has about his music—the very thing I was always looking for in a musician. Without Vangelis's encouragement, love, and support, I could never have written this book.

As for my sex life—except for one little tryst with a surfer half my age —I left it behind when I turned forty. That was over a quarter of a century ago, and I've never looked back. I'd already had so much sex in my life—maybe that's why I could put it aside. Truth is, I simply lost the desire. And I have never felt so free. I still occasionally suffer from my OCD, especially when I get nervous or stressed out. But I'm working on it homeopathically, and, like Pope John Paul II, I've come to think of it as "self-flagellation" and figure I too must be on my way to sainthood.

Because of a wall down the middle of my uterus, discovered during a third pregnancy, it turns out I never would have been able to carry a baby to term and the abortions probably saved me from even greater tragedy. Luckily, my life today is filled with young people (and even some formerly pain-in-the-ass ex-band members), who—because of everything I've seen and done and been so open about—feel they can confide in me and have come to regard me as their rock and roll fairy godmother, the role and the label I love best of all.

And no, I never did meet Van Morrison. But, hopefully, there's time.

Acknowledgments

THANKS TO everyone at Chicago Review Press, especially Yuval Taylor and Allison Felus; everyone at Foundry Literary Media, especially Peter McGuigan; everyone mentioned in the book, especially Andrew Hoy; all of the photographers; all of my friends; and everyone who helped me with this project, especially my firestarter Pamela Des Barres, my photo editor Arlene Pachasa, and my absolute rocks Tony Zanetta and Mr. Kalafatis. And special thanks to Rufus for the foreword and to Vangelis for more than I could ever mention here.

Index